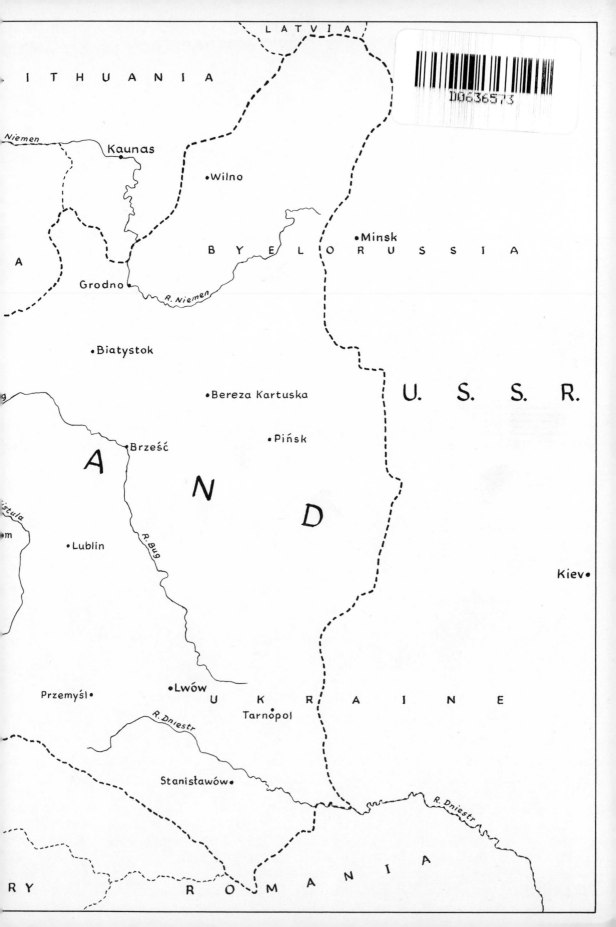

LATVIA

LITHUANIA

Niemen

Kaunas

•Wilno

BYELORUSSIA

•Minsk

A

Grodno

R. Niemen

•Białystok

•Bereza Kartuska

U. S. S. R.

•Pińsk

Brześć

A

N

D

Vistula

Lublin

R. Bug

Kiev•

•Lwów

Przemyśl•

U K R A I N E

Tarnopol

R. Dniestr

Stanisławów•

R. Dniestr

RY

R O M A N I A

The Struggles for Poland

The Struggles for Poland

Neal Ascherson

Michael Joseph London

First published in Great Britain by Michael Joseph Ltd
27 Wrights Lane, Kensington, London W8
1987

The television series *The Struggles for Poland* produced by
DNA 'Poland' Ltd, Executive Producer Martin Smith,
for Channel 4 in association with WNET/Thirteen New York
and Norddeutscher Rundfunk Hamburg

Ascherson, Neal
    The struggles for Poland.
    1. Poland——History——20th century
    I. Title
    943.8'04   DK4382
    ISBN 0-7181-2812-5

Printed and bound by The Bath Press, Bath, Avon

Contents

Acknowledgements

The author and publishers would like to thank the following for the use of photographs and other material in the book:

Archiwum Dokumentacji Mechanicznej, *pages* 66, 73; BBC Hulton Picture Library, 30 (bottom), 37, 53, 54, 55 (top and bottom), 140, 143, 145; Bundesarchiv, Koblenz, 95, 96, 110; Bundesbildstelle, Bonn, 180; Mrs Ciolkosz, 11; DNA 'Poland' Ltd, 163; Express Newspapers plc, 117; Franklin D. Roosevelt Library, USA, 128; Joanna Helander, 152; *Illustrated London News*, 43, 57; Imperial War Museum, 32, 125, 126; Independent Polish Agency, Lund, 224 (bottom), 226; Józef Piłsudski Institute, UK, 47, 64, 82 (bottom); Julien Bryan Collection, 88; Mary Evans Picture Library, 30 (top); Edward Mier-Jedrzejowicz, 199; The Photosource, 85; Piłsudski Institute of America, 69; Polish Images (Pictures), 182, 192, 195 (top and bottom); Polish Institute and Sikorski Museum, 116, 120, 124; The Polish Library, Posk, 123; Oxford University Press, 4 (the map on page 4 is taken from *God's Playground Vol. 2* by Norman Davies, © Norman Davies, 1981, published by Oxford University Press); Studium Polski Podziemnej, 105, 134 (bottom); Warsaw Museum, 21; Michael Yardley, 211; and Yivo Institute for Jewish Research, New York, 146.

Above all, the author's thanks go to the endless flow of encouragement, knowledge and advice supplied by the television team at David Naden Associates who made *The Struggles for Poland* series; in particular to Martin Smith, Executive Producer and driving force behind the whole project, to Bolesław Sulik, Dai Vaughan, Annie Dodds, Wanda Kościa, Maria Polachowska, Shelagh Brady, James Barker, Raye Farr, Paul Robinson and Angus MacQueen, to the staff of the Sikorski Institute, and to Jan Ciechanowski for checking the manuscript for accuracy.

Maps and endpapers by Boris Weltman. Picture research by Annie Dodds. While every attempt has been made to trace the copyright holders, this has not always been possible. The author and publishers would be glad to rectify any inaccuracies in future reprints. They would also like to thank those who lent pictures but whose names, for various reasons, cannot be acknowledged.

A Short Chronology

966 Baptism of King Mieszko I, of the Piast dynasty. The effective foundation of the Polish state under the Piasts, who rule until 1370.

1241 First Mongol invasion: the Poles defeated at the battle of Legnica.

1264 First statute of Jewish liberties, at Kalisz.

1386 The Polish princess Jadwiga marries the Lithuanian ruler Jagiełło. Foundation of the Jagellonian dynasty, on the throne until 1572. Beginning of the Union between Poland and Lithuania.

1410 Battle of Grunwald. The Polish–Lithuanian army defeats the Order of Teutonic Knights.

1466 Peace of Toruń. The power of the Teutonic Knights finally broken.

1505 Statute of *Nihil Novi*: the noble estate limits royal power and establishes the rights of parliament (the Sejm).

1573 Confederation of Warsaw: the guarantee of religious toleration.

1573 The nobles gain the right to elect the king.

1596 Union of Brest (Brześć): creation of the Uniate or Greek Catholic Church.

1600–1629 First period of wars with Sweden.

1648 Cossack rebellion of Hetman Chmielnicki in the Ukraine.

1652 First use of *Liberum Veto* – the rule of unanimity for decisions of the Sejm.

1655–60 Polish–Swedish War: 'The Deluge'.

1674 Election of John Sobieski as King John III.

1683 King John Sobieski defeats the Turks at the gates of Vienna.

1700–1721 The Great Northern War.

1733 Russian armies intervene, forcing the removal of King Stanisław Leszczyński.

1764 Election of King Stanisław August Poniatowski, last king of Poland.

1768 Confederation of Bar: nobles' rising against Russian influence.

1772 First Partition of Poland.

1791 Constitution of the Third of May.

1793 Second Partition.

1794 National insurrection led by Tadeusz Kościuszko.

1795 Third Partition: Poland disappears from the map.

1807–13 Napoleon creates puppet Grand Duchy of Warsaw.

1830–31 November Rising: war with Russia; the 'Great Emigration' takes place after defeat.

1846 Galician Rising: ends in massacre of landowners by peasantry.

1848 Attempted rising in Prussian Poland.

1863–4 January Rising, against Russia. Ends in defeat.

1864 Russia abolishes serfdom in Russian Poland.

1867 Birth of Józef Piłsudski.

1905 Revolution in Russia and in Russian Poland.

1914 Outbreak of First World War. Józef Piłsudski leads Polish Legions against Russia.

1918 (11 November) Poland regains independence.

1919–21 Polish–Soviet War. Battle of Warsaw won by Piłsudski's troops, August 1920.

1921 Treaty of Riga with Bolshevik Russia.

1926 (May) Piłsudski's coup d'état.

1934 Non-Aggression Pact with Germany.

1935 Death of Piłsudski.

1939 (23 August) Nazi–Soviet pact.
(1 September) Germany invades Poland.
(17 September) USSR invades Poland, which is then partitioned between Germany and USSR.

1941 Hitler attacks USSR. Polish government in exile (London) forms alliance with USSR.

1943 Discovery of mass graves at Katyń leads to break-off of Polish–USSR relations.
Warsaw Ghetto Rising.

1944 (August to October) Warsaw Rising.

1945 The West recognises Soviet-sponsored provisional government of Poland.

1948 Polish United Workers' Party formed. Poland a one-party state. Removal of Władyslaw Gomułka from party leadership. Stalinist period begins.

1956 (June) Riots in Poznań.
(October) Gomułka returns to power. Stalinism abolished.

1968 'March Events': student riots in Warsaw and elsewhere.

1970 (December) Warsaw Treaty: West Germany recognises new Polish western frontier.

(December) Riots and strikes in Baltic ports. Fall of Gomułka, replaced by Edward Gierek.

1976 Riots at Radom, Ursus (Warsaw) and elsewhere.

1978 Cardinal Karol Wojtyła of Kraków elected Pope (John Paul II).

1979 First pilgrimage of John Paul II to Poland.

1980 (August) Strikes in Baltic ports lead to Agreements of Gdańsk, Szczecin, etc., and appearance of Solidarity independent trade union.

1981 (March) 'Bydgoszcz Incident'.

(13 December) General Wojciech Jaruzelski declares state of war, imposes martial law, suspends Solidarity, arrests thousands of union supporters.

1983 Second papal visit; end of martial law: general amnesty.

1984 (October) Murder of Father Popiełuszko.

1986 Second amnesty for political prisoners.

Preface

'The action of this play takes place in Poland – that is to say, nowhere.'
Those words were written ninety years ago, by a French schoolboy called Alfred Jarry. The play – *King Ubu* – which he had written to mock one of his teachers was to make him famous, and, by a queer irony, to inspire the playwrights of Poland's Theatre of the Absurd many years later. But the question he raised – where is Poland? – has puzzled and agonised both the Poles and their European neighbours all through history.

At the time Jarry was writing, Poland was indeed 'nowhere'. For many centuries, it had been a large and famous state. Then, in 1794, it vanished from the map, partitioned between Russia, Prussia and the Austrian Empire.

In 1918 Poland appeared again: its three conquerors had all collapsed in defeat and revolution. But the 'where?' of Poland – the extent of its frontiers – remained a problem which caused international quarrels, several minor wars and much bloodshed.

In 1939 Poland once more became 'nowhere' for six terrible years, invaded and partitioned by Nazi Germany and Soviet Russia. In the Second World War, set off by Hitler's attack on Poland, Stalin, Churchill and Roosevelt spent more time arguing about the 'where?' of the next Poland than about anything else. In the end, they shunted Poland two hundred miles to the west, to the place and shape it still has today.

Foreign diplomats and generals had learned something about Poland by the end of the war. But most ordinary people, especially in the West, knew little about Poland except that it had a tragic history and a heroic tradition of fighting for its independence. When Polish troops were stationed in Scotland during the war, many Scots assumed the Poles were a sort of Russian and wondered why they became so angry when one told them so. (In return, the Poles assumed the Scots were really English, and wondered why they became so angry when one told them so . . .)

After the war, the ignorance was dispelled a little. Poland had become a Communist state, and the West – especially Britain – was full of Poles who had decided not to return to home but to live in exile. And, as the years passed, Poland was often in the news: the most unpredictable and turbulent satellite in the Soviet 'empire'. But few people had any real impression of what Poland and the Poles were like, or of the look of this land 'behind the Iron Curtain, somewhere between Russia and Germany'.

This changed in 1980, the 'year of Solidarity'. In that year, Poland flung open a long-closed door and – mostly through television – re-entered the conciousness of the West. For two years, the world watched not merely a succession of incredible images, the scenes of a popular uprising unlike any in modern history, but also the spectacle of a nation loudly claiming its full membership of the European family. Passionate interest in Poland was now added to sympathy. And with this interest came a curiosity which has still not been satisfied.

For with the image came a sense that this nation, reclaiming its right to be a member of the international community, was all the same a most unusual member. More perhaps than any other European nation, Poland is consciously connected to its own history, living in and through that history. The past, whether in the form of the classics of Polish literature or in the form of political chronicles and folk-lore, is continuously used to prompt action in the present. What happens now is sure to have happened before; the figures on the stage today are only fresh actors playing the limited number of familiar parts.

The Russian liberal exile Alexander Herzen, who lived in London in the nineteenth century, was very aware of this unique intimacy of the Poles with their past. Whenever he tried to organise a common front between Polish and Russian revolutionaries against their joint enemy the Tsar, this attitude towards the past and the future came like a shadow between them. Herzen wrote: 'The ideal of the Poles was behind them: they strove towards their past from which they had been cut off by violence and which was the only starting-point from which they could advance again. They had masses of holy relics, while we had empty cradles.'

Herzen thought that because Polish nationalism 'strove towards its past', it was always conservative, even reactionary. But this was a simplification. Professor R. F. Leslie has written that every Polish struggle for independence has also become a social struggle over which element in society should dominate an independent Poland.[1] Among the 'holy relics' were many radical democratic ideas: revolutionary projects in Poland often come dressed in archaic uniforms. One of the mainstreams of the independence movement in the first decades of this century was socialist, drawing its main support from industrial workers, even though its leaders planned to revive the anachronism of a Polish–Lithuanian federation. Solidarity, a trade union which was

---

1. See *The History of Poland Since 1863*, ed. R. F. Leslie, Cambridge University Press, Cambridge, 1980, p. 3 and elsewhere.

reluctant to call itself 'socialist' and enjoyed a close relationship with the Catholic Church, in fact stood for a programme of workers' control of production which orthodox Communists regarded as dangerously extreme.

The course of Polish history is not just a string of tragedies. It is extraordinary, rich and often very disconcerting. In this century and the last, for example, the Polish experience has often seemed like the experience of the rest of Europe seen through a looking-glass. The end of the First World War, for most peoples a moment of defeat or of victory too bitter to be enjoyed, was for Poland the joyful return of independence after over a century during which the country did not appear on the European map. The victorious outcome of the Second World War appeared to many Poles – whose nation had been a member of the coalition against Hitler from the first day to the last – as another defeat, exchanging one form of subjugation for another. Because of the part they played in that war, fighting – as the old Polish revolutionary slogan has it – 'for your freedom and ours', Polish exiles and their descendants now live scattered in almost every country of western Europe and the New World. No other nation has suffered so much in this century, and gained so little.

Polish history is disconcerting in a second way: because it does strange things to abstract ideas and political -isms. In most lands, an ideology is a cloud which hangs over the landscape for a season and then drifts away. In Poland, clouds precipitate in hail, rain or snow; the results of an idea are all to palpable, visible, and often absurd. Bismarck's *Culture Struggle (Kulturkampf)* against the Catholic Church came to earth as weals on the bottoms of Polish pupils caned for speaking their mother-tongue. 'Romanticism' means armed men in a forest, or chained men in the snow. 'Communism' is a word painted on a fence, beyond which abandoned machines whose tyres have been stolen rust away in puddles. 'Solidarity' means a trade union.

In Poland, then, ideas crash to earth and all that is visible is their impact on human lives, more evident in that country than in most. But 'the Polish question' has never ceased to trouble European politics and at times to dictate them. Britain and France went to war for Poland in 1939; the anti-Hitler alliance with Stalin nearly collapsed over the disputed future of Poland; the new Polish western frontier on the Oder and Neisse rivers after 1945 became one of the most intractable problems of the Cold War and paralysed West German foreign policy for twenty years. Today Poland – far the biggest, most self-confident and least intimidated society of all those within the Soviet alliance – has acquired the character of a smoking volcano, quiescent after its latest discharge in 1980 but capable at any time of yet another eruption which could shatter the whole landscape of East–West relations.

This book was written to accompany *The Struggles for Poland*, the television series on Polish history in the twentieth century which is a co-production between Channel 4 in Britain, WNET in the United States and Norddeutscher

Rundfunk in West Germany. I worked as a consultant to those who prepared the series, and I have made use of much of their many hours of interview film with witnesses – and principal actors, and victims – of the period. Series and book, naturally, stand independently one of another. But I hope through this book to offer more background to those whose imagination has been seized by the television series, and – perhaps – to encourage readers to turn to television and watch for themselves the newsreels, the images and the faces which print cannot evoke.

The twentieth century is not yet over, and for the first eighteen years of it there was no state called Poland. At the opening of the century, there were few statesmen – indeed, few Poles – who thought that the restoration of an independent Poland was imminent or likely. The trend of Europe in 1900 was moving away from the idea of the smaller nation-state towards the big, centralised empires. It looked as if the Polish cause would soon become an irrevocably lost one. But the First World War, destroying the whole European order and upsetting all calculations, suddenly opened the way to a Polish resurrection.

Improvised and often chaotic, the new Poland drew its own frontiers in a flare of border conflicts fought out on the rubble of three collapsed empires. Then there began the long struggle to create a stable society, and to maintain an independent state within secure frontiers. It is a tale of disaster and courage, of desperate wars and insurrections, of a succession of imperious leaders from Piłsudski to Gomułka, of spectacular destruction and reconstruction.

But Poland is not – as it sometimes must seem – a doomed country, whose every dawn of hope ends in tragedy. Seen in a true perspective, this nation which so many statesmen have tried to abolish has moved ahead through terrible setbacks on its journey towards justice and effective independence – and it is still moving. The story of Poland is a story of hope, against all the odds.

1

The Rise and Fall
of Independent Poland:
966–1900

Polskość: The Polishness of Poland

'Poland is a very strange country, in which I always feel at home.' So said the French director Claude Lanzmann, who spent a long time filming in the remote Polish countryside. Many foreigners agree with him, as they leave a land which – in spite of their affection for it – they find bizarre, even exotic, in its past and present.

But what exactly is this 'strangeness'? Too much emphasis on the oddity of Poland becomes destructive, hiding a nation under a crust of caricature. And in the end it is very misleading. In important ways, Poland – one of the older European states – has been more 'normal' than its younger neighbours.

This is specially true of its history. For hundreds of years, Poland was an open, tolerant country with many races and religions. The power of the kings was limited by charters and agreements, and great matters were frequently decided by debates and votes. But on either side of it there slowly grew up the more primitive states of Prussia (a military kingdom demanding rigid obedience from its subjects) and Russia, with its tradition of hopeless servility before God-given tyrants. Between these neighbours an enlightened and progressive Poland, in many ways having more in common with western Europe, tried but eventually failed to survive.

The modern Polish novelist Kazimierz Brandys once divided the world into countries with corpses under the floorboards – including Germany and Russia – 'and those like France and Poland which have no corpses to hide'. When a visitor commented that Poland was an abnormal country, he retorted: 'It is a perfectly normal country between two abnormal ones.' Brandys points out that for three hundred years, between the Renaissance and the Partitions which abolished Polish independence, Poland functioned without great upheavals, stable 'at a time when Europe was staggered by peasant revolts, the Inquisition, dynastic wars, religious wars, the Hundred Years War, the Thirty Years War.

I

Who knows, perhaps it was Europe that was sick, all Europe with the exception of Poland?'

This is why a visitor to Poland who falls into conversation at once feels – like Claude Lanzmann – that he or she is in a way 'at home'. Talk about politics or the world is spirited, well informed, full of speculation – like the same kind of talk in Paris or Rome. In Russia, outside a very small intellectual élite, there is a provincialism of mind. Even modern West Germany, in comparison to Poland, is introverted, tending towards *Nabelschau* – inspection of one's own navel.

Poland's 'strangeness' arises from this very same problem of being 'a perfectly normal country between two abnormal ones'. Polish history seems outlandish to us because – after the disappearance of Poland from the atlas in 1794 – Poland was cut off from the outside world and ceased to be familiar. And the plight of Poland during the Partitions drove Poles to patterns of behaviour and thought which were so extreme – the great patriotic risings of the nineteenth century, the almost religious forms which nationalism took – that to luckier peoples they seem unnatural and bewildering.

All the same, the impression of 'strangeness' and the unfamiliarity of Poland have become realities which can't be argued away. Before reading an account of Polish history, it may be useful to summarise some of the elements of that history.

The land of Poland: a peasant countryside, patterned by family-owned strips of soil.

The country people of Poland, whose views and methods change only slowly. Catholic and patriotic, their ancient motto is 'We Nourish and Defend'.

Where is Poland? The brief answer is: in different places at different times. The Poles themselves, as an ethnic group, are a West Slav people speaking a Slav language whose relationship to Russian is – very roughly – like the relationship of Dutch to German. They have ranged over the flat, originally forested plains of northern Europe between the Oder river and the Pripet Marshes in the east. To the south, they have been bounded by the Carpathian range of mountains; to the north, by the Baltic Sea. The spinal chord of these lands is the Vistula river, rising in the southern mountains, flowing through Kraków in the south and Warsaw in central Poland to the sea at Gdańsk (Danzig).

Most of Poland is level, and – especially in the east – there are large primeval forests where boar, elk, wolves and bison can still be seen. Both these facts are politically important. The flatness has meant that Poland lies on the natural invasion route for those entering Europe from the east and for those attacking Russia from the west. It also means that Poland has no 'natural frontiers' across that east–west axis. As for the forests, they have provided shelter for generations of partisan fighters, most recently for the guerrilla soldiers of the resistance against Nazi occupation.

Most of Poland has fertile soil, although towards the east and north-east it becomes poor and sandy, sometimes broken up by marshes and by constellations of lakes. But it is rich in minerals. From the earliest times, the salt deposits

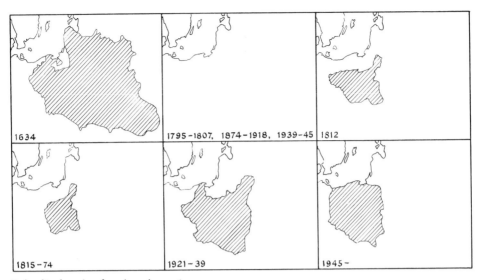

Poland's changing frontiers since 1634

near Kraków were a source of wealth and trade, and amber from the Baltic beaches was exported all over Europe. In modern times, first-class coking coal was discovered in Upper Silesia, in the south, and most recently mines for sulphur, copper and lignite (brown coal) have been opened up. But Poland depends on other countries for iron ore and for oil, although one of the first petroleum fields in Europe was established in East Galicia – a part of Poland annexed to the Soviet Union since 1945.

The climate tends to extremes, by European standards. There is usually bitter frost and deep snow in winter, and summer heat – in June, especially – can be intense. With these contrasts goes a tendency to natural calamities: droughts, floods and untimely frosts which kill spring crops. This, too, has political meaning, for Poland is a country where harvests are unpredictable. Feasting in abundance one year can be followed by famine the next. Poland must be the last country in Europe which still uses a word – *przednówek* – for the dangerous hunger gap in spring between consuming the remains of last year's crop and harvesting the next one.

Poland's frontiers have changed wildly throughout history. Sometimes Poland has been a sprawling empire stretching almost from the Black Sea to the Baltic. At other times it has been a little landlocked nucleus, or has vanished completely. At present, since the Allied leaders in 1945 decided to shift it bodily to the west, Poland is roughly where it was when it began a thousand years ago, in the time of the Piast dynasty. This series of changes led Bismarck, the supreme Prussian statesman of the nineteenth century, to dismiss Poland as a 'seasonal state', a sort of sandbank which grows larger or smaller depending on how the rains fill the river.

Who are the Poles? A state is not the same as a nation. This is where Bismarck went wrong, and why so many in the West – where nation and state have come to seem synonymous – find Poland puzzling. But the Poles never mix the two words up. A 'nation' is a group of people united by cultural or racial identity, often by both. Thus a Polish passport will describe somebody as 'citizenship: Polish; nationality: Ukrainian [or Jewish, or German]'. A state is simply the political superstructure which may contain several different 'nationalities'. A state can change its borders, or be suppressed altogether. A nation survives, even if it is moved to another place or unless – as in the case of Europe's Jews under Hitler – it is physically exterminated.

For almost all of Poland's history, it has been a multinational state. Until the nineteenth century, the statement 'I am a Pole' meant 'I am the subject of the Polish crown' and not 'I am a Polish-speaking Slav of the Polish race'.

The proper title of the Poland that was finally destroyed in 1794 was 'The Polish Commonwealth of the Kingdom of Poland and the Grand Duchy of Lithuania'. This state ruled not only people we would now describe as 'ethnic Poles' – Slavs speaking Polish and almost all of the Catholic religion – but also Lithuanians, Jews, Germans, Ukrainians, Byelorussians, Tartars and even some Scots. Their religions were Catholic, Judaic, Calvinist, Lutheran, Islamic, Eastern Orthodox and 'Uniate' (a section of the Orthodox Church which declared its allegiance to the Vatican).

Today, the picture is different. Almost all the inhabitants of modern Poland are Slav Poles who speak Polish, and most of them are practising Catholics. The new Poland created in 1945 is – for almost the first time – a state of one nation. A few small 'national minorities' remain. But almost all Poland's Jews were murdered by the Nazis; the Germans were expelled; the Lithuanians, Ukrainians and Byelorussians vanished behind the new western frontiers of the Soviet Union, leaving only a few thousand living inside Poland's borders. 'Who are the Poles?' is now a fairly straightforward question to answer. But in history the answer was very different and much more complicated.

The Partitions are the single most important fact of Polish history, and they helped to form most of the attitudes of modern Poles towards the world they live in.

In the late eighteenth century, after more than 800 years of existence, the Polish state was wiped off the map of Europe by violence, and divided between its three neighbours. There is nothing comparable to this in European history. The only parallels, which are remote, are the English conquest of Ireland, the Spanish conquest of Catalonia, and the crushing of Bohemia by the Habsburg Empire.

There were three Partitions, each reducing the size of Poland until the last one in 1795 abolished the state completely. From then until 1918 there was no independent Poland, although Napoleon set up briefly a puppet 'Grand

Duchy of Warsaw' between 1807 and 1813. For the whole of the nineteenth century, the period of the Industrial Revolution and of the greatest scientific and intellectual changes the human race has ever experienced, Poland as such was not present. Instead, there were Poles who lived in the Russian Empire, Poles who lived in Prussia (later the German Empire) and Poles who lived in the Habsburg Empire which became known as Austria-Hungary.

The Partitions lasted until 1918, when Poland regained its independence. This meant that they were still in living memory when Poland was partitioned again in 1939 between Hitler's Germany and the Soviet Union, who declared that the Polish state was an 'abortion' which had been abolished for ever. After Hitler's invasion of the Soviet Union in 1941, all Poland came under Nazi rule. This 'Fourth Partition', although it lasted for less than six years, brought with it more savagery and slaughter than all its predecessors. Hitler not only destroyed the state but – if he had not been defeated – would have proceeded to destroy the Polish nation as well by the same methods of mass murder which he applied to the Jews.

There were four major insurrections in occupied Poland during the Partitions, and countless national conspiracies. In a way, the 1944 Warsaw Rising against the Germans was a fifth insurrection. All the risings ended in

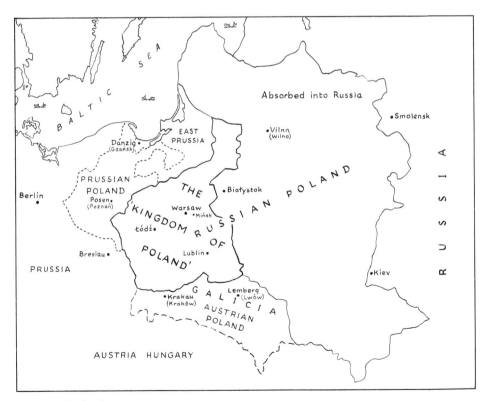

Partitioned Poland, 1815–1918

heroic defeat. But the Poles became practised conspirators, and developed a lasting disrespect for all authority – which for so long was foreign.

Russia and Prussia, especially, tried to suppress both Polish culture and language and the Catholic faith. In response, the Poles developed one of the most intense and self-sacrificing versions of Romantic nationalism ever seen in Europe. In its most extreme form – known as 'Messianism' – Poland was thought to be the collective reincarnation of Christ, to be crucified and then resurrected for the redemption of all nations.

During the nineteenth century, the definition of a 'Pole' gradually changed. The Partition powers – on the 'divide and rule' principle – played off the ambitions of the other nationalities against those of the Slav and Catholic Poles. As a result, the old idea of a multi-racial Poland decayed, as the ethnic Poles came to suspect other races – especially Ukrainians and Jews – of collaborating with the Partition powers and of lacking commitment to the fight to regain independence. The ethnic, Catholic Poles began to regard themselves as the 'real Poland', and their racial and religious prejudices against others – which had always existed – became much more intense. By the end of the century, the conservative wing of Polish nationalism had become sharply anti-Semitic.

During the Partitions, and especially after the November Rising in 1830, a large part of Poland's political, military and cultural leadership fled abroad. They settled in Paris, above all, where they became the recognised voice of their suppressed nation in the world. Much of the planning of the insurrections took place in Paris or London, and the best part of Poland's classic literature was composed in France. In the First World War, committees of Polish exiles in France and Switzerland were able to persuade Britain, France and the United States to restore an independent Poland after their victory. In the Second World War, the Poles followed the same tradition by setting up a government in exile near Paris and then in London.

In the later nineteenth century, there began an enormous economic emigration from the Polish lands, mostly of poor peasant families seeking a better life in North America or in the coal-mining areas of France, Belgium and Germany.

Out of these two very different currents of emigration there grew up the idea of *Polonia* – the notion that Poland did not exist only on the river Vistula but throughout the world, wherever Polish communities had settled. There is only one familiar parallel to this. It is the worldwide Diaspora of the Jews, and their attachment to the idea – and then the reality – of the land of Israel.

The period of the Partitions left the Poles with violent but sometimes very mixed feelings about the rest of Europe. It was natural enough that they learned to hate and distrust Russians and Germans. But there were differences even here. With the Prussians and Germans, seen by Poles as inhuman and mechanical, it was difficult to make any contact. Polish attitudes to Russia, though, were more contradictory. There was contempt for Russian 'barbar-ousness', but also a fascination with Russia's size and power. There was loathing for the Russian schoolmaster bullying children who spoke Polish in class, but there was also real affection – even a sense of Slav kinship – for the open-heartedness and generosity of simple Russians. This is a mixture of emotions that has lasted.

During the Partitions, the Poles came to see France as their truest friend in the outside world. There was some background to this: the French and Polish royal families had intermarried, French had become the polite language of the great Polish aristocrats, and Poland had drawn many ideas from the Enlightenment and the Revolution of 1789 before its fall. Afterwards, Napoleon supported the Polish cause (for his own ends), and for most of the nineteenth century French governments not only welcomed Polish exiles but loudly endorsed their calls for the restoration of independence.

Apart from words, though, not much was done to help. As the years passed, and the twentieth century began, Polish feelings not just about France but about the United States and Britain became ambiguous. These were 'free' countries in which – France especially – Poles felt at home. At the same time, Poles came to realise that these governments would offer their country little more than sympathy and applause. The Poles felt themselves to be culturally part of 'the Christian West', but the West did not reciprocate – would, indeed, betray Poland for the sake of a quiet life. As a result, attitudes towards the West became the queer compound they still remain: yearning admiration combined with sardonic mistrust. The Second World War, which left most Poles with a sense that they had been betrayed and abandoned by their Allies in the West, strongly reinforced this trauma.

After nearly two centuries of intermittent persecution the Catholic Church in Poland has emerged more influential in civil society than in almost any other country in the world. Well over three-quarters of the population, including many members of the Polish United Workers' Party (the Communists) regard themselves as believers. At the same time, the Church itself in Poland is unusual in its attitudes. It is highly conservative over matters like abortion and contraception, but at the same time 'classless': a church of the people. It is intensely patriotic and often openly 'political', claiming a special right to act as the voice of popular opinion about anything from working conditions in factories to the curricula of universities.

This is the result of the Partitions, and especially of that 'Fourth Partition' of the Nazi occupation. After 1795, the Catholic Church became the main institution which preserved and defended Polish culture, language and identity against foreign oppression. The 'Black Madonna', the ancient icon of the Virgin which is kept in Poland's holiest shrine, the monastery at Częstochowa,

The Black Madonna of Częstochowa, Poland's most beloved icon. The scars on her cheek are said to have been made by the swords of Hussite heretics.

became – with her sad, scarred face – the symbol of Poland's suffering and hope. Many priests and some bishops took part in the patriotic conspiracies and risings of the nineteenth century. As in Ireland under the English, the Catholic faith and the struggle for independence became fused and inseparable in the minds of the population.

Although many priests saw themselves as 'Polish soldiers in black uniform', most of the bishops at first did not. In the first patriotic risings in 1794, the Warsaw revolutionaries hanged two bishops as traitors, and the Primate committed suicide. The Vatican through most of the Partition period condemned all the efforts to restore Polish independence, and supported the Russian Tsars even though they were systematically persecuting the Catholic Church in their Polish lands. An example was the fate of Father Ściegenny, a priest who encouraged peasants to resist the Tsar. When the Tsar protested to Rome, the Pope unfrocked Father Ściegenny and allowed him to be imprisoned. This pattern repeated itself in the Second World War, when Pope Pius XII shocked the Poles by his reluctance to condemn the Nazi occupation in strong terms, even though over 3,000 priests, monks and nuns were murdered. Today, with a Polish Pope, relations between the Vatican and the Church in Poland are intimate. But they have never been so before.

Lastly, the Partitions gave a special, mystical quality to Polish nationalism. 'Messianism', the idea of Poland as a new Christ, has been mentioned. With it went the idea – still voiced by Pope John Paul II – of the sanctity of a nation. Polish Catholics talk as if God created Man in three concentric circles: the individual, the family, and the nation. Any earthly ruler who raises his hand against the independence of a free nation is violating God's law as plainly as a ruler who destroys the rights and the moral independence of a single man or woman. This is why this Polish Pope kisses the ground of each nation that he visits, and why Poles consider their struggles for justice and independence not only as a political cause but also as a moral crusade.

Kingdom, Commonwealth and Partition

On 21 February 1900, the Russian police broke into a first-floor apartment on Wschodnia (East) Street, in the industrial city of Łódź. Here they found two items which they had been seeking for six years all over the Russian-occupied part of Poland, and even in the capital of St Petersburg itself. One was a small but lovingly maintained British printing-press, the source of the underground newspaper *Robotnik (The Worker)* which had carried the views of the Polish Socialist Party, the call for national revolution and social justice, to tens of thousands of Poles throughout the Russian Empire and to their fellow countrymen abroad.

The first number of *Robotnik (The Worker)*, the clandestine newspaper of the Polish Socialist Party which Piłsudski edited. Dated June 1894, it carries as its masthead the slogan of Karl Marx: 'Proletarians of All Lands, Unite!'

Pierwszy numer „Robotnika"

The second was a young man with a moustache and fierce grey eyes. At thirty-three Józef Piłsudski was already regarded as one of the 'elders' of the Polish Socialist Party (PPS), a bold and experienced conspirator who had spent five years in Siberian exile. He has been described as 'the most formidable leader of revolt in all the story of Polish revolution'. He was an overwhelming personality and a natural leader, but also a professional genius in the patient, detailed and often ruthless work of clandestine resistance.

Eighteen years later, Piłsudski was to take charge of his nation and organise its independence. By then, he had shown still more talents: as a military commander of troops on the conventional battlefield, and as a remarkably gifted and vivid writer. Only then did it become apparent that there was one skill that he lacked. Piłsudski, whose whole life had been spent in the peremptory, authoritarian world of resistance to tyranny and of armed struggle, never found his feet in the conduct of democratic politics. He was not a conciliator.

He was born in a country manor in Lithuania, to a family of the Polish squires who had dominated that country for centuries, only four years after the suppression of the last great Polish insurrection which began in January 1863. He grew up in a land helplessly exposed to the Russian vengeance that followed the January Rising: executions, torturings, arrests, deportation to Siberia, the confiscation of estates, the suppression of Polish culture and language, and the persecution of the Catholic Church. At school, Piłudski's teachers were Russians who sneered at his Polishness and treated him as an alien in his own country. `

Józef Piłsudski acquired a hatred and fear of Russia which never left him. The Polish gentry in Lithuania were little affected by the doctrines of compromise, of a sort of patriotic adaptation to foreign rule, which became widespread in other parts of the divided nation in the years after 1863. They remained true to the older tradition of romantic conspiracy, which looked to yet another armed insurrection to liberate Poland.

For all his hostility to Russia, Piłsudski was a child of the Russian Empire whose conditions largely formed his own political outlook. Traditions of the Polish gentry contributed to his views. But so, too, did the fact that he grew up in an autocratic state ruled by force, in which the possibility of bringing about change by open political activity did not exist – and had never existed. The dissenter was condemned to become a revolutionary. It has been rightly pointed out that there were parallels between Piłsudski's background and that of Lenin, his near-contemporary. Both came from families of the minor aristocracy. Both were involved through their brothers in the attempt to assassinate Tsar Alexander III in 1887; Lenin's brother was hanged, while Bronisław Piłsudski was sentenced to fifteen years' imprisonment. Both spent years in Siberian exile; Lenin's spell came some seven years later, but Józef Piłsudski was banished for his marginal part in the plot of 1887. Both took their political style from the desperate necessities of conspiracy. Both became socialists – but here the comparison ends. For while Lenin's Marxism was a profound and permanent conversion grounded upon ideological acceptance, Piłsudski can be called a 'socialist of convenience'.

He studied socialist literature, and in Siberia read *Das Kapital* to the end. But it was essentially the style of socialist struggle that appealed to him, rather than its class analysis. National liberation remained his real priority. Socialism – in Russian conditions – appealed to him as simply the most professional and pitiless form of conspiracy against the Tsardom.

The problem of Polish insurrections in the past had been to mobilise the peasant masses behind leaders who generally sprang from the landowning class. By the end of the nineteenth century Poland was still basically rural, far less industrialised than most of western Europe. But an urban working class had developed in many of the Polish cities, harshly exploited and ripe for revolt. Through a socialist programme, the proletariat could be enlisted in the national cause. As Piłsudski and many of his contemporaries saw it, liberation from the foreign oppressor would at the same time mean liberation from enforced poverty and helpless exploitation. The social question and the national question were interdependent, and there was no way to solve them separately. Here was the thinking behind Piłsudski's remark that 'a Polish socialist must aim for the independence of the country, and independence is the indispensable condition for the victory of socialism in Poland'.

On that February day in 1900 Piłsudski stood in the Łódź apartment, watching the police take away his printing-press and waiting to be taken away himself to prison, perhaps to death. Some days later, his interrogator remarked that his newspaper was finished at last. 'But, Captain,' Piłsudski replied, 'I am quite sure that the next number of *Robotnik* is being printed at this moment.' And he was right, although it was being produced in London and would be delayed by the problems of smuggling it across several frontiers.

'At the beginning of the twentieth century, as zoologists relate, there broke out in the region of Wilno a war between the native rats and a tribe of rats from the upper Volga, who gnawed their way through our good old rats and conquered their territory. It was a holy war conducted underground, a war which took place beneath the floorboards, and the people walking on the boards knew nothing about it.'[1]

So wrote the editor and historian Stanisław Mackiewicz, reflecting on the phase of Piłsudski's struggle which ended with his arrest in 1900. Piłsudski himself remembered those times as 'mole-work' or 'rat-work'. As his captors led him off, he could be proud that his own energy had produced an illegal newspaper with a circulation far higher than that of any other revolutionary

1. Stanisław Mackiewicz, *Klucz do Piłsudskiego*, published by the author, London, 1943, p. 68.

sheet in the Russian Empire. And yet an impartial observer of the condition of partitioned Poland in 1900 would not have shared his confidence in the future. Most Poles walking on the floor of ordinary life knew nothing of him or his work, although they were aware that something was going on beneath the planks.

The situation at the turn of the century was a strange one. Poland had lost its independence just over a hundred years before, and remained partitioned between Russia, Austria-Hungary and the German Empire, which had inherited the conquests of Prussia. On the one hand, the profound discourage- ment which had fallen upon the Poles after the failure of the January Rising in 1863 was rapidly wearing off. The sober doctrines which gained support in the decades after the Rising, suggesting that the true patriotism was to avoid head-on conflict with the occupiers and build up the economic and cultural strength of the nation by hard work, agricultural improvement and social organisation – this cautious approach was out of fashion. Political parties were being founded, some operating openly in the relatively tolerant conditions of the Austrian partition, others underground. Higher education, some of it clandestine, was reviving even under the Russians. In the Prussian partition, a vigorous and quite successful struggle was being waged on the land to resist German colonisation. The economic turn-down at the end of the century, which had reached the dimensions of a severe slump in Russia, was spreading bankruptcies and unemployment and undermining the case for patient, constructive work. The new generation, which had not experienced the devastating consequences of 1863, was disinclined to be patient.

But even if Polish nationalism was reviving, the condition of Europe in 1900 offered little opening for the restoration of Poland. In many ways, it looked as though a tide had turned, and that the Poles had missed their historical opportunities.

In the first half of the nineteenth century, Polish independence had been high in the priorities of European liberalism. Revolutions then were 'national' revolutions, the liberation of peoples from an 'international' league of reactionary Popes, Emperors and Kings. France, above all, had given moral support to the Polish cause, and had welcomed the Polish exiles after the failed insurrection of 1830–31; they were given state pensions corresponding to their rank. Even in Germany, a young revolutionary generation had given its heart to the Poles as the bravest fighters in the struggle for national liberty and constitutional government. But after the revolutionary wave of 1848, in which Polish exiles fought on the barricades in France, Italy and Germany, in Prague, Vienna and in the tremendous national uprising in Hungary, the climate slowly changed. The surge of 1848 failed to overthrow the systems in Austria and Prussia, and did not touch Russia. Germans, faced in 1848 with the threat that Polish independence would mean the partial dismemberment of Prussia, withdrew their sympathy.

By 1900, a 'realistic' assessment of Polish chances could only be discouraging. Prussia had become the controlling element in a German Empire. Russia had begun to industrialise, enforcing an even more centralized and repressive regime on its dominions. The Habsburg Empire had become a 'dual monarchy' of Austria-Hungary in 1867, but attempts by Galicia, the Polish province under Austrian control, to win an autonomous status like that of Hungary had been weak and unsuccessful.

The trend in Europe seemed to be towards consolidation into a few vast supranational powers, towards a new epoch in which the aspirations of small, suppressed nationalities would become anachronisms. Both Germany and Russia had embarked on policies designed to eradicate what remained of Polish cultural and political identity. The huge scale of modern armies and the power of their weapons, now rapidly mobile along railway lines constructed principally for military reasons, reduced the chances of any old-fashioned national uprising.

In the Polish lands themselves, there were signs that the old cause of independence was beginning to disintegrate. Industrial capitalism, developing most rapidly in the Russian partition, established its markets and its finance within the separate framework of the three empires, and – even where its owners were Polish – saw its interests in gradual change and reform rather than in the violent upheaval of national revolution.

Socialism, too, led in new directions. Piłsudski and the Polish Socialist Party (PPS) were isolated in their belief that national liberation and the emancipation of the working class were a single, indistinguishable issue. The mainstream of Marxist thinking and politics in Russia and Germany was internationalist, treating the resentments of subject peoples in multinational empires merely as a means towards an end: the universal proletarian revolution, in which differences of nationality would be transcended. The first socialist movement in Poland, *Proletariat*, had been internationalist and had collaborated closely with Russian revolutionaries before it was crushed and its leaders hanged or imprisoned in 1884. One of its orators had proclaimed: 'Down with patriotism and reaction! Long live the international social revolution!' The same attitude to Polish independence, even more forcefully argued, was now being taken by the Social Democratic Party of the Kingdom of Poland (SDKP), founded in 1893, the same year as the PPS.

Finally, even the ideology of nationalism itself was beginning to create problems for Polish patriots. By the end of the nineteenth century, Ukrainians living in the east of what had once been independent Poland were beginning to assert a political identity of their own. Inevitably, a divide-and-rule policy was attempted by the partitioning powers. The Polish landowners of Galicia, in regions with a Ukrainian majority, were alarmed by this development, and it confirmed their view that Polish interests were best protected by a loyalist, conciliating policy towards the Austro-Hungarian authorities. Here was a vicious circle. The Polish identity was now under challenge from above and from below as well, from the assimilationist policies of the Empires and from the ambitions of those whom the Poles had tended to look upon as 'subject peoples'. The more the Polish gentry asked for Austrian protection against the Ukrainians, the stronger became their dependence on the survival of the Empire.

But what was it, anyway, that Polish patriots wished to restore? This was not a simple question. Poland had not been an island, but a multinational state with no natural boundaries except the Baltic Sea to the north and the mountain wall of the Carpathians in the south. In its 800 years of existence, ending with the Third Partition in 1795, its frontiers had shifted all over the map of eastern Europe. To demand the 'restoration of Poland' was to meet the question: 'Which Poland, of what kind?'

Two elements had dominated most of Polish history. One was the relationship between Poland and Lithuania, the huge and more primitive dukedom to the north-east which remained pagan until the end of the fourteenth century. The second was the exceptionally strong position of the Polish nobility and gentry, which became the dominant class in society in the late Middle Ages and which prevented the development of an absolute monarchy.

The Polish state was founded in 966. It was in the tenth century that tribal groups all over eastern Europe began to settle and consolidate into relatively stable kingdoms. One of these groups, the Polane, established its area of control in 'Great Poland' (the lands around Poznań), and under King Mieszko I extended its influence as far as the mouths of the Vistula on the Baltic Sea, where the city of Gdańsk now stands. Mieszko's acceptance of the western form of Christianity in 966 is held to mark the origins of the Polish state. The Piast dynasty, which he founded, ruled until 1138.

After the Piast period, in the thirteenth century, Poland began to suffer the foreign invasions and encroachments which have plagued the nation ever since. Two Mongol hosts swept in from the east, devastating the land and slaughtering the Polish armies which tried to halt them. Near the end of the century, the German crusading order of the Teutonic Knights conquered eastern Prussia, a region inhabited at the time by pagan peoples of Baltic origin, which was beyond the limits of Polish control. This was an aspect of the great colonising movement of Germans towards the east; Poland benefited in many ways from this movement, which brought her immigrant craftsmen and scholars and led to the foundation of new villages and town settlements under German law. There was nothing peaceful about the Teutonic Knights, who were soon in conflict with the Poles along the Baltic coast. But Poland continued to develop as a remarkably multinational structure, especially in the towns, a trend which was further advanced in the brilliant reign of Casimir the

Great (1333–70). Casimir gave Poland its first written laws, rebuilt Kraków into a magnificent capital and – an act with great consequences – welcomed into Poland thousands of Jews fleeing from persecution in the Rhineland.

In the fourteenth century, the Kingdom of Poland entered a historic partnership with the Grand Duchy of Lithuania, a union which transformed the whole extent and future of Poland. The Lithuanian union began in 1385, when Jagiełło of Lithuania, prince of the only pagan nation left in Europe, was persuaded to marry the eleven-year-old Princess Jadwiga in Kraków. In return, he accepted baptism and ordered his people to adopt Roman Catholic Christianity. He was elected king the following year by the Polish nobility.

In outline, the Polish–Lithuanian union went through much the same stages as the union between England and Scotland several centuries later. It began as a union of crowns: Jagiełło and his successors were at once kings of Poland and Grand Dukes of Lithuania, while the political systems of the two nations remained separate. Finally, after nearly 200 years of association, the Union of Lublin in 1569 brought Poland and the Grand Duchy together into a single 'Commonwealth' with one united parliament (Sejm). The Polish–Lithuanian Commonwealth was to last for over 200 years, binding together races of entirely different origins and language. After the Lublin Union, the Lithuanian nobility and gentry – originally a warrior caste speaking an East Slav dialect but ruling a population of Baltic language – became steadily 'polonised', reinforced by immigration and intermarriage from Poland proper until by the late eighteenth century the landowning and dominating class in Lithuania was *'plus polonais que les polonais'* – the main source of Romantic Polish patriotism.

The Jagiełło dynasty ruled Poland until just after the Lublin Union. At the outset, especially, these were dangerous years. The threat of the fanatical and aggressive Teutonic Knights had to be confronted.

At the great battle of Grunwald in 1410, the Order was defeated by the combined Polish and Lithuanian armies. The Teutonic Knights were not finally subdued until the Peace of Toruń over fifty years later, but the breaking of their power allowed Poland to gain control of the Baltic seaboard around the city of Gdańsk. By dazzling good fortune, the whole length of the Vistula river, stretching from the fertile plains of central and southern Poland to the seaport of Gdańsk at its mouth, had now returned to Polish possession just as the growing populations of northern Europe were looking for fresh supplies of grain. Through the 'Vistula grain trade', Poland was to feed the soaring prosperity of western Europe in the Renaissance as North America's prairie wheat was to feed the Industrial Revolution in Europe three centuries later.

The Jagellonian dominions expanded. They reached their maximum after 1490 when, for a brief period and through dynastic marriages, not only Poland and Lithuania but the kingdoms of Hungary and Bohemia owed allegiance to the Crown of the Jagiełłos. They were the princes of almost all central and eastern Europe. Only the duchy of Muscovy, far to the east, remained beyond their control, labouring to unite the territories of what would become modern Russia.

But the victory over the Teutonic Knights, which made the Jagellonian kings mighty, also began the process of limiting their royal power. The Polish nobility was seeking to entrench its rights against the monarchy. Even before the Peace of Toruń in 1466, the nobles had struck a bargain with the king, selling him their military support in the war in return for privileges which included the establishment of provincial and national assemblies. Here were the origins of the Polish parliament, the Sejm, and the seeds of a 'noble democracy' which was to put bounds on the power of the crown. But here, too, was the beginning of a fateful segregation in society, lifting the aristocracy to the status of a class so self-confident and powerful that it came to identify itself as 'the nation'. The gentry – ranging from magnates with huge estates to petty squires with only a patch of land, composed not only of Poles but of Lithuanians, Germans and eventually a number of Jewish nobles – was 'the nation', while the burghers of the towns and the peasantry on the land were merely subjects.

This was not as outrageous as it sounds. In much of Europe at the time, a nation was defined as a series of 'estates': nobles, the Church, the burghers and commoners, and so on. But there was always a large mass of the poor 'below the line' who belonged to no 'estate' and were not considered to be part of the political nation at all, even though they usually formed a majority of the population. The Polish 'noble estate' merely pulled the line upwards until it excluded from 'the nation' almost everyone but its own members.

There was good and bad in this 'gentry power'. It meant that the Commonwealth was a primitive and limited democracy, in which no king could ever attain absolute control – a contrast to the grimly autocratic systems soon to arise on either side of Poland in Prussia and Russia. The gentry, perhaps ten per cent of the total population, enjoyed their 'golden freedom' by developing a high-spirited, generous, often wild and hard-drinking style of life; their proud impulsiveness and touchy independence have left their mark on Polish behaviour to this day. On the other hand, the Commonwealth was not only difficult to govern but – more importantly – almost impossible to adapt to changing conditions.

The sixteenth century was Poland's 'Golden Age'. All through the period, the privileges of the gentry continued to accumulate. They had personal immunity against the law, freedom to follow any faith and – from 1496 – a monopoly on landholding; the burghers had to sell what land they possessed. They acquired increasing power over the peasants on their land, who were steadily reduced to the condition of serfs, forbidden to leave the estate.

Here was a real divergence between the histories of eastern and western Europe. In the West, rural slavery or serfdom was rapidly vanishing by the late Middle Ages, partly due to the shortage of labour caused by plague, and was being replaced by wage labour. But in central and eastern Europe – not only in Poland, but in the whole region from eastern Germany to Russia, from the Baltic south to Hungary – serfdom became far more common in the same period, and survived until the nineteenth century. The cause seems to have been the increasing monopoly of political power by the noble classes, reinforced by the new wealth of the great estates which exported grain to the West.

In 1505, the nobles extorted from the Crown the *Nihil Novi* (Nothing New) statute, a pledge that no new taxes or laws would be applied without the consent of both chambers of the Sejm. In 1573, when the last of the Jagiełło kings died, the nobility finally secured the right to elect the monarch – not through their representatives in the Sejm but at a vast, often chaotic, rally of the entire gentry at Warsaw.

In the sixteenth century, the Polish gentry – and not just the bigger landowners – prospered as the rye and wheat from their estates was floated down the Vistula on rafts and sold at Gdańsk to German, Dutch and Scottish merchants. But this was an agricultural boom. The urban development and the rise of a native middle class which was taking place so rapidly in western and northern Europe at this period was only stunted in Poland. Especially in smaller towns, jealous local landowners controlled trade and prices; serfdom meant that it was almost impossible for peasants to move off the land, find work in towns and enter trade, and most commerce stayed in the hands of Jews, Germans and Scots. Some of the money rubbed off on the towns; cities like Kraków or Toruń acquired magnificent buildings and became centres of craftsmanship, high art and science. But no coherent middle class emerged in Poland, as it did in the West, to challenge the old landed nobility for economic and political influence.

The sixteenth-century Reformation came to Poland mostly from Bohemia. Today, the overwhelming mass of Poles in almost all layers of society are fervently Catholic, and allegiance to the Roman Catholic faith – and loyalty to the Vatican – is commonly regarded as an integral part of Polish patriotism. But this was not always so. Lutheranism, Calvinism and other Protestant faiths made rapid headway in Poland, while some forty per cent of the total population of the Commonwealth, mostly in the Lithuanian lands, already belonged to the Orthodox Church. The Reformation scarcely affected the mass of the Polish peasantry, who held to their old Catholic faith, but Lutheranism was strong in the towns, especially among the Germans, and a part of the nobility adopted Calvinism: more, perhaps, as a way of outflanking and reducing the ecclesiastical jurisdiction of the Catholic church than out of passionate conviction.

Poland escaped the religious wars that racked Germany and the West. In 1573, the Confederation of Warsaw declared that 'we who differ in matters of religion will keep the peace among ourselves'. In comparison to most other

European states, the Commonwealth was a haven of amazing toleration. There were confrontations and riots between Protestant and Catholic, principally in the towns, which have led the historian Norman Davies to describe Poland as a place where 'toleration, as distinct from tolerance' prevailed. But even the arrival of the Counter-Reformation, slowly converting the majority of the population back to a more intense and inward version of the Catholic faith, did not lead to an era of religious persecution and martyrdom. Witch-hunting, rising to an appalling peak in the early eighteenth century, sent tens of thousands of innocent women to the stake. But Protestantism, unable to compete with the missionary energy of the Jesuits, above all, declined almost without bloodshed. The Protestant nobles lost much of their interest in the Reformation once they had achieved their aims through the Confederation of Warsaw.

The seventeenth century brought war to Poland. Central Europe was devastated by the Thirty Years War, in which the Commonwealth was only marginally involved. But Poland repeatedly invaded Muscovy, and in 1648 was faced with a huge Cossack rising in the Ukraine led by the Hetman Chmielnicki whose troops massacred both Jews and Protestants in the territories they controlled.

In 1655, there took place the catastrophic Swedish invasion remembered as 'the Deluge', which conquered most of Poland and laid it waste. The Swedes were not driven out of Poland until the Peace of Oliwa in 1660; a renewed war against Russia followed, and then, in 1672, Poland became the first victim of Turkey's final and greatest onslaught on the heartlands of Europe.

In 1683, King Jan Sobieski of Poland won the battle of Vienna, ending for ever the Turkish threat to Catholic Europe. Sobieski had been elected king for his prowess as a general, commanding the forces of the Commonwealth against the Turks in intermittent wars which raged for nearly ten years. Now, as the Turkish armies besieged Vienna, he led the combined Polish and Austrian forces to a total and legendary victory. A heavy, bluff man who carried his glory lightly, talking to his subjects with a directness and simplicity rare among kings, Jan Sobieski became immortal in Polish folk-memory as the saviour of the Christian West from the heathen. He deserves the honour. But it is also true that by his triumph at Vienna, Sobieski removed from the scene the only military power which might have checked the rise of Russia to imperial strength.

The Commonwealth now entered a period of decline. Further wars in the early eighteenth century ensured that the damage of the previous fifty years was never made good. The political system fell into decay. The 'democracy of the gentry' came inevitably to mean the predominance of a few great families,

King Jan Sobieski (1674–96). At Vienna in 1683, he routed the Turkish armies and saved the city, ending for ever the Turkish threat to central Europe. In the background can be seen the battle, with the spire of St Stephen's rising over Vienna.

fiercely competing for influence and increasingly ready to ally themselves with foreign powers to attain their ends.

The Sejm had now adopted the *Liberum Veto* system, the rule of unanimity, which allowed a single member to halt all proceedings with a cry of *nie pozwalam* – 'I do not permit'. The invitation to corruption, obvious enough, was accepted eagerly by outsiders; Russia, in particular, presented herself as the guarantor of the 'noble democracy' which kept the Commonwealth so conveniently weak.

The eighteenth century is the focus of intense arguments about Polish history. One school of thought sees it as a shameful time, in which the nobility deliberately allowed the Commonwealth to lapse into anarchy and into fatal dependence on its hostile neighbours for motives of blind egotism and greed. Others point out that Poland was the victim of its virtues. Only Britain had developed a more effective system of early democracy and constitutional monarchy, and Poland–Lithuania remained in some respects more tolerant than Britain. It was hardly Poland's fault that its neighbours to east and west were the absolutist states of Russia and Prussia, politically and culturally far less advanced.

The old saying *nierządem Polska stoi* – roughly, 'the essential thing about Poland is unrule' – was not contemptuous. Given a chance, this fluid combination of the King, the Sejm and the gentry could have evolved towards an enlightened parliamentary democracy. Poland's tragedy is that it did so, but only when it was already too late.

Poland's weakness was made manifest in 1733 when Russian armies intervened to depose the elected king, Stanisław Leszczyński, and replace him by a more pliable monarch. But there followed a period of relative peace, in which intellectual energy revived: a season of new ideas for the political and economic revival of the Commonwealth. It was in this atmosphere that, in 1764, Stanisław August Poniatowski was elected to the throne. He was to be the last king of an independent Poland.

Nobody expected much of him. He had been the lover of Catherine II of Russia, and she, through her Polish contacts in the Czartoryski family, engineered his election. But almost at once this apparently feeble courtier began manoeuvering to increase the power of the Crown, to reform and modernise the political structure of Poland by reducing the influence of the magnates, and to restore some of the Commonwealth's lost independence. A crisis with Russia opened when he attempted to curtail the Sejm's unanimity rule. The Russians responded by cynically organising the Orthodox and Protestant interests against him. Stanisław August survived this challenge, but in 1768 there broke out what was in effect the first Polish insurrection in the cause of independence, the Confederation of Bar.

This was a nobles' rising, strongly Catholic in character, and directed not only against Russian interference but against the King's apparent compliance with Russian pressure. It failed, after four years of war against both Russian and royal forces, and in 1772 Frederick the Great of Prussia was able to persuade Catherine and Joseph II, the young Austrian Emperor, that the 'chaotic' condition of Poland justified a forcible and drastic reduction of the Commonwealth. Through this 'First Partition', Russia, Prussia and Austria annexed almost a third of Poland's territory and thirty-five per cent of its inhabitants. In the style of many future crimes of aggression, the Partition was proclaimed to be a high-minded action designed to secure the stability of Europe. But, as Norman Davies has put it, the Commonwealth 'was not destroyed because of its internal anarchy. It was destroyed because it repeatedly tried to reform itself'.

In his mutilated kingdom, Stanisław August did his best to press forward with reforms. The army was reorganised and an attempt was made to relieve the condition of the peasantry. In 1773 the National Education Commission was set up, in effect the first ministry of education in Europe. In 1788 there met the Four-Year Sejm, dominated by men of high intellectual calibre who had absorbed with enthusiasm the ideas of the Enlightenment in the West.

The Constitution of the Third of May, one of the proudest achievements of all Polish history, was their work. It was drafted and passed in 1791, at a moment when most of the reformers' parliamentary opponents were absent from the Sejm. It was the zenith of Poland's astonishing revival at the end of the century. The Constitution's provisions, had they ever been applied, would have transformed the nation. The Sejm's disastrous unanimity rule was to be dropped, the throne was to be made hereditary rather than elective and a Cabinet (including the king and the Roman Catholic primate) was to be established: three reforms which would have given the state real authority at last. The town citizens were to be given the same civil rights as the nobility, and the peasantry was declared to be under the protection of the law of the land.

But almost all these changes were to remain on paper. It was inconceivable that Russia, above all, would allow a strong and radical parliamentary democracy to emerge from the mutilated rump of the old Commonwealth. Russia invaded Poland in 1792, supported by the Confederation of Targowica, a conspiracy of Polish magnates organised in Russia and committed to overthrow both the Sejm and the new Constitution. Stanisław August won some early victories against the Russians but then, foreseeing defeat and anxious to spare Poland total destruction, gave in. While a stream of reforming intellectuals and officers left for the West, shattered by the King's collapse of will, Stanisław August signed the Confederation of Targowica. Meanwhile, a Prussian army entered Poland from the other flank. There followed the Second Partition of 1793.

Austria did not take part this time. But Russia annexed another immense slice of what had belonged to the Grand Duchy of Lithuania, while Prussia took Gdańsk on the Baltic and a swathe of western Poland stretching from the

Poznań region to Toruń on the middle Vistula. The Sejm, meeting at Grodno, was forced to recognise the Second Partition and repeal the Constitution of the Third of May.

But Stanisław August had lost his authority; the only power now visible in the land was the Russian army. As in France in the same period, the mood in Poland which had begun with constitutional reform in the name of Reason was stoked up by foreign invasion into a blaze of radicalism that was revolutionary and patriotic at once.

An army mutiny in March 1794 exploded into national insurrection. On 24 March, in the ancient market square of Kraków, Tadeusz Kościuszko took the oath to restore the independence of Poland and establish 'general liberty'.

Kościuszko, a professional soldier who had trained in France and fought in the American War of Independence, was well aware of the revolutionary surge in Polish opinion and saw that his only chance was to enlist the peasant masses in the national cause. On 7 May, he issued the *Manifesto of Polaniec*, abolishing serfdom and promising that the new insurrectionary government would defend the peasants against their landlords. At the battle of Racławice, the charge of peasants armed with scythes and pikes stormed through the Russian guns and put the enemy to flight. Warsaw rose against the occupiers, led by the tailor Jan Kiliński and by a committee openly supporting the ideas of Jacobin revolution in France. In both Wilno and Warsaw, leaders of the Confederation of Targowica were hanged – including a bishop – and there were massacres of those suspected or rumoured to support Russia.

But the desperate courage of the Poles and the skill of their beloved Kościuszko were not enough to hold the combined armies of Russia and Prussia. Kościuszko was defeated, wounded and captured at the battle of Maciejowice in October 1794. On 4 November, General Suvorov captured Praga, the suburb of Warsaw east of the Vistula, and the Cossacks massacred its inhabitants. The capital surrendered, and the King was taken off into exile, finally abdicating in November 1795.

Tadeusz Kościuszko (1746–1817), who had fought in the American War of Independence, led the rising of 1794 in a vain attempt to save Poland from partition and destruction. Few Polish homes lack a picture of him.

The Third Partition, sealed by treaty in January 1797 but dating in practice from 1795, ended the independence of Poland. The Commonwealth vanished from the map of Europe. Austria took Kraków and the surrounding region, Prussia occupied central Poland as far east as Warsaw, the Russians advanced their frontiers to a line which – in its northern trace – ran close to the present Polish–Soviet border along the Bug river. A secret clause in the Partition treaty – the first of many such secret clauses in Poland's history – laid down that 'the name or designation of the Kingdom of Poland . . . shall remain suppressed as of now and for ever'.

A hundred and twenty-three years were to pass before a sovereign Polish state reappeared. Poland had 'descended into the grave', as the Romantic poets were to put it, but it was an unquiet grave. Poland was not dead, and it was not only the Poles who tried to resurrect her.

France, at war with all Europe, did not abandon the Polish cause, though ruthless calculation was as important as fraternal emotion in French actions. Napoleon allowed General Jan Henryk Dąbrowski to raise two legions of Polish exiles in Italy (their 'March, march, Dąbrowski' song became Poland's national anthem) and another legion was organised in Germany. They served France loyally, in part by helping to combat the national insurrection in Spain, and in 1807 Napoleon established the Grand Duchy of Warsaw, a satellite state carved out of the Polish territories annexed by Prussia which soon included not only Warsaw but Kraków and a part of the Austrian zone.

Although the Grand Duchy seemed to Poles only a prelude to the restoration of full independence, the great process of reform which had begun in the time of King Stanisław August Poniatowski was revived and carried further. The Napoleonic Civil Code of law was imported from France, and has shaped the Polish legal and administrative tradition ever since. Serfdom was again abolished, and a modern constitution gave equal rights to all but the poorest peasants. Hope returned; Napoleon seemed a liberator; and the Poles gave their treasure and their young men to help his disastrous invasion of Russia in 1812.

But with Napoleon's defeat, Poland again left the map. The Congress of Vienna in 1815 changed the Partition boundaries: the Prussians fell back some way to the west, Kraków became a 'free city' in practice subject to the partitioning powers, and most of the old Grand Duchy of Warsaw, including the capital, became a semi-autonomous region of the Russian Empire, the so-called 'Kingdom of Poland'.

Abroad, all those who opposed the Holy Alliance, the block of three reactionary powers which not only suppressed Poland but seemed to threaten liberty throughout Europe, gave at least sentimental support to the Polish cause. It was the sense of belonging to a 'liberal international' that encouraged a series of Polish national conspiracies, especially in the Congress Kingdom.

Matters came to a crisis in 1830; the July Revolution in France spread waves of democratic unrest and turbulence across the Continent, while the Tsar prepared to send Russian troops (with Polish regiments) to suppress the new and liberal state of Belgium.

The November Rising began on the night of 29 November 1830 when a small party of officer-cadets attacked the Belvedere Palace, residence of the Russian viceroy, and another group captured the Arsenal with the assistance of the Warsaw population. The rising rapidly developed into a national insurrection, and the armies of the Congress Kingdom fought Russian troops in open warfare for almost a year before going down to defeat. But the leadership of the rising, ill-prepared, proved divided and confused; the liberal nations of the West, Britain and France, did not come to Poland's aid, although thousands of Poles secretly crossed frontiers to join the insurrection; and the strategy of the generals did not match the courage and professionalism of their soldiers. Warsaw was recaptured by the Russians in September 1831, and by late October organised resistance was over.

The consequences of the November Rising were grim and long-lasting. General Paskievitch in the Kingdom and General Muraviev in Lithuania carried out their own versions of 'pacification': hundreds were executed, and some 180,000 Poles were deported, many in irons to Siberia. The civil service was purged, and the Kingdom lost its relative autonomy, to be ruled by decree. Polish institutions like the Bank, the army, the Sejm and the Commission for National Education were systematically abolished.

The 'Great Emigration' was Poland's response to the failure of the November Rising. Most of the intellectual and political élite of Poland fled abroad, some 10,000 in all, establishing their exile centre in Paris around Prince Adam Czartoryski in the Hotel Lambert. This outflow of politicians, writers, musicians, philosophers and generals was the most extraordinary block of talent ever to transfer itself from one country to another until the Jewish intellectual emigration from Germany and Austria to the United States a hundred years later. Adam Mickiewicz and Juliusz Słowacki wrote verse and drama, mystical and moral and yet intensely political, that still suffuse and inform the Polish imagination; Joachim Lelewel wrote Poland's history; Frederic Chopin composed; Cyprian Kamil Norwid developed a new poetry whose innovation and genius was only recognised in the following century.

This was a Romantic culture. Neither the old Age of Reason nor the optimistic, liberal mood of the contemporary West could answer the questions the Poles now put to themselves: why had Heaven allowed the martyrdom of their country when it sought only justice, and how – when – could it be resurrected from the tomb? Against the background of intense Catholic faith, there developed the haunted idea of Messianism which – in its extreme form – presented Poland as the collective Christ, crucified to redeem the nations, one day to be resurrected by a new embodiment of the Holy Spirit.

At home, the earth continued to heave over the buried nation. Another national rising was planned for 1846, but ended in multiple disaster. In Prussian Poland, the leaders were arrested; Kraków rose, but the rebellion was rapidly crushed by Austrian and Russian troops. In Galicia, the portion of southern Poland held by Austria which stretched from Kraków eastwards to the fortress city of Lwów and on into the Ukraine, 1846 did not just fail but turned into a slaughter of Poles by Poles. In this overcrowded province, nearly five million Polish and Ukrainian peasants worked the lands of a tiny class of great landowning magnates. As the rising began, the Austrians were able to provoke a peasant rebellion against the landlords which turned into a massacre; some two thousand estate owners and their families were murdered, and their manors burned down.

The fiasco of 1846 was a turning-point in the history of the Partitions. From Kościuszko's rising onwards, Polish leaders had been able to rely on peasant support, promising an end to rural servitude in return for military service. Now, after Galicia, the Powers saw that they could cut off this source of strength by exploiting social divisions in Polish society. In 1848, Count Franz von Stadion, the Austrian governor of Galicia, offered the peasants possession of their own land and the abolition of feudal labour services. The Russians took a similar course in 1864.

As a result of the failure two years before, the Polish national leaders were too demoralised and disorganised to take a major part in the liberal revolutions which blazed across Europe in 1848. Minor rebellions in Kraków and Lwów were bombarded into surrender by the Austrians. In Prussian Poland, a National Committee sprang up in Poznań seeking autonomy within Prussia, but the movement was suppressed a few months later as the Hohenzollern monarchy regained control in Berlin. But Polish exiles fought 'for your freedom and ours' in almost every other nation in Europe during 1848–9. The poet Mickiewicz raised a legion in Italy, General Ludwik Mierosławski (who had led the ill-fated 1846 rising in Poznań) fought in Sicily and in southern Germany, General Henryk Dembiński and the legendary General Józef Bem commanded armies in the Hungarian national revolution. In the 1848 'springtime of nations', European sympathy with the Polish cause – rising all through the idealistic and revolutionary movements of the first half of the century – reached a peak, from which it then declined. Europe now entered a period of huge wars between empires and of internal class struggle, in which the fate of a 'failed' nation-state seemed steadily less relevant.

To write about 'Polish history' in this period inevitably distorts proportions. There was a common language, a common Polish version of Catholicism, a common culture whose strength and content could vary greatly between regions and social classes. There were 'Polish events', generally conspiracies which with great effort and luck could be made a shared experience for some Poles in two, if not always three, of the Partitions. But most of the 'history' that Poles made or suffered in the nineteenth century was – naturally enough – an aspect of the history of Austria, Prussia or Russia. And these were very distinct experiences.

The Austrian Partition – Galicia and Austrian Silesia – was the most lenient. Here the ever-changing efforts of a multinational empire to reach a stable relationship with its subjects – Germans, Czechs, Magyars, Croats, Poles and Ukrainians, to name only the larger population groups – allowed the Poles to acquire considerable autonomy in Galicia where they numbered about three million, almost half the population of the province. They – or rather the highly conservative Polish landowners – ran their own internal affairs, fostered Polish culture without much hindrance, and for much of the period used Polish as an official language. As the Empire was itself Catholic, Polish religion raised no problems. Galicia was economically backward and rural, and the Polish nobility, nervous both about peasant radicalism and the rise of the Ukrainian minority (about forty-one per cent of the province's population in 1880), relied on the Austrians to protect them and became thoroughly nervous about ideas of national resurrection.

In Prussia, by contrast, the Poles – just under three million of them – were a minority. Up to the 1848 crisis, they had been handled with tolerance. But in the second half of the century, as the policy of Germanisation set in, they were treated increasingly as a threat.

Their position became far more exposed in 1871, when Germany united into an empire under Prussian leadership. Bismarck, who had been the chief minister to the Prussian King, now became the first Chancellor of the Hohenzollern Empire. Within a few years, the Prussian Poles were embroiled in the *Kulturkampf* – Bismarck's attempt to break the influence of the Vatican and bring the Catholic Church throughout the German dominions under the control of the state. Bismarck did not launch the *Kulturkampf* simply to break the national spirit of the Catholic Poles – though he certainly hoped for such a result. Neither did he attack the Church simply because he, like the rest of the Prussian ruling class, was a Lutheran Protestant. His central purpose was to destroy or at least disable any institution which challenged the absolute authority of the German state. But the effect of Bismarck's onslaught against their church, coupled with his violent contempt for the very idea of Poland, faced the Poles in Prussia with the most serious danger to their cultural survival that they had yet encountered.

They became the target of campaigns not only against their faith but against their education and finally against their land. Government-financed waves of German farmer-colonists were sent east to buy out the Poles and settle. On all three fronts the Poles of the Poznań region and West Prussia successfully defended themselves through a generally defiant Catholic leadership (Cardinal Ledóchowski was imprisoned for two years), and through a network of self-help organisations which not only blocked the German colonisation plans but in some areas bought back farms that had been purchased from Poles.

Bismarck regarded Poland as a 'seasonal state', a sort of sandbank which appeared in times of international crisis but which had no title to be considered a nation. The keystone of his European strategy was the maintenance of peace between the German and Russian Empires through their common interest in the partition of Poland. After his fall in 1890, when he was succeeded by Chancellor Caprivi, German policy changed towards a hostility to Russia that was to reach its climax in 1914, but this brought no relief to the Prussian Poles, now regarded as a security risk in a military frontier zone.

Of all three fragments of Poland, the Russian partition was easily the most oppressive. It contained the largest block of Poland's former population: there were over five million Polish subjects of the Tsar, of whom about 4.3 million lived in the 'Kingdom of Poland' and the remainder either in the old Lithuanian territories or in the eastern Ukraine.

After 1831, the Kingdom was in effect under military occupation. Polish culture was treated as subversive, and the Catholic religion was regarded as a disqualification from official employment. The modest political liberty allowed in Prussia and still more in Galicia was unthinkable in Russian Poland. Polish politics, to the extent that there were any beyond an unfocused hatred of anything Russian, could only develop as conspiracies prepared to use violence to maintain themselves and armed revolution to achieve their ends. Between the Russian tradition of total, utterly centralised and despotic authority and Poland's history of free speech and limited power, no stable compromise was possible.

After the Russian setback in the Crimean War (1854–6), conspiracies were formed among the thousands of Polish students studying at Russian universities and there was a new restiveness in the Kingdom. The new Tsar Alexander II, who had come to the throne in 1855, warned the Poles that they would win no concessions, but in 1860 patriotic demonstrations took place in Warsaw, followed by more in the following year which were crushed by the gunfire of Russian troops. Plans were laid for another national insurrection, which exploded prematurely in January 1863.

The January Rising was in some ways a contrast to the rebellion of 1830–31. Politically it had been carefully prepared and its underground leadership was highly organised, but its military strength was weak. There was no collision of armies; instead, partisan bands fought a guerrilla war throughout the Kingdom which soon spread to the huge forests of Lithuania and regions of Byelorussia and the Ukraine. The partisans were supported by an 'underground state', running central and local government, foreign policy, a press and an arms industry.

The odds, however, were hopeless. Feeble attempts by France, Britain and Austria to mediate with the Tsar were ignored. As in 1830, thousands of Poles came from Austria and Prussia and from all the emigrations in the west to fight

The rising of 1863 against the Russians. Insurgents, some of them peasants with pikes made out of scythe blades, have ambushed a Russian passenger train.

A parade of victorious Cossacks in Warsaw, after the Russians had subdued the 1863 rising

and die, but the Rising itself did not spread beyond the Russian partition. After fifteen months of desperate courage, the insurrection crumbled away, and its last leadership, headed by Romuald Traugutt, was hanged outside the Warsaw Citadel.

The January Rising failed mainly because, without the intervention of a foreign power, partisans could not defeat a Russian army which came to number nearly 350,000 men. But its collapse was hastened by a clever stroke of politics. The underground 'government' had – as usual – promised the peasants full ownership of their land and an end to labour duties for the landlord. But in March 1864, Alexander II proclaimed a version of these reforms as his own, on behalf of the Russian government, depriving the Rising of much of its appeal to the rural poor.

A thick darkness of repression now fell on the Kingdom. Again, there were executions; again, thousands of Poles were herded off in long convoys to Siberia. The Kingdom lost its name and its last shreds of autonomy, becoming the 'Vistula Territory' of the Russian Empire. Poles were excluded from almost all official positions; Russian became the language of education and government; the Catholic Church was persecuted and the spread of the Orthodox faith encouraged; a stream of Russian bureaucrats, teachers and policemen moved in. The policy of 'Russianisation', the deliberate extermination of the Polish identity, was applied even more severely after the murder of Alexander II in 1881.

Under the Partitions, two broad strategies were open to patriotic Poles. One was the Romantic tradition of armed insurrection, a course which turned out to be hopeless in practical terms unless there was full-scale support from other European nations – which never materialised. The other was to preserve and build up the cultural and economic strength of the nation, which involved a degree of compromise and collaboration with the partitioning Powers.

This second strategy, known as 'Organic Work', dominated the decades after the failure of the 1863 Rising. In Galicia, the agrarian slum of Europe, there was little industrial development before the end of the century. In Prussian Poland, the self-help policies of the Poles, combined with the economic dynamism of Germany, gave them a prosperous farming interest and useful experience in finance and industry. But it was in Russian Poland, in spite of ferocious political and cultural suppression, that the most vigorous changes took place.

Polish society there had been shattered as much by the land reforms of 1864 as by the defeat of the Rising. The easy-going old life of the rural gentry came abruptly to an end, with the loss of unpaid labour. A part of the petty nobility left the land and moved to Warsaw where – barred from any responsible post – they became the embryo of the turbulent, independent Warsaw intelligentsia that survives today. Others, however, went to Russia itself, to study, to work as managers and – often – to encounter the new Russian generation of

revolutionary conspirators. Professor Leslie records that the Polish population of St Petersburg rose from 11,000 in 1864 to 70,000 by 1914.

In 1851, the tariff barrier between Russia and the Kingdom had been
abolished; in the years after 1863, Russia's protectionist policies cut off the
supply of industrial goods from the West. This was the opportunity for
Russian Poland, still economically far more advanced than the rest of the
Empire. There were few Polish capitalists, but German investment poured in
to finance industrial development; large-scale industry appeared not only in
the boom town of Łódź, whose textiles clothed all Russia, but in the coal and
iron basin of the Dąbrowa and in Warsaw in the form of heavy and light
engineering.

By 1900, Poland accounted for an eighth of all Russian production. Organic
Work, at a first glance, seemed to be paying off. But in fact it was already a
discredited creed.

There were two reasons for this. One was social: the new Polish working
class was underpaid and atrociously housed, and – in Russian Poland – almost
totally deprived of trade union protection until 1906. Revolutionary socialist
ideas spread rapidly, accelerated by the slump at the end of the century. On the
land, the end of serfdom and land reform had only created further problems as
a rural population with a soaring birth rate tried to fend off starvation on tiny
plots of soil. Many gave up the struggle and emigrated, from Prussian Poland
to the United States and to the Ruhr in western Germany, then from the old

Jewish craftsmen, in a poor district of Warsaw, in the early years of this century. In Warsaw the Jews
formed forty per cent of the population.

Kingdom, and finally in an enormous exodus from overcrowded Galicia which took over one million – Poles, Jews and Ukranians – abroad, mostly to the Americas, between 1870 and 1914.

The second reason for the fading of the Organic Work strategy was political. If it was not to degenerate into mere opportunism, only making life easier for those with money and position, it had to show returns – an appreciative readiness of the partition Powers to allow the Poles to run their own affairs. But the opposite was true: in Russia and Germany, above all, imperialist russianising and germanising policies were growing rapidly more oppressive.

It was at this stage in Polish history that Józef Piłsudski entered the struggle. As the nineteenth century ended, the Poles looked back on a hundred years of humiliation and martyrdom and swore that there would not be another hundred. Internationally, the outlook for restoring an independent Poland was bleak. But the tightening vice of foreign repression, added to the miseries of the economic slump, was breeding up a fresh militancy in all the Polish lands. The emergence of coherent political movements, like the Polish Socialist Party, gave resistance and struggle a quite new staying-power. Piłsudski was typical of the young Polish generation, impatient to renew the struggle, hoping against all reason for a sign of weakness in one of its imperial enemies.

Conspirators for Polish independence: a rare photograph of some of the underground leaders of the Polish Socialist Party, 1896, London. Józef Piłsudski, who was to dominate Poland between the world wars, sits at the centre, a pen in his right hand.

2

Poland Resurrected:
1900–1921

In August 1914, the novelist Joseph Conrad decided to take his family on a Continental holiday. He wanted to show his English wife and children the city of Kraków, where he had grown up and where he had buried his father, the revolutionary Apollo Korzeniowski.

The Archduke Franz Ferdinand, successor to the imperial Austro-Hungarian throne, had been shot at Sarajevo a few weeks before. Like most ordinary Europeans, Conrad paid little attention to this. As a result, the outbreak of the First World War caught the Conrads in Kraków, in what was now the enemy territory of Austria-Hungary, and it was only with the greatest difficulty that they managed to escape internment and make their way back to Britain.

On the night of the general mobilisation, as army cars rushed hooting through the streets and crowds of unwilling young men slouched to the barracks to have their hair cut off and their uniforms fitted, Conrad and a group of Polish friends gathered in the smoking-room of his hotel and contemplated the future.

'The big room was lit up only by a few tall candles, just enough for us to see each other's faces by. I saw in those faces the awful desolation of men whose country, torn in three, found itself engaged in the contest with no will of its own, and not even the power to assert itself at the cost of life. All the past was gone, and there was no future, whatever happened; no road which did not seem to lead to moral annihilation.' Conrad, recalling the scene a year later, wrote: 'I am glad I have not so many years left me to remember that appalling feeling of inexorable fate, tangible, palpable, come after so many cruel years, a figure of dread, murmuring with iron lips the final words: Ruin – and Extinction.'[1]

1. Joseph Conrad, *Notes on Lifes and Letters*, J. M. Dent & Sons, London, 1921, p. 229, p. 238.

Four years later, Poland regained her independence. The war which seemed to promise only ruin and extinction led to the collapse of all the three partitioning empires. But there are lessons in that memory of Conrad's which should never be forgotten. Only hindsight or the bravest contemporary guess could identify those baleful days of 1914 with the beginning of Poland's resurrection. Only the most absurd nationalism could attribute that resurrection to the actions of the Poles themselves. There was nothing inevitable about Poland's revival in 1918, which was the result of an incredible stroke of fortune. In 1914, there was no lack of Polish politicians struggling for the independence of their country, openly or underground, at liberty or in prisons. But Conrad in that Kraków hotel, like most Poles, shared only their aspirations, not their optimism.

By the opening of the twentieth century, the new generation of 'activist' politicians in Poland had acquired long-lasting divisions. There was a conservative-nationalist wing, whose ideas were to prove permanently influential but which – in spite of its strength – never gained control of events. And there was a socialist wing, hopelessly split on fundamental issues, which none the less contrived to seize the chances offered by history.

The National Democrats were the first genuinely modern party in Polish history. The *Endecja* (their Polish acronym) emerged mainly from the cold but fertile mind of Roman Dmowski, the most impressive political thinker of his age in Poland. Dmowski, in his origins and attitudes, was a complete contrast to Piłsudski. He was the son of a suburban Warsaw family. A diligent science student, he might never have become a professional politician if he had not been arrested and imprisoned by the Russians after a street demonstration in 1892, when he was nineteen years old.

His ideas, as they slowly took shape, owed much to the new German nationalism, and broke entirely with Polish tradition. He looked forward to a racially united 'Poland for the Poles', and though he began as an anti-clerical, he came to regard Catholicism as one of the definitions of a 'true Pole'. Dmowski resented the presence of Ukrainian, Byelorussian, and above all of Jewish populations in the Polish lands as a hindrance to the nation's destiny. He taught the fashionable doctrines of state-worship and argued that the cause of the nation was morally supreme: almost any deception or even treachery could be justified if it served the nation, while sympathy for other races was a cardinal sin against 'national egoism'.

The National Democrats took pains to establish themselves in all three partitions as an 'all-Polish' party. They developed a powerful youth move-ment, and – especially in Galicia – a peasant wing. Although they began as a socially radical party, they were gradually drawn into much more conservative attitudes as they attracted the support of the upper classes (impressed by the

Endecja's hostility to socialism), of the Polish middle class and intelligentsia, and eventually of the hierarchy of the Catholic Church.

Dmowski's strategy was equally cold-blooded. In spite of the German flavour to his thinking, he came to regard German imperialism as the most dangerous threat to Poland, and adopted a policy of wary collaboration with the Russians who, he thought, might be persuaded to restore some internal autonomy to Poland. Dmowski was not personally pro-Russian in any emotional way; it was, after all, his arrest by the Russians in 1892 that had radicalised him as a student. His attitude was opportunistic. His middle-class support still craved for a compromise with the Tsar and dreaded revolution. And in Dmowski's view, a Russian grant of internal self-government to Poland would lead irresistibly towards sovereign statehood.

The Polish Socialist Party (PPS) was established in 1892–3. The PPS was active mostly in Russian Poland – which meant that it was an illegal, banned formation operating in clandestinity. It was the biggest left-wing movement in the Polish lands, drawing its support largely from the big workforces of the factories and mines. However, the conditions in which the PPS had to work meant that its capacity to defend working-class interests was very limited. Instead, the PPS developed a collective genius for conspiratorial organisation and publishing. *Robotnik* first appeared in 1894. Lively, inspiring and full of uncensored news, *Robotnik* was distributed by a network of party members, students and even Polish soldiers in the Russian army. It soon became the most successful underground paper in the Russian Empire.

There was a left-wing element in the party, tending towards the internationalism of the suppressed *Proletariat*, but the arrest of most of its leaders allowed the group around Piłsudski, including other men who were to lead Poland between the wars like Stanisław Wojciechowski and Stanisław Grabski, to take effective command. Their view was that the fights for national independence and socialism were one and the same; the PPS at this period was much more like a national liberation movement in Africa or Asia of our own times than an 'orthodox' Marxist party.

Socialist though he was, Piłsudski's own outlook was astonishingly old-fashioned compared to that of Roman Dmowski. The new vogue ideas about racial superiority and national egoism had simply passed him by. A man who habitually looked eastward, rather than to the ideas of the West, Piłsudski hoped for a revolutionary collapse of the Russian Empire out of which, like a phoenix, would reappear a modernised version of the old Commonwealth: a multinational federation of Poland with Lithuania, Byelorussia and the Ukraine.

The Social Democracy of the Kingdom of Poland and Lithuania (SDKPiL) was a socialist party founded at the same time as its rival, the PPS. But the SDKP (Lithuania was only added to its title in 1899) sharply rejected the emphasis that the PPS laid on the recovery of Polish national sovereignty. The smallness of its membership, mostly among self-employed and craft workers, was to some extent compensated by the intellectual brilliance of its leaders, most of whom were of Jewish origin. The party's most conspicuous figure was Rosa Luxemburg, the most independent and original of all early Marxists, who divided her energies between the Polish and German socialist movements and was to be murdered in Berlin at the end of the Spartacist rising in 1919.

Rosa Luxemburg, a small, neat person whose principles were as uncompromising as her courage, spent even more of her life in Russian and German prisons than Piłsudski did. The daughter of a Jewish businessman from Zamość, in south-east Poland, she was still only a clever schoolgirl in Warsaw when she discovered politics and joined a secret splinter group of the *Proletariat* party. In her time, Marxism had not yet been deformed into a rigid dogma, and Rosa Luxemburg became famous throughout the European socialist movement for the way in which she used the ideas of Karl Marx to construct her own doctrine of spontaneous revolution by the masses.

Although her parents were Jewish, they were thoroughly assimilated into Polish society, and she grew up in a social and political background that was Polish rather than Judaic. Rosa Luxemburg did not, as is often said, underestimate the elemental force of Polish nationalism among the masses. But she came to argue that, in an age of worldwide capitalism and imperialism, the cause of national independence had become irrelevant to a socialist revolution. Thus any socialist party – like the PPS – which put independence first would lose its 'proletarian' and revolutionary edge, and degenerate into a mere tool of 'petty-bourgeois' politics and interests. It was a striking theory. But even Lenin, who greatly admired her, thought that Luxemburg's approach to the Polish question was unrealistic.

Peasant politics remained a separate affair: the various socialist movements made little headway in the Catholic and traditional countryside. But no single, unified peasant party emerged during the Partitions. The sheer weight of repression in Russian Poland prevented any coherent political organisation on the land. In

Rosa Luxemburg (1871–1919). Born into a Jewish family at Zamość, she divided her political energy between the German Social Democrat Party (SPD) and the Social Democracy of the Kingdom of Poland and Lithuania (SDKPiL), the small Marxist party which was the ancestor of Polish communism. She was murdered by right-wing German soldiers in Berlin after the Spartacist rising in January 1919.

Prussian Poland, the dogged battle to defend the soil against German colonisation produced a much more intense political awareness among the farmers, and gave rise to elaborate networks of 'self-help' institutions. However, no distinct political party appeared.

In Austrian Galicia it was different. There, the far more tolerant conditions of Austrian rule allowed a whole series of peasant movements to arise in the second half of the nineteenth century, and in 1895 a Polish Peasants' Party (PSL) was founded. The shocking rural misery and inequality in Galicia helped the PSL to flourish, but in the early twentieth century splits appeared between a radical wing led by Jan Stapiński and a more moderate group whose central figure was Wincenty Witos – the man who was to dominate peasant politics in later years. In spite of these divisions, the PSL provided the biggest single block of Galician deputies in the Vienna parliament when Austria-Hungary finally granted the Empire universal suffrage.

The development of party politics among Poland's Jews formed yet another separate world, distinct from the mainstream of Polish socialism and nationalism. Over three-quarters of the total Jewish population of Europe (according to some estimates) lived in the lands which had formed the old Commonwealth. Through the centuries of its existence, the Polish–Lithuanian Crown had gathered to itself Jewish settlers from all over Europe until, at the time of the Partitions, some 800,000 Jews inhabited its lands – far the largest Jewish settlement in the world.

Like the different Christian denominations during the Commonwealth, they lived in a climate of toleration rather than of tolerance. The Jews dominated village and small-town life and trade, and they were not loved by the Christian Slav peasantry, although they were fairly consistently protected by the landowning class. Christians and Jews were mutually mystified, often repelled, by their very distinct ways of life, and yet there was a kind of unwilling symbiosis: neither found it easy to imagine existing without the other.

The Partitions brought this toleration to an end. All three Powers scrapped the extensive system of Jewish self-government which had existed during the Commonwealth, and tried in different ways to force the Jewish population into their own political frameworks. There were relatively few Jews in the part of Poland annexed by Prussia. Far the largest Jewish population remained in Austrian Galicia or in the lands occupied by Russia: the Kingdom of Poland and the vast Lithuanian territories directly absorbed into Russia. Soon after the Third Partition in 1795, the Empress Catherine II applied to the Jews her policy of persecuting all faiths save that of Russian Orthodoxy by establishing the Pale. This was a crude form of apartheid, designed to keep the Jews out of the Russian heartland. The Jews were confined to the Pale of Settlement, roughly limited by the old eastern frontier of the Commonwealth, and were forbidden to migrate beyond it.

The ideal of assimilation into Gentile society imported from the West, affected a part of the Jewish population in the nineteenth century. Jews took a vigorous part in the insurrections. The Jewish Light Horse, commanded by Colonel Joselewicz, defended Warsaw in 1794, while Jews fought in the risings of 1830 and 1863. But the movement never went very deep, in a highly conservative community, and by the end of the century very different tides were running. In the 1880s, the Russian authorities tried to divert opposition by encouraging pogroms against the Jews. A combination of fear of persecution and rising poverty, especially in overcrowded Galicia, led to an enormous emigration which was to last through the first half of the twentieth century. The emigration reached its peak before the First World War; the Jewish population of Galicia was halved.

Three main political currents appeared: Zionist, conservative and socialist. They were not exclusive. The Poale Zion (1901) was a popular movement that tried to reconcile socialism with Zionist emigration. Orthodox Jews created a variety of groups which were conservative (in both the social and religious senses) and opposed to Zionism, but no conservative party with staying power appeared until Agudat Israel was founded in 1912. The most militant and vivid of all these parties, defying both Zionism and the traditional Jewish approach to politics, was the Bund – the General Jewish Workers' League of Lithuania, Poland and Russia. The Bund, set up at a secret meeting of Jewish socialists at Wilno in 1897, was the first mass socialist party in Russia and – as one of the movements which joined to establish the Russian Social Democratic Party – a direct ancestor of the Mensheviks and Bolsheviks. Marxist in ideology, internationalist in outlook, the Bund became a powerful revolutionary force among the Jewish working class, above all in the Pale territories to the east.

The Jews lived scattered throughout Poland, claiming no territory as their own. Much the biggest of the settled minorities, concentrated in lands they regarded as their birthright, was the Ukrainian population. By 1900, Ukrainian nationalism was well established, angry and ambitious. It raised for Poles that most difficult and divisive question: Poland yes, but which – and where? Old-fashioned Polish patriots still regarded the assortment of East Slav peoples who now called themselves Ukrainians as natural subjects of a Polish state whose rightful dominions extended almost as far east as Kiev. Ukrainian politicians, looking in the opposite direction, contemplated an independent state which would include the ancient Polish city of Lwów and stretch on westwards halfway to Kraków.

The 'Ukrainian idea' had brought together peoples of very different origins: the independent Cossacks, who were free descendants of escaped serfs; the 'Ruthenian' family of peoples, who formed a majority of the population in eastern Galicia; and several small 'mountain' tribes living on the north slopes of the Carpathian range. Many of these peoples were 'Uniates' by religion: this was the new faith which had appeared in 1596–7 when the Orthodox Church within the Commonwealth had accepted union with Rome. Under the Partitions, this 'Greek Catholic' church survived in Galicia, but – true to form – the Russians suppressed it with terroristic violence in their part of Poland.

It was natural that the idea of a 'Ruthenian' cultural nationalism should take hold under the more tolerant rule of Austria. And it was equally natural that the Austrians, helped by some of their Polish viceroys in Galicia, should encourage this nationalism as a way of holding Polish militancy and unrest in check. But, in the end, this sort of manipulation only inflamed the situation. The Poles came to see Ruthenian–Ukrainian nationalism as a deadly threat to their own hopes. The Ukrainians, absurdly under-represented in Galician and Austrian politics through a battery of gerrymandering devices, became more suspicious than ever of Polish intentions.

No tidy line divided the two populations and their languages. They lived on top of one another, the top being usually Polish. The ancient fortress-city of Lwów was inhabited mostly by Poles and Jews, while in the countryside around, a Ruthenian peasantry touched its cap to Polish nobles and landowners. As far east as Kiev itself, Polish families could be found living on estates which had been theirs for centuries. Much the same pattern existed in the 'Borderlands' to the north, where Polish squires and Jewish traders living in Jewish *shtetl* villages ran the rural economy among a Ruthenian peasant population that eventually came to be known as Byelorussian. Far weaker than the Ukrainian movement in 1900, a Byelorussian nationalism existed too, claiming the lands between Minsk and the river Bug. The Russians, who considered Ukrainians and Byelorussians to be errant members of the great Russian family, treated both nationalisms with brutal contempt.

In 1904, the Russian Empire blundered into war with Japan, and the world – incredulous – saw for the first time the defeat of a great Power by a non-European nation. Though Polish soldiers and sailors were obliged to fight in the Far East, Poland had no conceivable interest in a Russian victory. On the contrary, the possibility of a Russian defeat – a sign that the great oppressor was growing old and weak – gave new energy and conviction to Polish revolutionaries. Józef Piłsudski set off for Japan in 1904, offering to raise Polish legions to fight Russia. He met a polite refusal; disconcertingly, he also met Roman Dmowski, who had travelled to Tokyo in order to head him off. All that Piłsudski gained was a secret compact with Japanese intelligence, and Japanese officers attached to the embassy in Paris began to give courses in bomb-making to selected militants from the PPS.

The disaster in the Far East hit Poland in several ways. While conspirators rejoiced, the Polish 'Establishment', committed to compromise with Russia, offered vows of loyalty. But the war intensified economic crisis and unemployment in Polish cities, and open protest demonstrations were seen again in Warsaw. There was a large, threatening workers' demonstration on

May Day, 1904. Unrest persisted, and that autumn the PPS organised a demonstration in Grzybowski Square in Warsaw, at which armed revolutionaries opened fire on the Russian police.

Turmoil and now bloodshed in Russian Poland lit up sharply the differences between Piłsudski and Dmowski. For Piłsudski, the signal for all-out underground armed struggle against the Tsardom had been given. Dmowski, on the other hand, saw this as his chance to urge the Tsar towards a more liberal policy towards Poland. A shower of memoranda flew from 'responsible' figures in Warsaw to St Petersburg, suggesting reforms for Poland. Nicholas II turned them down.

He had more urgent problems. In January, the Japanese captured Port Arthur. In St Petersburg, a strike at the Putilov engineering works led to an enormous but peaceful march to the Winter Palace with demands for land reform, an eight-hour working day and an elected constitutional assembly. The Tsar ordered the troops to open fire, and the 'Bloody Sunday' massacre that followed pitched the Russian Empire into its first revolutionary crisis.

Poland exploded. Both the PPS and the SDKPiL put their energy behind the general strike which began a few days after Bloody Sunday, but the PPS were able to broaden the strike into a national uprising. Their gunmen drove the police off the streets and fought Russian troops in the cities. Hundreds died as workers all over the Kingdom went to the barricades. The revolution spread to the countryside, where peasant strikes against landlords became a demand for

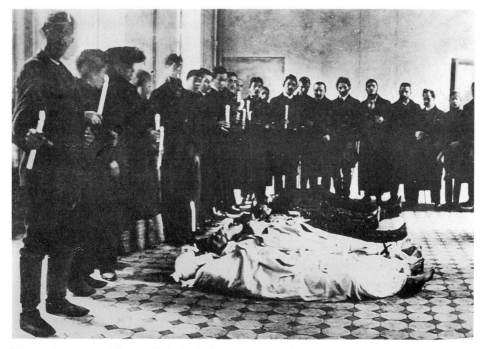

Warsaw, May 1905. Victims of Tsarist bullets during a violent May Day demonstration.

the restoration of Polish liberties and language. School pupils joined a total boycott of Russian schools which was to last, its front unbroken, until 1908, and which survived in many places until 1914.

Professor Wacław Jędrzejewicz was a twelve-year-old pupil at one of the Warsaw high schools. 'In the school strike of course, with great joy, I took an active part throwing inkpots around the class and all sorts of pranks like that. We stopped going to school. Private study groups of teachers and pupils were formed, and we worked through our school curriculum in private homes, often at our house on Natolinska Street. The Revolution came, and martial law in Warsaw, and workers' demonstrations – one very strong PPS demonstration – and of course for that I wasn't allowed out of the house. My brother was eight years older and a student at the University which was also on strike; he took part in those demonstrations. And we heard shots very close to Natolinska Street. In the evening, we saw Cossacks on the streets. It was winter. There were bonfires lit in the middle of the road. No public transport; the streetcars weren't running . . .'

The Tsarist régime retaliated with arrests and executions. It was indirectly supported by Dmowski who – although he had allowed his followers to join the school boycott movement – formed armed groups from his own working-class supporters to murder and intimidate socialists.

The climax in Russia arrived in October, with another general strike and the appearance of the Soviet of Workers' Deputies in St Petersburg, where Leon Trotsky proclaimed the social revolution. A fresh strike in Poland paralysed the country. On 30 October, the Tsar finally issued a manifesto promising a parliamentary constitution and elections in April 1906, and after more bloody uprisings in Moscow and in several Polish centres, the tide of revolution began very slowly to fall back.

For some years, Russian Poland remained in turmoil. Rosa Luxemburg, in the thick of it all, wrote to German friends from Warsaw in January 1906: 'My dears, it is very nice here, every day two or three persons are stabbed by soldiers in the city; there are daily arrests, but apart from these it is pretty gay. Despite martial law we are again putting out our daily *Sztandar* [the newspaper of the SDKPiL], which is sold on the street . . . For the present, the production and printing of *Sztandar* has to be carried on in bourgeois printing-houses by force, with revolver in hand. Our meetings too will start again as soon as martial law is ended. Then you will hear from me! It is savagely cold, and we travel about exclusively in sledges . . .'[2]

The workers' struggle carried on, against increasingly savage repression which reached its peak in a strike of Łódź in December 1906, when hundreds were killed or executed. Meanwhile, the post-mortem on 1905 began to reopen bitter divisions in the underground Left.

2. Quoted in J. P. Nettl, *Rosa Luxemburg*, Oxford University Press, Oxford, 1966, Vol. I, p. 331.

November 1905: the white eagle of Poland is raised during a demonstration in Warsaw. The slogan at the left reads: 'For Fatherland and Freedom'.

Like all authentic revolutions, 1905 had taken the revolutionaries by surprise. Nobody planned it; instead, huge masses of ordinary men and women spontaneously took events into their own hands, leaving the parties to chase frantically after them. No party was more astonished than the Social Democracy (SDKPiL), whose intellectuals – Rosa Luxemburg in particular – had developed a whole theory of spontaneous revolution.

The PPS was in confusion. The events of 1905 faced the PPS squarely with the question: would they work whole-heartedly with Russians for an all-Russian revolution, or were they going to stop when they had wrested an independent Poland from the flames? The left wing of the party took the first option. Piłsudski and his comrades, in charge of the terrorist organisation of the party still waging its frantic war with bomb and revolver, leaned instinctively to the second: revolution was only a means to the end of national independence.

The PPS finally split in 1906, unable to agree on the sort of revolution it wanted. One wing, the so-called 'PPS-Left', set off in an internationalist, Marxist direction. This group eventually converged with Rosa Luxemburg and the SDKPiL, and in 1918 they fused to form the first Polish Communist Party. The other fragment of the PPS stuck to the doctrine of armed struggle for independence. Over the years, it became as much a nationalist party bound to the personal charisma of Józef Piłsudski as a socialist movement.

Roman Dmowski and the National Democrats, in contrast, tried to use the chance of parliamentary influence offered by the new Russian constitution. The elections of 1906 to the first Duma (parliament) were boycotted by the Polish left, and twenty-five out of the thirty-six deputies elected from the Polish lands were National Democrats. They achieved little. Minor relaxations and concessions for Poland had mostly been promised before the Duma met, and owed little to parliamentary pressure. In the second Duma (October 1906), Dmowski himself sat as a deputy for Warsaw, but a draft bill for Polish autonomy incensed the Tsar and was rejected. None the less, the *Endecja* was able to use its position as the main 'official' party in Russian Poland to build up support at home in every legal form of social organisation, including the peasantry and the industrial working class. Wherever it put down roots, the party infected the soil with its doctrines: the biological superiority of Poles, the inferiority of foreigners, the menace to the 'Polish way of life' presented by socialism, and the treacherous, alien nature of the Jews.

No revolution took place in Prussian or Austrian Poland, but the 1905–6 eruption in the Kingdom inspired and excited Poles everywhere. There were demonstrations of sympathy in all the Galician towns. More significant, because it formed attitudes in the next generation, was the reverberation of the great school strike, especially in the German lands. There had already been a pupils' strike which had passed into legend at Września, near Poznań, in 1901, when schoolchildren refused to come to religious-instruction classes in the German language and had been collectively punished by caning. In 1906, this boycott was renewed, and many schools remained closed for a year. In Galicia, a torrent of boys and girls arrived from Russian Poland to continue their education under the Austrians, and they spread their own eager militancy through the schools they joined.

The torpor of Galicia was at last breaking up. A small but politically turbulent working class was appearing, especially in the east of the province where oil-fields had been opened up near Drohobycz. The grip of the conservative landowners, already shaken by a peasant strike in 1902, was beginning to loosen, and they hindered but could not suppress the agitation for democratic reform which was renewed in 1905. In 1907, the Austrians conceded universal suffrage (limited to men of twenty-four and over), and in the elections that year to the imperial parliament in Vienna, the conservatives lost their overall majority of Galician seats.

Socialism, which had become the standard-bearer of the Polish cause in the Kingdom in 1905, was still very weak in the other two Partitions. The Galician elections of 1907 returned only six socialists – themselves divided – out of 105 deputies. In Polish Prussia, where industry was still rare, the National Democrats attracted wide support: they were anti-German, and they took a 'safe' view of religion and property, the two elements of Polish society under direct attack from Berlin. This attack was renewed in 1907, when the German

Empire, impatient with the failure of the twenty-year campaign to colonise the Polish lands, decided to allow the compulsory purchase of Polish estates for German settlement. The National Democrats also made headway in Galicia, where they had no difficulty in appealing to Polish fear of the Ukrainians and resentment of the Jews.

The whole international situation in these years after 1900 lent strength to the National Democrat appeal. For most of the nineteenth century, Europe – as the Poles saw it – had been divided in two. At the eastern end sat the three empires, all highly conservative and all agreed that Poland had been abolished for good. Apart from occasional ruptures like the Austrian–Prussian war in 1866, they had stuck together. At the western end were liberal nations, who sympathised with the Polish struggle but provided only Notes, tears, and charity for Polish refugees.

Now, everything had changed. The empires had quarrelled. Germany and Austria-Hungary were challenging Tsarist Russia, which in turn was now allied with liberal and republican France, Poland's traditional friend. Europe had become unpredictable; conflict was burning up the Balkans, and threatening to spread into the sort of continental war which had not been seen since the time of Napoleon.

Dmowski and his friends were seductive when they argued that Poles should now back a liberalised Russia and its French ally against Germany. Unfortunately, Russia did not stay 'liberalised'. Nicholas II was beginning to take back the concessions wrung from him in 1905, and restrictions of the franchise made each Duma less independent than the last. Nobody paid attention to the demands of the Polish deputies, and it became painfully clear that Dmowski's strategy of 'loyalism' was not paying off. There was a split within the *Endecja*, and Dmowski resigned his seat in 1909.

Russia continued to tighten the screw on Poland. In 1907, the Russian government horrified all Poles by publishing a plan – carried through in 1912 – to remove eleven districts from the 'Vistula Territories' (the old Kingdom of Poland) and incorporate them in Russia proper. The following year, Russia bought out the main railway line from Warsaw to Vienna, sacked all the 16,000 Polish railway workers, and replaced them with Russians.

These events helped to revive unrest in Russian Poland, which had died down after the failure of 1905. Piłsudski and his armed-struggle bands, now disavowed by the majority group in the PPS, at first refused to give in and fought on with a campaign of murder, harassment and 'expropriations' (armed robberies). In 1908, Piłsudski himself and his future wife Alexandra Szczerbińska took part in a reckless but spectacularly successful mail-train robbery at Bezdany, near Wilno; escaping in a speed-boat down the river Niemen, they carried off a fortune in rouble notes to be used to buy weapons and printing equipment.

But in spite of Bezdany, Piłsudski now came to the conclusion that guerrilla war and terrorism were getting nowhere. The Russians could not crush him, but they could contain him; after 1905, their grip on Poland had become so tight that there was no chance of extending his struggle into another mass movement. Piłsudski therefore moved down to the relative freedom of Galicia, and embarked on an entirely new tack: the 'Austrian Orientation'.

This resembled Dmowski's tactics only in that both counted on using the growing tensions between the partitioning Powers to sell Polish support in return for concessions. But while Dmowski traded in politics, Piłsudski – typically – tried to bargain with armed force. Brooding on the reasons why 'the nation does not believe in the possibility of victory', he concluded that national self-confidence would never be restored until Poland regained the proudest of all its institutions – a Polish army. He would make one. An army would not only revive the patriotic spirit; it could persuade the Austrians to accept Polish regiments as allies, rather than cannon-fodder, in a future war with Russia.

The army began as a few young men drilling secretly in backyards. Within a few years, however, there were *Strzelcy* (riflemen) paramilitary units all over Galicia, and talks about their use in wartime had begun with the slightly sceptical officers of Austrian military intelligence. Nobody in Vienna supposed that Piłsudski and his lieutenants were inspired by selfless loyalty to the House of Habsburg, and the riflemen were kept short of weapons. Among their officers were men with a future in Polish history: Kazimierz Sosnkowski and Władysław Sikorski.

Piłsudski's riflemen drilling: Austrian-occupied Poland in 1913. From these patriotic volunteers, Piłsudski created the Polish Legions of the First World War.

(1915)   w KOŁKACH (POLESIE)

Józef Piłsudski, at war. When this photograph was taken in 1915, he was commanding the Polish Legions in the campaign against Russia.

Austria-Hungary and the Russian Empire went to war on 6 August 1914. The same day, while Joseph Conrad sat with his family in a Kraków hotel and pondered his new situation as an enemy alien in his own country, Józef Piłsudski marched out of the city and invaded the Russian Empire on his own. He took with him three companies of Polish riflemen, armed with ancient rifles throwing a bullet 'the size of a potato' and so badly equipped that some of the cavalrymen carried their saddles across the Vistula, hoping to find horses on the other side.

Piłsudski hoped to touch off a national insurrection. Two years later, he wrote: 'In 1914 I was not concerned with settling the details of the military question in Poland, but simply with this – was the Polish soldier to remain a mystical entity deprived of flesh and blood? In a great war fought on Polish soil, when a soldier with his bayonet and uniform would penetrate to every cottage and farm of our countryside, I wanted the Polish soldier to be something more than a pretty picture often looked at secretly in corners by well-brought up children. I wanted Poland, which had forgotten the sword so entirely since 1863, to see it flashing in the air in the hands of her own soldier.'[3]

This march, which later became a heroic focus of the Piłsudski legend, was by normal standards a futility. Piłsudski had meant to head for the Dąbrowa industrial area, where the PPS had strong support, but it had already been occupied by advancing German forces, so he made for the town of Kielce instead. Here, too, he found German troops already ensconced, and after two weeks he was obliged to retire to Kraków again, without the chance to fire more than a few shots at Russian patrols. Piłsudski's vision had been that the nation would rush to the standards of a free Polish army, acting as an independent ally of the Austrians. Nothing of the sort happened. He was well received in Kielce, but the population had no inclination to join the war on the German and Austrian side. Neither empire had made Poland any promises of liberty in return for loyalty. The Russians, on the other hand, promptly did so.

On 14 August the Grand Duke Nicholas, as commander-in-chief, issued a manifesto promising a reunited Poland, within the Russian empire but self-governing, if the Tsarist armies were victorious. This made a great impression in the Kingdom, putting wind back into Dmowski's sails and leaving Piłsudski's 'Austrian Orientation' becalmed. There was no longer any hope for an independent Polish army. Instead, 'Polish Legions' were raised in Galicia around the nucleus of his original riflemen, but placed firmly under Austrian military command.

Piłsudski led the First Brigade whose proud marching song – 'We, the First Brigade' – still catches at all Polish hearts; they fought skilfully and energetically for the next year in the fast-moving campaigns in southern Poland, while the Second Brigade, later commanded by Colonel Józef Haller,

3. *Józef Piłsudski: The Memories of a Polish Revolutionary and Soldier*, ed. Darsie Gillie, Faber & Faber, London, 1931, p. 186.

was in action far to the east in the Carpathians. Meanwhile, Piłsudski detached some of his best officers to run the Polish Military Organisation (POW), a secret force operating behind the Russian lines.

In the spring of 1915, a German–Austrian offensive broke through and drove the Russians back beyond the old frontiers of the Kingdom in the east. The headquarters of the German zone was now in Warsaw, and the Austrians occupied Lublin. A Russian counter-offensive in 1916 pushed the Austrians back some way in Volhynia, but then came to a halt.

With these huge shifts of power, 'the Polish question' at last came back to international life. Foreign statesmen on all sides laid plans to exploit Polish discontent – and manpower – against their enemies. Roman Dmowski left Russia after the defeats of 1915 and turned his attention to the Western powers; in London and Paris, he presented himself as the natural leader of the Polish nation and denounced Piłsudski as a mere German agent. In 1916, Austria and Germany, still – like their enemies – trying to define their war aims two years after the killing had begun, played their own Polish card against Russia. They proclaimed the establishment of a Polish Kingdom, without naming either its king or its frontiers, and established a provisional Council of State in Warsaw. A few days after the proclamation, the Germans announced the creation of a 'Polish army' to be 'temporarily' under German command.

To the tens of thousands of Polish soldiers already fighting on both sides against their will, and to the Legions, this offer was not impressive. Poland had been devastated by the war, not least by German bombardments and

Polish cavalry entering Warsaw, December 1916. In fact, these men were under German command.

exactions, and the new 'kingdom' scheme looked to them like a pretext for an even more ruthless exploitation of Polish wealth and blood by Germany and Austria. None the less, Piłsudski thought something might be made of it. He accepted the job of organising the Council of State's military committee, and the Legions were brought back from the front to form the cadres for the new army.

A competition to offer Poland a future was beginning. The Russians started talking about full independence, and raised separate Polish divisions out of their armies. President Wilson, impressed by the appeals of the famous concert pianist Ignacy Paderewski, told the Senate in January 1917 – well before the United States entered the war – that there must be a free Poland with access to the sea. Dmowski, on the other hand, was making little progress with Britain and France, anxious not to offend their Russian war ally by interfering in the Polish question.

They could have spared themselves their anxiety. In March 1917, revolution broke out in Russia and the Tsardom collapsed. The Petrograd Soviet called for the complete independence of Poland, and the new provisional government promised a free Polish state associated with the new democratic Russia. Russia, however, was no longer in a condition to carry out its promises. Its armies were disintegrating, and German forces were moving forward deep into its western borderlands.

Back in Warsaw, the Germans were methodically wrecking their chances of gaining Polish popular support. Quarrels in the Council of State came to a head in the summer of 1917, when the Germans made an attempt to enforce an oath of loyalty on the legions. Piłsudski seized this pretext to show his independence. Most of the First and Third Brigades of the Legions refused the oath, and were interned. Piłsudski resigned from the Council, and in July he and Kazimierz Sosnkowski were arrested by the Germans and imprisoned in the fortress at Magdeburg. A Regency Council was organised by the Germans in September, composed of 'responsible' figures and including the Archbishop of Warsaw, but the German attitude to Polish interests was now becoming so alarming that the Regency never gained credibility with the population.

Any revived Polish state was certain to lay claim to the territories in the east which had once belonged to the Commonwealth: Lithuania, Byelorussia and the Ukraine. But these were now under German military occupation. As the Russian Empire dissolved, the German generals in the east found themselves masters of a huge, chaotic region of Europe in which independence movements struggled to establish themselves and militias of every kind ravaged the countryside.

Germany sponsored a Lithuanian state, and in February 1918, at the negotiations at Brest-Litovsk, agreed to the emergence of a Ukrainian state which was to include eastern Galicia and the largely Polish district of Chełm. The Galician Poles rebelled in protest: the Polish corps commanded by Józef

Haller deserted the Austro-Hungarian flag and crossed the lines into Russia. After fighting their way past the Germans and the Bolsheviks, a remnant arrived with Haller at Murmansk on the White Sea. Here they took ship to France, where Haller was appointed commander of the Polish army being formed on the Western Front.

In November 1917, the Bolshevik rising in Petrograd had seized power and finally removed Russia from the war. This did nothing to improve Polish–Russian relations; its first impact on them was a violent revolutionary surge against Polish landlords and settlers in Byelorussia and the Ukraine, and Polish troops which had once formed part of the Tsarist armies were soon defending estates against Bolshevik raids. In Poland itself, the PPS (Left) and the SDKPiL tried to organise workers for a Bolshevik rising (Feliks Dzierzyński, one of the SDKPiL leaders, was to join Lenin as his first head of the political police – the Cheka). But most underground activity went into a growing struggle against the Germans, whose police chief in Warsaw was murdered in October 1918.

By now, a situation all too common in Polish history had arisen: the Poles abroad had lost touch with the mood of the nation at home. In Warsaw and Kraków, patriots dreamed of the absent hero Piłsudski fuming in his Magdeburg cell. In France, however, Roman Dmowski was winning recognition as the leader of the Polish cause. With Russia out of the war, the Western powers could now address themselves to using the Polish struggle as a lever against Germany and Austria. Dmowski's Polish National Committee in Paris was nursed as the embryo of a government in exile by the French, although the British and Americans became doubtful about his real authority within Poland. In January 1918, President Wilson included the establishment of an independent Poland as the thirteenth of his Fourteen-Point war aims, and Britain, France and Italy took up the call for a Poland with access to the Baltic Sea.

The old problem of 'which Poland – where?' was left open. Wilson, true to his principle of 'nationality states', said that the state should 'include territories inhabited by an indubitably Polish population'. This directly contradicted Piłsudski's vision of a resurrected Commonwealth of many nations, and came much closer to Dmowski's 'modern' conception of a Poland for Poles only. But it did not face the appalling complexity of deciding what 'indubitably Polish' meant in the borderlands where Poles, Ukrainians, Byelorussians and Germans lived together. Before the Allies could stumble any further into this thicket of definitions, events imposed their own solutions.

Defeat, despair, hunger and revolutionary unrest in Germany and Austria–Hungary finally took effect. In October 1918, the Austrian armies in southern Poland began to fall apart; the men simply set off home. In November, revolution broke out in Germany with a Fleet mutiny, and spread rapidly to the cities. In Warsaw as in Berlin, German troops refused their officers' orders and elected 'soldiers' councils' on the Bolshevik pattern.

After a century and a quarter, foreign authority over Poland had suddenly dissolved. But no effective Polish authority stood ready to take over. In the small industrial region of Austrian Silesia (Cieszyn), a 'Polish National Council' had been in charge since October. Then the socialist leader from Galicia, Ignacy Daszyński, proclaimed a 'Popular Government' at Lublin in what had been the Austrian military zone. In Warsaw, the Council of Regency – respected by nobody – dithered and looked frantically for a way of handing over its responsibilities. Far off in Paris, Dmowski and the Polish National Committee watched in impotence.

The power vacuum was soon filled. The Germans released Piłsudski so suddenly that he only had time to wrap a razor and toothbrush in a sheet of paper. He and Sosnkowski were rushed by car to Berlin. Two days later, they were put on a special train for Warsaw. The Council of Regency, with relief, instantly appointed Piłsudski commander of the armed forces. It was 11 November 1918, the day of the Armistice on the Western Front and the day which Poles still celebrate – when they are allowed to – as the restoration of independence.

A few days later, the Council of Regency declared that Piłsudski was head of state, and dissolved itself. Daszyński's government at Lublin collapsed, and a provisional Cabinet was formed in Warsaw led by the socialist Jędrzej Moraczewski, the first prime minister of independent Poland. Piłsudski, who had persuaded the German 'soldiers' councils' to go home and take their revolution with them, was trying to build a coalition government on as wide a political base as possible, including the National Democrats if he could get them.

In practice, he was dictator. The word has a better ring in Polish than in other languages; *dyktator* is used in the sense the Romans used it to denote a leader who is given all powers at a moment of supreme national danger. Kościuszko in 1794 was only the first of several to carry the title. But Piłsudski, for all his romantic sense of history, had no such ambition. If the new Polish state was to have a chance of stability and unity, the game must be played by democratic and republican rules as far as possible. A decree announced that he would remain provisional head of state only until elections had produced a parliament (which in fact, when it met early in 1919, asked him to carry on).

The whole architecture of central and eastern Europe was now thundering down in ruins. Surrounded by chaos and revolution, Poland's option for democracy had many enemies. In December 1918, the PPS (Left) and the SDKPiL fused into the Communist Party of Poland, and tried to launch a workers' revolution which challenged the very concept of Polish independence. In January 1919, a cabal of officers attempted a right-wing coup d'état and managed to arrest the prime minister before they were persuaded to surrender. But the real problem of internal politics that faced Piłsudski was what to do about the National Democrats. Somehow they must be drawn into sharing responsibility, if Poland were not to split into two camps so hostile that they might slide into civil war. Messengers came and went between Warsaw and Paris in an effort to soothe Dmowski's injured feelings.

A compromise was reached in January. Ignacy Paderewski, who had worked closely with Dmowski in the West but was not actually a National Democrat (and disliked Dmowski's streak of anti-Semitism) was persuaded by Piłsudski to take over as prime minister. It was agreed that the Polish National Committee in Paris, with the addition of some Piłsudski supporters, would be transformed into the Polish delegation to the coming peace conference at Versailles. When the elections were held later in January – confined to central Poland and western Galicia, as the other Polish areas were still embroiled in frontier struggles – the National Democrats emerged well ahead of the socialists as the strongest single party, but the peasant parties of the centre held the balance in the Sejm and the Paderewski compromise survived. Piłsudski himself remained as head of state and commander of the armed forces.

Piłsudski had not liberated Poland. Neither, indeed, had the Poles themselves. If anyone deserved gratitude, it was the millions of anonymous soldiers and civilians in the three partitioning empires who decided that they

The great pianist Ignacy Paderewski (1860–1941), seen here–with his famous mane of hair–on a tour of the United States in 1902. Paderewski became the most respected advocate of Polish independence in the West, and helped to represent Poland at the 1919 Peace Conference.

had suffered enough from wars and crowns. On the other hand, it was the Poles and nobody else who were now to decide the 'Poland – where?' question. The Allies at Versailles considered that they were entitled to draw the frontiers, after hearing and judging all claims and counterclaims. But in the event the Poles drew most of their own borders, often in blood and often in places which shocked the statesmen at Versailles.

The Western world was familiar enough with Poles as 'unfortunates', as exiles and refugees considered to deserve charity, sympathy and the occasional hearing. Now, as the Versailles conference opened in January 1919, President Wilson and the British and French prime ministers, Lloyd George and Clemenceau, confronted free Poles uninhibited by feelings of gratitude or enforced humility. Lacking imaginative sympathy for a nation whose political reflexes had been determined by over a century of violent cultural and political strangulation, the Western statesmen were appalled. With the exception of the noble Paderewski, the Poles struck them as extreme, irresponsible and – in their natural gaiety and high spirits – frivolous.

Dmowski set the tone. Delegates at the opening session were meant to speak for ten minutes at a time; Dmowski spoke without a text for five hours, switching merrily from one language to another. Count Sforza, the Italian

Poland was one of the battlefields of the 1914–18 war. Poles in the various contending armies suffered over a million casualties.

Versailles, 1919: Allied officers peer to see the signing of the Peace Treaty

The architects of Versailles. Left to right: David Lloyd George (British prime minister), Vittorio Orlando (Italian prime minister), Georges Clemenceau (French prime minister), Woodrow Wilson (President of the United States).

foreign minister, recalled: 'We saw the Poles reappear . . . still the delightful and impractical Poles of old. Their public men flooded the Cabinets of the Entente with memorials, reports, plans, historical reconstructions, juridicial theses without end. According to them, half Europe had been Polish and might become Polish again.'[4]

But in the gap between the end of the war and the beginning of Versailles, the new Polish frontiers were already being set. Fighting had broken out between Poles and Ukrainians at Lwów in November 1918, ending with all Galicia under Polish control seven months later. In December 1918, there was a victorious Polish rising in the German province of Poznań. The Lithuanian capital of Wilno was taken first by the Bolsheviks and then by the Poles. Czechs and Poles fought each other in the Cieszyń region, the small industrial area which had been Austrian Silesia. That struggle ended in July 1920 when the Allied powers enforced a partition – a solution never accepted by the 140,000 Poles who found themselves on the Czechoslovak side of the frontier.

The Allies managed to exert some control over the new borders with Germany. The Poznań region and much of West Prussia went to Poland, which was given access to the Baltic by a 'corridor' of territory running to the sea. The port city of Danzig, mostly German in population, was made a 'Free City' under a High Commissioner appointed by the newborn League of Nations. The corridor cut East Prussia off from the rest of Germany; Polish claims to the southern part of East Prussia subsided when a plebiscite gave them only a fraction of the vote.

The toughest problem on the western borders was Upper Silesia. With its concentration of coal-mines, many producing high-grade coking coal, and its iron and steel mills, this was the most valuable industrial area in central Europe. Under German rule, its population had become a dense mixture of Catholic Poles and Catholic German Silesians under a crust of Prussian Lutheran administrators and industrial capitalists who were usually German or German–Jewish. Many 'Germans' were of Polish descent and had relations who considered themselves Polish.

About the only problem modern Poland has been spared is regionalism. Minorities of other nationalities are a different matter; the Poles themselves share a remarkably uniform culture. The exception was – and to some extent still is – Upper Silesia, separated from the Polish state long before the Partitions and conscious of a distinct identity. The Polish mining villages had given their hearts to the charismatic Wojciech Korfanty, who had represented them in the German Reichstag and who was to be the only politician in independent Poland with a local support so strong that he could defy the influence of Warsaw. Korfanty belonged to the Christian Democrats, a Catholic party formed in 1902 to block the advance of socialism in the working class.

---

4. Carlo Sforza, *Makers of Modern Europe*, Bobbs-Merrill, New York, 1930, p. 375.

Nobody was going to abandon Upper Silesia without a fight. The economy of central and eastern Germany depended on it; but without Upper Silesia, Poland would be a poor rural country lacking a primary industrial base. After two Polish insurrections in the region, the Allies intervened and held a plebiscite. This produced a German majority of votes, inflated but not decided by trainloads of Germans ferried in for the poll. The result, on 3 May 1921, was a third Polish rising led by Korfanty and helped by the passive support of the French occupation troops, which ended after several months of savage fighting with the Poles in possession of most of Upper Silesia. The League of Nations drew a final partition line in October, giving the best part of the industrial districts to Poland.

These fights around the frontier were overshadowed by the Polish–Soviet war of 1920–21, an event which for a brief but terrifying moment seemed to threaten the whole of Europe and whose baleful consequences were to determine not only the nature of the Polish state but the fate of the next generation.

Here, Piłsudski was the moving spirit. It is still often said that he attacked Russia in order to suppress Bolshevism, that he acted as a mere tool of Britain and France who had already intervened on the White side in the Russian civil war. But this is a false account both of what happened and of Piłsudski's motives. Paderewski in Paris had once suggested that Polish armies could be used to overthrow Lenin, but nothing had come of it. Piłsudski's aim, in contrast, had always been to restore something akin to the old Common-wealth, by detaching the Ukraine from Russia and bringing it into a federation with Poland. He failed to reach any agreement with the Whites, who could see no point in helping Poland to demolish the empire they hoped to restore.

The Polish–Soviet war, 1920. General Józef Haller (bearded, on the left) being shown Bolshevik positions.

Ever since the Armistice, the Germany army stranded in the east had formed a buffer between Poland and Russia. In February 1919, it finally withdrew, and Polish and Bolshevik units began to collide. Slowly the old Commonwealth outlines began to reappear, as Polish troops took Wilno in April 1919 and Minsk, the main city of Byelorussia, in August. The Bolsheviks, preoccupied with the civil war, were ready to be flexible over frontiers with the Poles, but talks between the two sides broke down in December. Meanwhile, the Allies were becoming alarmed by Piłsudski's march to the east. They had no love for Bolshevik Russia, but neither had they expected Poland to turn into the enormous revival of historical dominions which was now taking shape.

Piłsudski turned his attention to the Ukraine, which had a precarious government of its own under the Hetman Petlura. He was able to force Petlura to agree that eastern Galicia – in spite of its Ukrainian majority in population – should be merged into Poland, in return for Polish protection for Petlura's authority in the rest of the Ukraine. But the deal did not stick; most Ukrainian patriots rejected the surrender of Galicia as unpardonable treachery. However, Polish troops supported by Petlura's forces went ahead with their attack on the Bolsheviks in the Ukraine, on 8 May 1920.

By now the Bolsheviks saw the Polish advance as a threat to the survival of the Revolution itself. A huge army was assembled, and in the summer of 1920 a double counter-offensive, led by Budyonny's cavalry army in Galicia and the talented young General Tukhachevsky in the north, burst through Piłsudski's defences and poured westwards towards Poland.

It seems to have been Lenin, normally the coolest of men, who decided – against the opinions of his colleagues, including Trotsky and Stalin – that this offensive should go forward until it carried the Revolution into the heart of Europe. Tukhachevsky proclaimed: 'Over the corpse of White Poland lies the road to worldwide conflagration.' By August, the offensive was nearing Warsaw; Cossack cavalry crossed the Vistula north of the capital, and the Bolsheviks were approaching the German frontiers of East Prussia. If Poland fell, the way to Berlin would be open.

Confident of victory, the Soviet government had set up a revolutionary committee, the nucleus of a Polish government, at Białystok under Julian Marchlewski, a Polish Communist who had been one of the SDKPiL leaders. But Lenin and his generals had made a double misjudgement.

In the first place, the Polish workers and peasants put nation before class and fought stubbornly to defend the new independence of their country. All classes and parties rallied to the defence of Warsaw (the Jews volunteered, too, but many of them were interned by the police on suspicion of 'unreliability').

The second misjudgement was military. Tukhachevsky's armies surging across northern Poland were leaving an undefended flank, and the Poles – outmanoeuvred but not defeated – took their chance. A strike force was hastily put together, and on 13 August it tore across Tukhachevsky's rear and cut him off. A hundred thousand prisoners were taken, and the Soviet armies fled out of Poland with Piłsudski's men at their heels.

Marian Żebrowski was a young cavalry officer; his regiment headed the Polish counter-offensive as it hit the left flank of Tukhachevsky's advance. 'Army people know what it means when one is attacked across the line of one's advance. That means the complete destruction of an offensive – and that's just what happened. The third and fourth squadrons destroyed everything ahead of them. The second squadron rode round the right wing, crossed a bridge and covered our right. The first squadron was sent to deliver a cavalry charge on the left, where larger groups of the enemy had been seen. In the last phase of its attack, the squadron got into some marshland and in this marshy ground there were small units of the enemy. Our men fired on them, but the horses began to sink into the soft ground and the charge came to a standstill. The enemy redoubled their fire, and the squadron took heavy casualties . . . My friend, an officer-cadet called Suchodolski – his horse was killed and he fell, and was stabbed seven times with a bayonet. I helped to carry him to the ambulance cart and he just said to me: "Marian, we won such glory today, though I won't see the results of it . . ."'

This was the battle of Warsaw, or the 'Miracle on the Vistula'. It was one of the most dazzling operations in European military history. It saved Poland's independence, and it forced Soviet Russia to abandon for ever the idea that November 1917 had been only the prelude to world revolution; from now on, Lenin was to adopt a more defensive policy which was to end in Stalin's formulation of 'socialism in one country'. Many people, then and now, have concluded that in 1920 Poland saved Europe from Communism. It would be more prudent to say that the 'Miracle' probably saved Germany from Soviet invasion. The revolutionary tide in Germany was ebbing fast by the summer of 1920, and any Red Republic established there by Soviet troops would have been swept away by the combined armies of the West.

Other consequences of the 1920 war were more ominous. At the Treaty of Riga, signed in March 1921, Poland's frontiers were finally set far in the east. Too far, and yet not far enough. They gave Poland neither the federation of smaller nations which Piłsudski had dreamed of reviving, nor the tight, ethnically compact Poland for the Poles that Dmowski wanted. Instead, the frontiers split three communities entirely against their will and without their consent: Lithuanians, Byelorussians and Ukrainians. Poland between the wars included not only 22 million Poles, but nearly 5 million Ukrainians, 1.5 million Byelorussians, 80,000 Lithuanians and the same number of Russians, as well as some 700,000 Germans, mostly in the western provinces. The 1931 census, based on language, found that Poles were less than 70 per cent of the population: the next largest group was Ukrainian-speaking (14 per cent), followed by Jews speaking Yiddish as first language (8.7 per cent).

This was the shipwreck of Piłsudski's hopes. In place of a great community of nations liberated from the Russian Empire, with Poland at its head, Poland had ended up as a single state containing large and often bitterly resentful minorities.

The second consequence of the war, even more sinister for the future, was to reinforce powerfully the prejudices of Poland's eastern neighbours. Soviet Russia, which had begun by proclaiming Poland's right to independence and revoking the Partition Treaties, now reverted to traditional suspicion of Poles as a race of aggressive, fanatically Catholic landowners dedicated to the overthrow of the Russian state. The Lithuanian Republic, robbed of Wilno, had no reason to trust Polish policies. The Germans might have been expected to feel gratitude after the battle of Warsaw. Far from anything of the sort, they never forgave the loss of their eastern territories, and right-wing German opinion carried on the Bismarckian view that Polish independence was an absurd disaster to be put right at the first opportunity.

The third consequence was related to the second. The Poles themselves also fell back on past attitudes. Soviet Russia seemed after all to be the old Russia, the arch-enemy of Polish liberty and independence. Poland saw itself once again as the 'bulwark' of Western Christianity against the hordes of the East, and acquired a faith in Polish military strength that was not really justified. Internally, the war crippled the chances of the Polish Communist Party, which had supported the Soviet invasion and was now branded with the mark of disloyalty to the very existence of a separate Poland.

With this went a new wave of anti-Semitism. There had been abuse and violence directed at Jews in the first year of independence, stoked up by the soldiers of Haller's army – politically close to Dmowski and the *Endecja* – when they returned from France in 1919. This was a hangover from the last Partition decades, when the National Democrats, especially, had encouraged Poles to suspect the Jews of Russian or German sympathies. But it was the universal, international perspectives of Marxism which had an appeal for Jewish intellectuals in Poland, repelled by the narrow, racial nationalism of Dmowski. In consequence, the leadership of the Polish Communist Party, much of it inherited from the old SDKPiL, was largely Jewish. Communist support for the Soviet invasion thus made it easier to create the image of a hate-figure who was Jew, Red and traitor all in one.

The new Poland had few friends. One exception, as in the nineteenth century, was France. General Weygand had led an Allied military mission to Poland at the time of the Polish–Soviet war (and there was a young, impressionable officer on his staff named Charles de Gaulle). On the whole, however, Western statesmen regarded this bumptious, quick-tempered young state with a dislike that its victory over Soviet Russia did little to diminish.

But the real tragedy of the Polish–Soviet war lay deeper. The Revolution of 1917 had raised real and marvellous hope that, with the fall of the Tsardom, the relationship between Russians and Poles might escape its terrible past and be transformed into a lasting friendship. This hope was now extinguished.

3

Independent Poland between the Wars: 1921–39

While Poland's 'where' question was being settled by great and little wars around the frontiers, the 'what sort of Poland' questions also remained to be solved. The new state had to create a working economy and select a constitution. Above all, Poland had to find a political system which balanced the need for strong central authority with the democratic demands of a bewilderingly wide fan of interest groups, national minorities and ideologies.

The first task was to overcome the chaos left by the collapse of the Partitions. The three reunited fragments of Poland had different laws, different educational systems, and different economies facing outwards towards markets which had mostly ceased to exist. The railways were an example of the confusion. There were three incompatible signalling arrangements, three kinds of brake (which meant that wagons of the various regions could not be run in a single train), 160 types of locomotive and, in addition, the tracks in Russian Poland were of a wider gauge than the others.[1]

Much of Poland had been devastated by war, and a gaudy variety of currencies – roubles, marks, Austrian crowns, even some dollars and British gold sovereigns – was in circulation. Over seventy per cent of the population worked on the land, ranging from the well-organised farmers of the Poznań region to the overcrowded and underemployed peasants of Galicia. The coal revenues of Upper Silesia were frozen by recurrent fighting and uncertainty, while the industries of the Kingdom, above all the textile mills of Łódź, had lost the old Russian market which had been the reason for their existence. By 1920, production was only forty per cent of its pre-war level, and the economy was further burdened by the imposition of part of Austria-Hungary's war debts upon Poland. The first Polish governments took the easy way out by simply printing more money. The result was steady inflation, which cut the already

---

1. See Antony Polonsky, *Politics in Independent Poland 1921–39*, Oxford University Press, Oxford, 1972, p. 8.

miserable living standards of working people but which – in its early stages – helped industry to revive.

Binding the fragments of Poland into a single political system proved equally difficult. The intelligentsia had inherited much of the old *szlachta* (nobility) tradition of zigzag independence and individualism. Stifling a doubt or filing the edge off a sharp opinion in order to reach consensus was no part of that tradition. Under the Partitions, there had certainly been doctrines of compromise, practised by many of the powerful land-owning families, by the Church, and by some of the political formations that arose in the later nineteenth century. But these had been compromises with the authorities of the partitioning Powers, not between Poles. By the time of the first post-independence elections in 1922 there were no fewer than ninety-two political parties.

The Upper Silesian coalfield and industrial area: Germans and Poles fought each other for its possession after the First World War (when this photograph was taken). Its coal is still today Poland's single most valuable asset.

At first sight, the eight years of parliamentary government between 1918 and 1926 seem anarchic, a whirl of short-lived coalitions, petty crises and tumults in the Sejm. But there were underlying patterns, revealing three main political camps and four main issues of conflict between them. And throughout this period, Józef Piłsudski remained the central figure in Polish life, at first directly involved as head of state or as commander of the armed forces, later as an unofficial kingmaker in retreat at his country house at Sulejówek, near Warsaw.

The three main political blocs were the Right, the Centre and the Left. Roman Dmowski, back from France, and the National Democrats dominated the Right. The leading personality of the Centre was Wincenty Witos, head of one of the two larger peasant parties, the PSL-Piast; his sturdiness and popularity brought him to the head of the all-party government which took the impact of Bolshevik invasion in July–August 1920. The Left was divided between a more radical peasant party (PSL-Liberation) and the PPS – the Polish socialists. Although the PPS regarded Piłsudski's commitment to socialism with growing doubt, he still retained great influence in the party; many of its best-known people were his old comrades from prison cells and underground struggle.

The March Constitution, which came into effect in late 1922 although it was passed the year before, was modelled in many ways on that of France. Allowing for pro-French sentiment and for memories of the debt owed by the 1791 Third of May Constitution to the French Enlightenment, this was not a very appropriate choice. The administration was tightly centralised: Warsaw was to run everything, allowing almost no room for democratic local government. The president was in theory a weak figure, elected by both chambers of the Sejm with only limited powers to dissolve parliament and call elections.

The first elections under the March Constitution took place in November 1922. No bloc, let alone any single party, won an absolute majority. Right and Centre gained about the same number of seats, the Left rather fewer. But – and here was a fourth bloc which was to be the focus of much political hatred – the national minorities won almost a quarter of the seats. As many Ukrainians boycotted the elections in protest, the biggest group of minority deputies was composed of Galician Jews from the Zionist parties.

After the elections, Piłsudski gave up his powers as head of state with relief. His successor, chosen after an obstinate struggle in the Sejm, was Gabriel Narutowicz, a rather unpolitical professor who had been teaching in Switzerland before independence. He was Piłsudski's candidate and the socialists' candidate, but his election was clinched by the votes of the national minorities who – as they generally did – put their weight behind the Left.

Led by National Democrat militants, the Right instantly raised an outcry against Narutowicz, protesting that Jews and Ukrainians had imposed a president on Catholic Poles. A few days later, Narutowicz went to open an exhibition of paintings in Warsaw. As he was standing near the British ambassador, making polite conversation, a member of the exhibition committee produced a gun and shot him.

The murder of the president appalled Poland. Eligiusz Niewiadomski, the killer, was a painter unbalanced by political excitement who was not a member of any party, but most Poles put the blame on the *Endecja*. Piłsudski in particular was distraught. Always impatient of politicians, he now began to speak as if the parties – and the National Democrats especially – were a mere excrescence on Polish life. Wacław Jędrzejewski, who was close to him, recalls: 'Piłsudski stopped talking to people – he chose only those with whom he wanted to talk. It was a different, different Piłsudski.'

Piłsudski retreated in disgust to Sulejówek. But his influence over the Left and the army remained, and contributed to shaping the pattern of politics after the murder of Narutowicz (who was succeeded as president by Piłsudski's old PPS comrade Stanisław Wojciechowski). The key to this pattern was simple: the socialists and Piłsudski himself were determined to prevent the National Democrats governing. This was ensured by a series of Centre–Left coalitions.

Achilles in his tent. Józef Piłsudski *en famille* at his country retreat at Sulejówek, after leaving the political scene in disgust. Aleksandra, the veteran conspirator, is darning for the camera. The Russian samovar, a very unpretentious one, was part of the lifestyle of those brought up in eastern Poland.

And on the only two occasions when a Centre–Right coalition appeared, with *Endecja* members in the Cabinet, Piłsudski and the Left drove Poland to the brink of revolution or civil war through either political strikes or military rebellion.

The four main issues in domestic politics were: land reform; the constitution and how control of the army fitted into it; the treatment of the national minorities; and the handling of the economic and financial crisis.

Several of these problems converged in 1923. The German hyperinflation swiftly infected Poland, and the Polish mark – at 50,000 to the dollar in the spring – crashed to a rate of five million to the dollar by December. While a government headed by Władysław Sikorski was trying to beat down the inflation, Wincenty Witos and his Piast peasant movement unexpectedly struck a deal with the National Democrats over land reform. Sikorski resigned, and a Centre–Right coalition took office under Witos – with Roman Dmowski himself becoming foreign minister a few months later. One of Dmowski's conditions for the pact was that the new government should take a tougher policy towards the Ukrainians, in particular, and settle colonies of Polish farmers among them.

Wincenty Witos (1874–1945), dominant figure of peasant politics. Although he was far more sophisticated than this picture suggests, he left Warsaw when he was prime minister at the crisis of the 1920 war to get his harvest in.

Nothing much came of the settlement plan. Nor did Witos manage to do anything effective to speed up the purchase of land from the big estates and its redistribution to the rural poor. Instead, his government was soon paralysed by the resistance of the Left, backed by a working class which faced starvation as the firestorm of inflation burned away their wages. A violent railway strike in October 1923 was followed by a general strike, in which the PPS and the workers took over the city of Kraków.

Lidia Ciołkosz, a PPS member whose husband was one of the Socialist leaders, remembers that 'in Kraków General Czikel sent army troops against the striking workers, which was absolutely intolerable for the PPS. The first shots were fired by the police. General Czikel foolishly sent in mounted troops, and the asphalt sprayed with water made the horses slip. Later a tank was brought in. It ended in bloody riots; some strikers as well as soldiers were killed. And the memory of this strike, the riots, the use of troops against workers, all put Witos in a very bad light as far as the workers were concerned . . .'

Polish heavy industry, much of it state-owned, consisted of a very few, very large plants. Rather than staying away from work at home, the workers occupied and fortified their factories – the so-called 'Polish Strike' technique which was to re-emerge in Communist Poland nearly fifty years later.

When Poland regained independence, more than a quarter of the land belonged to large private estates. Though their methods were traditional, the estates were much more productive than the small strips of the peasantry.

The Witos government collapsed in December 1923. With the first Centre–Right experiment over, there followed a government under the independent Władysław Grabski, an economist who was one of the few capable men on the political stage. His government lasted almost two years, to general surprise and relief, and Grabski made a valiant effort to rescue the economy by cutting expenditure, establishing a new Bank of Poland and – in April 1924 – bringing in a new currency, the zloty, whose value was tied to that of the stable French gold franc.

Grabski hoped that his reputation as a man above party would help him to deal with the other unsolved problems. He persuaded the Sejm to accept a land reform measure, by which 200,000 hectares would be bought and redistributed each year. He reached agreement with the Catholic Church, and a concordat with the Vatican was signed in February 1925, allowing for religious education in state schools: nobody but Grabski could have achieved this, for the Church was closely identified with the National Democrats, and was – accordingly – regarded with bitter suspicion by the Piłsudski clique and by the Socialists. He was less successful with the national minorities, and had to abandon a more liberal policy towards the Ukrainians and Byelorussians because of Polish opposition.

But it was the economy which finally wrecked Grabski. Old-fashioned as they were, his methods reduced inflation for a time; however, events outside his control frustrated them. Nobody wanted to lend money to Poland, and the prices of agricultural exports slumped. The decisive blow came when Germany, still vindictive over her territorial losses, announced a tariff on imports of Upper Silesian coal from Poland; when the Poles rejected this, Germany declared a full-scale trade war and banned over half Germany's imports from Poland. The new zloty began to slip. The Bank of Poland warned Grabski that it would not prop up the currency any longer, and he resigned in November 1925.

An all-party government led by Alexander Skrzyński, a diplomat with a good reputation in the West, tried to restore the economy. For a few months, Skrzyński's policies seemed to work. Unemployment fell slightly, and the British mining strike – which soon became the 1926 General Strike – allowed Polish coal to seize many British markets. But the zloty went on falling against the dollar, and the government decided on further cuts in state spending. When it came to reducing pensions and firing 18,000 railway workers, the PPS ministers could take no more and walked out of the Cabinet. Skrzyński himself resigned on 5 May 1926.

It was a bad moment for Poland. The Poles had flung themselves into the adventure of rebuilding their state and their nation with brilliant hopes, much sacrifice and unexpected energy. But now, eight years on, Poland was still neither stable at home nor safe abroad. At the Treaty of Locarno, signed in 1925, Britain and France had been among the states which guaranteed to keep Germany's western frontiers where they were – but there was no such international guarantee for Germany's eastern frontier with Poland. Instead, an ominous relationship of outlaws between defeated Germany and the new Soviet Union, which had begun with the Rapallo Agreement of 1922, was growing steadily stronger, and a German–Soviet neutrality pact was signed the month before Skrzyński's government fell. There were few Poles who did not see this unlikely friendship as a threat to Poland's independence.

At home, there was ill-feeling and intolerance. The workers were exasperated by 'recovery programmes' which seemed to benefit only the rich. The rural poor, their overcrowding made steadily worse both by their birth rate and by the American 'closed door' which prevented emigration, were impatient for the land they had been promised. The Ukrainians were resorting in despair to terrorism and were beginning – equally desperately – to look towards the Soviet Union for support. The main political parties were not just mutually intolerant; they considered one another a menace to the nation. The National Democrats feared the PPS would take the country into a sort of Jewish national Bolshevism; the Left was convinced that the Right, given power, would tear up the constitution and install a form of Fascism.

For all this, Piłsudski himself was partly to blame. This was not the Poland he had dreamed of, the morally pure nation for which the men and women of 1863 had striven. After 1922, when he left the presidency, Piłsudski retained enormous authority but used it mostly in negative ways. He was not at all the type of a European dictator. Off the battlefield, he was a hesitator. Complaining in violent, barrack-room language about the narrow selfishness of party politicians, he none the less resisted a whole series of attempts to draw him back into positions of responsibility. He intervened constantly in army affairs, so that the officer corps became divided between amateurs bound to him by personal loyalty – the old Legionaries – and those with professional training in the armies of Austria–Hungary, Germany or Russia. If little could be done with Piłsudski, yet nothing could safely be done without him.

The resignation of Skrzyński's government led to a crisis. President Wojciechowski approached one politician after another to form a fresh administration. All failed, usually because of Piłsudski's obstruction. Finally, the impatient Wojciechowski turned to the Right. Wincenty Witos offered to form another Centre–Right government in coalition with the National Democrats, and his offer was accepted.

It was 10 May 1926. The Left and its supporters in the army, believing that democracy was about to be extinguished, beseeched Piłsudski to act. For months Piłsudski and officers loyal to him had been laying plans for a possible coup d'état, and on 12 May he left Sulejówek and marched to Warsaw at the

13 May 1926. Piłsudski crosses the Poniatowski Bridge in Warsaw to confront President Wojciechowski. Second from the left is Lt Marian Żebrowski, the only surviving witness of their conversation.

head of several regiments. In his own mind, this was to be only a 'demonstration': he expected his old friend Wojciechowski to give way and dismiss the Witos Cabinet at once. But the President defied him. Piłsudski's men had occupied Praga, the Warsaw suburb across the Vistula; he now confronted Wojciechowski in the middle of the Poniatowski Bridge.

It was an extraordinary scene. At either end of the bridge, soldiers in full battle order stood and waited. Piłsudski, in his marshal's uniform, strode out along the roadway with a small group of his officers. Near the Warsaw bank of the river, drawn up across the bridge to receive him, stood President Wojciechowski in his top hat, surrounded by ministers and loyal army commanders. Lieutenant Żebrowski, Piłsudski's young liaison officer, remembers the moment well. 'They bowed to each other. The President tipped his hat and said haughtily: "Marshal, I request that you immediately return your troops to barracks."'

Piłsudski walked back to the Praga side in a fit of despair. To cross the river meant doing battle with troops loyal to the government. It could provoke a full-scale civil war, which he might well lose. Other officers with him were less reluctant. They crossed another bridge, and shooting broke out as Piłsudski's troops entered Warsaw. Three days of street fighting ensued, at a cost of 379 lives. The railway workers' union, strongly socialist, called a strike which prevented units loyal to the government from reaching Warsaw, and on 14 May, the PPS ordered a general strike. But President Wojciechowski had already decided to stop the bloodshed, and surrendered to Piłsudski that evening.

Roman Dmowski (1864–1939), Piłsudski's great rival. Although the National Democrat movement he led never took power, its right-wing nationalist ideas still influence Polish thinking.

The coup of May 1926 was a turning-point in Polish history between the wars. But its consequences were not as dramatic as they might have been in another European country. For all their effervescence and verbal extremism, the Poles – including the Marshal himself – instinctively avoided violent and sudden change. There was no 'White Terror', no fascistic 'New Era'. Government under Piłsudski's influence became steadily more authoritarian and intolerant, but many of the period's best achievements, in economic development and in intellectual life, were still to come.

Everyone knew by 1926 that a political explosion of some kind was near. Roman Dmowski was in Paris at the time, trying to raise support in western Europe for a right-wing coup or 'national revolution' of his own. Professor

Stahl, one of his supporters, was in Paris with him and learned of the May coup from the newspapers. He rang Dmowski, who was naturally enraged that Piłsudski had forestalled him but then commented: 'It is good the ulcer has finally burst.'

The real losers of May 1926 were the parties of the Left. The PPS and the socialist trade unions – even the Communists – had backed Piłsudski, assuming that by overthrowing Witos and the National Democrats he was clearing the way for a left-wing government. They soon began to understand their mistake, and to see that their assumption that Piłsudski was still essentially a man of the Left had become an illusion. Now fifty-eight years old, he was concerned with authority and the state rather than with any political creed.

Piłsudski, in fact, seems to have had no clear idea of what he wanted to do. He believed that Poland needed a stronger form of government, in order to cut a more impressive figure in foreign policy and to allow the army to be developed without political interference. On domestic policies, beyond demanding less corruption and more hard work, he had few plans.

His first move was to allow himself to be elected president, and then at once to resign, opening the way for the pliant Ignacy Mościcki to succeed him. The PPS were shocked and alienated by this imperious trick, and opposed constitutional changes which strengthened the powers of the presidency. In October, Piłsudski himself took over as prime minister, keeping the additional posts of minister of war and chief of staff. The democratic forms remained, but the centre of power in Poland was no longer in the Sejm: Piłsudski and his 'boys' – officers from the Legions notable for loyalty rather than intelligence – took the real decisions in the Marshal's study or around his dining-table.

Walery Sławek, Piłsudski's most devoted follower, was given the job of organising a mass movement which would support the régime and outflank the existing parties. The result of his efforts, some eighteen months later, was a ramshackle body known as the Non-Party Bloc for the Support of the Government (BBWR), consisting largely of old Legionaries faithful to the Marshal with a sprinkling of conservative nobles and defectors from other parties, including some from the national minorities.

And yet the Sanacja (Moral Renewal), as the new régime called itself, started off with an air of success. The whole European economy was recovering by 1926, and foreign investment began trickling back into Poland. The long general strike in Britain continued to help Polish coal exports, and more than compensated for the losses of the German trade war. The new government was lucky, moreover, to have a pair of talented men: Gabriel Czechowicz, the finance minister, and Eugeniusz Kwiatkowski, minister of trade and industry. It proved easy to reawaken public enthusiasm for 'building a strong homeland', and the whole nation dug into its pocket to help Kwiatkowski's development projects. New industries were seeded with state funds, and a fishing-village on the beach of Poland's corridor to the Baltic was transformed into the port city of Gdynia. The Danzig Germans, who had been helping to obstruct Polish exports in line with the German boycott, now raised agonised protests against the loss of trade they expected. But after nearly two hundred years, Poland was again a maritime power.

There were no elections until 1928. When they were finally held, the Non-Party Bloc gained only a quarter of the vote, in spite of much surreptitious support and money from the administration. The Left did well. It was a recipe for trouble in the Sejm, which had given the government a relatively quiet ride up to then, apart from a running struggle against attempts to muzzle the press. Against Piłsudski's wishes, the Sejm now elected as its speaker the socialist Ignacy Daszyński, a firm democrat and a political veteran who had been a Galician representative in the Austrian parliament. A further series of bruising collisions with the Marshal convinced his old party, the PPS, that he and his clique of colonels were a menace to the democratic system. The parties of the Left drew together into a committee 'for the defence of the republic and democracy'.

It was an absurd situation. An authoritarian régime, led by an elderly and short-tempered soldier, was trying to operate within the rules of a parliamentary democracy although it had no majority in parliament. Something was bound to give way, and the first signs of collapse came in 1929 when the Sejm indicted Czechowicz, the finance minister, for corruption. Czechowicz seems to have been relatively guiltless, trying only to conceal Piłsudski's use of government money on the election, but the affair burned on as the Marshal tried to protect his minister and denounced his critics in the Sejm as the scum of the earth. That autumn, when the Sejm session opened, Piłsudski came to the ceremony accompanied by a squad of armed officers. Ignacy Daszyński refused to open the session until the officers left. 'Idiot!' said Piłsudski. But Daszyński stood firm, and the Marshal retired frustrated.

By now, the international fair weather which had helped the Sanacja through its first years was turning to storm. The Wall Street Crash of October 1929 set off the world slump of the 1930s, and no country was worse hit by it than Poland. In part, this was because of the old-fashioned methods the régime used to cope with recession, sticking blindly to an overvalued currency and cutting state spending to the bone. (Kwiatkowski, an early Keynesean who suggested reflating the economy by government expenditure, was sacked in 1930). But Poland suffered mostly because of the sort of society it was: a backward agricultural country with a narrow industrial base which was trying to compete on open terms with the highly developed capitalist world outside.

The figures are shocking. A nation less basically tough and patriotic might have disintegrated under such blows, or panicked into Communism or Fascism. National income fell by a quarter in the first four years of the Depression, and unemployment rose to at least twenty-five per cent (counting the 'hidden' unemployment of the rural poor, the true figure may have been as high as forty per cent). The small peasants had far the worst of it. Agricultural prices fell so much faster than industrial prices (the 'scissors' effect), with the money return per hectare falling to one twenty-sixth of what it had been in 1928, that the peasants were unable to buy fertiliser or machinery, let alone pay their debts or afford to buy fields through the land reform. Meanwhile, the population grew, from twenty-six million in 1919 to nearly thirty-five million in 1939, and some estimates of the 'surplus' population on the land run as high as eight million. Neither was there anything like a modern capitalist industrial economy. Over half the company stock was foreign-owned, while almost half the rest was state investment. Polish private capitalism was still in its infancy.

Against this background, the tensions between the régime and all the currents of opposition came to a climax in 1930. The socialists and the peasant parties, now acting as a loosely united movement known as the Centrolew (Centre–Left), began a nationwide agitation against 'the dictator Piłsudski' and 'the May system'. After an enormous Centrolew rally at Kraków in June 1930, Piłsudski lost patience with the opposition. In September, after months of preparation, he struck.

Eleven Centrolew leaders were arrested at once. Within a few weeks, the numbers of those detained ran into thousands, including sixty-four members of the Sejm. They were held in grim conditions in the old fortress at Brześć. Lidia Ciołkosz and her husband Adam had both been at the Kraków rally and

Kraków, June 1930. On the spot where Kościuszko proclaimed his insurrection in 1794, the opposition Centrolew parties proclaim their resistance to Piłsudski's 'dictatorship'.

had taken part in the mass demonstration demanding the resignation of the President that followed. In September, three policemen called on Adam Ciołkosz, showed him an undated arrest warrant signed by the minister of the interior, and took him away. At Brześć, Lidia remembers, 'prisoners were starved, prisoners were beaten; they were treated like dirt. They were humiliated; ordered to scrub lavatories with tiny brushes. Not everyone was as young as my husband, and for old people it was even harder . . .'

In October of the following year a group of opposition leaders was brought to trial in Warsaw and condemned for attempted subversion. Wincenty Witos, Piłsudski's old adversary, chose not to wait for the verdict and went into exile in Czechoslovakia with a handful of his followers.

With his opponents out of the way, Piłsudski organised elections in November 1930. Unrest among the Ukrainians of East Galicia was answered by a brutal 'pacification', as Polish cavalry rampaged through the villages, wrecking Ukrainian cooperatives, dairies and reading-rooms. Government intimidation, and some fiddling of the election results, brought a good result for the BBWR, and Sławek, as prime minister, took wide powers to govern by decree. Press censorship was imposed, and prominent members of the opposition were purged even from the universities.

A melancholy period now opened. Poland was not exactly a dictatorship, but it was no longer a democracy. Power lay in the hands of the Marshal's 'boys' – nine out of fifteen members of Sławek's Cabinet were soldiers – and Piłsudski himself was growing old and sick. One night – so Professor Jędrzejewicz recalls – an aide-de-camp heard voices in Piłsudski's bedroom and found the Marshal talking to himself. The ADC asked if his master was feeling ill. Piłsudski stared at him, and exclaimed: 'Do you know what will happen when I'm not here? Who will be able to stand up against the future that is awaiting Poland? Who will find the strength I still have, to resist that future?' And he spread his arms in despair.

His own authority still held the nation in awe, but most Poles now thoroughly disliked the Sanacja he commanded. Active opposition, however, was becoming increasingly dangerous: in July 1934, a concentration camp was opened at Bereza Kartuska, its first occupants mostly Ukrainians, right-wing extremists and Communists.

The opposition grew steadily more radical. On the Left, the PPS made cautious contact with the small Communist Party (KPP). But the most stout-hearted resistance to the régime from now on came from the Peasant Party (SL), formed from the rival peasant groups which had at last united in 1931. While the Depression years dragged on, workers drifted back from the cities to their villages, bringing with them methods of direct action never seen before in the countryside. Peasant strikes broke out in 1936. They were renewed on a huge scale in August 1937, as farmers calling for social justice and an end to the Sanacja tried to stop all food supplies reaching the towns. The régime hit back: forty-two people were killed in disturbances and over a thousand arrested. With Witos abroad, the inspiration of the peasants in this great trial of strength was Stanisław Mikołajczyk, a man who a few years later was to play a hard and tragic part in Poland's destiny.

Józef Piłsudski died on 12 May 1935. Setting aside their disillusion with his followers, the Poles came out on the streets in their millions to mourn him, and weeping crowds lined the railway line as his coffin was taken from Warsaw to be buried in the Wawel cathedral at Kraków beside the kings of Poland. An intelligent Pole in 1935 could imagine a much better Poland. Without Piłsudski, however, no independent Poland might have survived at all.

He left unsolved problems behind him. One was how Poland should now be governed. As he lay dying, the Sejm, on his instructions, adopted the April Constitution of 1935, which was meant to install an invincibly strong presidential system. The president was to be elected only every seven years, by universal suffrage, with power to appoint prime ministers and in emergency to govern by decree. Purged of opposition parties, the Sejm lost much of its importance.

Piłsudski had intended the faithful Walery Sławek to take this supreme post. But Sławek, an amiable but unsophisticated officer, was thought by his colleagues to lack the necessary authority. Once the Marshal was in his grave, President Mościcki refused to step down and was encouraged to stand firm by his old friend Eugeniusz Kwiatkowski. Piłsudski, however, got his post-humous way in military matters: General Edward Śmigły-Rydz was appointed Inspector-General of the Armed Forces.

A much better choice, from the point of view of vigour and political awareness, would have been the fire-eating General Sosnkowski, the man who shared Piłsudski's prison at Magdeburg. But Sosnkowski distrusted the Sanacja, and so it was Śmigły-Rydz, a stiff and unimaginative officer, who inherited Piłsudski's mantle as 'the Commandant'. Although the régime expended much propaganda on his supposed virtues, the mantle always remained much too large for him.

Foreign affairs were the most dangerous piece of unfinished business. When the Marshal died, Hitler had been in power for over three years, but the elderly Piłsudski never really took his measure. Piłsudski's policy had always been 'Eyes East!' – Russia as the historic enemy. It was a policy which had served him well in the past, and he was disinclined to rethink it.

France had a treaty of alliance with Poland, and had guaranteed the Polish western frontiers in 1925. But Piłsudski was not the only European in the early 1930s to suspect that France was growing unreliable. Justifiably sceptical of the West's will to construct a collective security arrangement in Europe, he took the opposite course and decided that Poland would only find safety through the expansion of its own military strength. Poland itself would become an uncommitted 'Great Power', balancing between Russia and Germany on its own.

Piłsudski seems to have regarded Hitler as a buffoon leading a movement of windbags. The story that he was so prescient that he suggested to the French a preventive war against Germany when Hitler became Chancellor is almost certainly a myth. Poland had signed a non-aggression pact with the Soviet Union in November 1932, and this gave Piłsudski and his foreign minister Józef Beck the confidence to defy both Hitler and the League of Nations when a crisis blew up over Danzig in March 1933.

Under its strange League of Nations status as a 'Free City', the magnificent old port of Danzig remained essentially a German town, open to all the political currents of Germany itself. The Poles, however, had a strong formal presence there, including a Polish post office, rights over the railways and the port, and a small garrison – its numbers limited by League regulations – at Westerplatte, near the harbour mouth. Now, egged on by the new Nazi government in Berlin, the Danzig Senate – the Free City's government – tested Polish determination by reducing the rights of the Polish harbour police. Piłsudski retorted by sending a regiment to reinforce the Westerplatte garrison, defying both Germany and the League of Nations.

It was a proud, provocative gesture. But Hitler, who had been in power for less than two months, was not ready for a showdown with Poland. Busy demolishing democracy at home and terrorising his opponents, it suited him to buy an interval of calm in the east. In January 1934, Germany and Poland signed a declaration that they would settle disputes only by peaceful means, while Beck went to Moscow to reassure the Soviet Union that the Poles would not join any anti-Soviet alliance with Germany.

In the short term, Poland gained: the Germans reduced their agitation for a revision of the frontier, and cut off support for Ukrainian terrorism. In the long term, though, this pact with the Nazis did much harm. It weakened the chances for any European coalition to contain Hitler. It broke ranks with Britain and France, whose diplomatic support had helped to make Polish independence possible. It gave the world the quite misleading impression – especially after a much-publicised visit by Hermann Goering to Poland – that Piłsudski and Beck welcomed Hitler and his gang as kindred spirits. Finally, it encouraged the Poles to take seriously the illusion of 'balance'.

It was an illusion because Poland's military strength was not – and could never have been – enough to make it a reality. The armed forces were large and their morale was high. But under Piłsudski's personal stewardship, loving but eccentric, they had failed to modernise. He had resisted plans to motorise cavalry, to introduce anti-aircraft guns, to form a bomber force, to organise armoured units. Efforts made after his death to close these gaps were too little and too late. At the outbreak of war in September 1939, the Poles had 313 tanks in the field. The Germans had 3,200.

No stable compromise was reached, during the Marshal's life or afterwards, with the five million Ukrainians and the two million Byelorussians. The growing influence of the Polish nationalist Right on the Sanacja, agitating for the subjugation and assimilation of the Slav minorities, broke down all attempts to reach a settlement. Split between Poland and the Soviet Union, these two unhappy peoples were unable to react with any coherence as their masters played politics with them across the border.

The plight of the Ukrainians of East Galicia (where Poles formed only a third of the population) was worse than it had been under the Austrian Empire. Then, at least, they had been one of many small nations under the Habsburg crowns, and their cultural development had been fostered. Now they were a minority in a hostile Polish state, which had shown in 1920 that it would never permit East Galicia and Lwów to rejoin the rest of the Ukraine, and which mistrusted Ukrainian culture as a training-school for subversives.

In the 1920s, the Soviet Union was relatively tolerant to its Ukrainians once the disasters of war and famine had passed. This encouraged envious unrest among the Ukrainians in Poland. From 1921 on, guerrillas of the Ukrainian Military Organisation, run from Vienna by a certain Colonel Konovalets, had been attacking Polish estates and inciting resistance. In 1929, the Colonel, now in Berlin, began to receive a secret subsidy from German intelligence; he rechristened his group the Ukrainian National Organisation (OUN), and expanded its operations. Less extreme nationalism was represented by UNDO (Ukrainian National Democratic Organisation), a party of the moderate Left, and by the Uniate 'Greek Catholic' church, the confession which had splintered away from Orthodoxy in 1596 and which now had most of its adherents in Galicia.

But after 1929, the whole picture changed. Stalin now began his drive to collectivise Soviet agriculture, and it was above all the rich and middle peasants of the Ukraine who were deported to exile and death as *kulaks*, accompanied to the labour camps by most of their cultural and religious leaders. Deeply shaken, the Ukrainians in Poland began to look for a compromise with Warsaw, and even the 1930 'pacifications' by Polish cavalry did not interrupt their efforts. UNDO, which had once demanded Ukrainian independence and nothing less, was by 1933 asking only for internal autonomy and promising that Polish state interests in Galicia and Volhynia would be respected.

At the extremes, both the Ukrainian Communist groups and the OUN went into decline. After the German–Polish understanding of January 1934, German military intelligence cut off the money and told the OUN to stop fighting. The OUN's desperate response was to murder the Polish minister of the interior, Bronisław Pieracki, on 14 June 1934. But this crime only made moderate Ukrainians more anxious to reach a settlement, and UNDO was allowed to run candidates in the dubious elections of 1935 which all other opposition parties boycotted. A chance of lasting reconciliation had arrived. It

'Pacification'. A Ukrainian co-operative store after a punitive raid by Polish troops in the autumn of 1930.

was not taken. The needless arrogance of Polish commanders and officials in Galicia and Podolia, coupled with the miseries of the Depression, led to a revival of violent nationalism in the later 1930s.

Relations with the Byelorussians took much the same course. A polonisation campaign in the 1920s provoked terrorist resistance and induced Byelorussians to look for support to the Soviet Union. However, after 1929 almost the whole Byelorussian leadership in the USSR was arrested and shot as 'Polish spies' or counter-revolutionaries, while their language was demoted to the status of a 'dialect of Russian'. Militancy among the Polish Byelorussians then subsided, although anti-Polish resentment remained and smouldered in the peasant countryside.

The German minority in Poland remained sour and disaffected. Relations were at their worst in Upper Silesia, where the rule of a particularly oppressive Polish governor led to constant German petitions to the League of Nations. Germans, of course, were in a far stronger social position than the Slav minorities, but their complaints that they were the victims of illegal discrimination both at elections and in their business lives were justified. Both the main German political groups, the Volksbund and the Jungdeutsche Partei, were fiercely nationalist; they refused to accept Poland's western frontier as just or permanent and backed German claims to regain the territory lost after the First World War. Both parties felt a natural sympathy for National Socialism, and rejoiced over Hitler's victory in 1933 as a token of their coming 'liberation'. The German–Polish thaw of 1934 obliged them to use more cautious language for a period. But for the most part the 750,000 Germans remained dangerously unreconciled to the very existence of the Polish state.

The story of Poland's Jews between the world wars was a complicated mixture of growing poverty, vigorous and hopeful social change, and of increasing anti-Semitism which finally began to infect the behaviour of government. The Jewish population grew phenomenally in numbers from some two million in 1919 to well over three million in 1939. At the same time, the Depression hit the Jews particularly hard as shopkeepers and small-business craftsmen in the towns and in the cities where they formed nearly a third of the population. The emergence of a Polish middle class, coupled with the development of peasant cooperatives which bypassed Jewish merchants in the countryside, increased the pressure and generated friction.

In spite of these problems, the Jewish community began to transform itself. The younger generation especially plunged with enthusiasm into the modern age, breaking down traditional patterns of life and organising education (Jewish schools were not subsidised by the state), sport of every kind, and self-help groups. Zionism caught the imagination of the young, but there was vivid and intense debate between a bewildering variety of political parties, from the conservative Agudat Israel to the socialist Bund, supported by a wealth of newspapers and periodicals in Yiddish or Polish. Faced with this new confidence and pride in Jewish identity, the nineteenth-century movement for assimilation withered. And yet it was assimilated Jews – writers like Julian Tuwim, Antoni Słonimski, and Leon Schiller in the theatre – who helped to give Warsaw its brilliant, non-conformist intellectual life in these years.

While Piłsudski was alive, the Jews received respectful treatment and some favours from government – neither then nor after his death were Polish Jews ever exposed to the state-sponsored violence and repression used against the Slav minorities. The Marshal in his revolutionary days had taken little account of which comrade was Jewish and which was not, and his sense of history led him to recognise the Jews as a part of Poland's heritage. The Jewish bloc in the Sejm struck a pact with the government in 1925, which led to government support for a variety of Jewish social and commercial organisations, and a number of Jewish personalities joined the Non-Party Bloc (BBWR) in 1928.

Anti-Semitism in Poland took several forms. One was ancient Catholic prejudice, especially among the peasantry, which was more religious than political. The other, more dynamic and dangerous, was the modern national-ism of the *Endecja* and its allies which used the 'alien' Jewish presence as a scapegoat and sought to exploit rising economic rivalries during the Depress-ion. The hierarchy of the Catholic Church, which tended to support the National Democrats, formed a bridge between the two. In the later 1930s, even the Peasant Party began to demand more 'Christian morality in public life' – a euphemism for reducing Jewish influence.

After Piłsudski's death, anti-Jewish agitation increased. Young supporters of the Sanacja, attracted by extreme nationalism and impressed by Nazi Germany, incited peasant boycotts of Jewish traders in 1936 and 1937 which turned into violence. The new student generation was intensely nationalistic, and small Fascist groups were active in the universities; after riots which closed many universities, a 'ghetto bench' for Jews was introduced in most law and medicine faculties.

Most Jews refused to use these benches and preferred to stand during lectures. Iza Ehrlich was a law student at Warsaw University. 'I had a friend called Wanda, who was not Jewish. We both stood in the back of the auditorium, and when the class was over a group of students, all men, came up to us. They asked why we were standing there; I think they assumed that neither of us was Jewish. I said that I was standing because I was a Jew. And Wanda said she was standing because she was a Pole. That enraged them. I think they were more enraged by Wanda than me – they expected me to stand – so they beat us up. There were six or seven of them, and they started hitting us ... there was this horrible feeling of being totally overwhelmed and helpless. I didn't believe that anti-Semitism was somehow native to Poland. I thought it was a political, economic issue, and once we had a different sort of politics there would be no anti-Semitism.'

Around half Poland's lawyers and doctors of medicine were of Jewish

origin. In 1937 the legal and medical professions banned further Jewish entry –
although, in practice, an unofficial *numerus clausus* had been operating against
Jews for years.

The Sanacja régime dithered. Unwilling to pass anti-Jewish laws on the Nazi
pattern, it was equally reluctant to defy the new wave of militant racial
nationalism among its young supporters or the frankly Fascist outbursts of its
ultra-right opponents. The government took the feeble course of condemning
the physical attacks on Jews during the peasant boycott campaign, but stating
that it had no objection to the boycotts themselves. A show was made of
looking at schemes for Jewish emigration, first to Palestine (with the
government opening talks with the Zionists) and then, when it became obvious
that the British would not dream of admitting any significant number of Polish
Jews to the Palestinian Mandate, to Madagascar and other improbable
destinations. Now, however, just as Nazi persecution of Jews in Germany,
Austria and soon Czechoslovakia reached new heights, the world was closing
its doors on Jewish emigration.

By the outbreak of war, the economic plight of Poland's Jews was desperate,
and something like a million Jews were existing on foreign relief – mostly from
Jewish organisations in the United States. A few years later, the Nazi
occupation was to 'solve the Jewish problem' in Poland with the gas chambers,
a course inconceivable to all but a handful of the most brutish Polish
anti-Semites. There were signs that, if the peace had lasted for a few more years,
the Sanacja or the semi-Fascist groups who might have succeeded it would
have adopted a drastically anti-Jewish policy, leading at least to the loss of civil
rights. It's an 'if' of history which cannot be answered. All that can be said is
that such a policy would have been fiercely resisted by the Polish Left,
especially by the Socialists of the PPS, and by all those who belonged to the
tradition which stretched back beyond Piłsudski to the old Commonwealth,
recognising the Jews – in spite of all animosities – as a permanent feature of
Polish society.

After the death of Piłsudski, the old ruling group of ex-Legionaries fell apart.
Śmigły-Rydz, appointed a Marshal, set about constructing a replacement for
the Non-Party Bloc and in 1937 launched OZON (Camp of National Unity),
a thoroughly authoritarian movement whose youth wing fell into the hands of
one of Poland's few genuine Fascist groups, the Falanga, led by Bolesław
Piasecki. Mościcki remained president, increasingly uneasy about the drift
towards dictatorship. Józef Beck, as foreign minister, carried on Piłsudski's
'Great Power' politics of non-alignment and balance, in a Europe where the
plain signs of imminent catastrophe made such a course irrelevant and
dangerous.

The outbreak of the Spanish Civil War in 1936, in which many Poles made
their way to Spain and fought in the International Brigades against Franco, was

BELOW: Edward Śmigły-Rydz (1886–1941) became Inspector-General of the Armed Forces on the death of Piłsudski, and was made a marshal in 1936. Though upright and patriotic, he did not make a convincing successor to Piłsudski, and was blamed for the failures of politics and strategy in the years leading up to the German–Soviet invasion of 1939.

followed by Hitler's annexation of Austria and then, in late 1938, by the Czechoslovak crisis. In France, a Socialist-Communist 'Popular Front' took power. These events helped to make Polish politics increasingly turbulent and extreme.

At the elections of September 1935, the opposition's call for a boycott was followed by over half the voters. In the following year came a wave of militant 'Polish strikes' in the industrial cities, in which fourteen people died, and a few months later the first outbreak of peasant strikes revealed the growing anger and militancy on the land. On the Right, Roman Dmowski was growing old and losing control of his younger supporters; perceiving that the government's attitudes were steadily converging with their own, they were encouraged to start a series of vicious attacks on Jews and on Jewish property.

From abroad, an older generation of 'responsible' conservatives watched this degeneration of politics with alarm. In 1937, at Morges in Switzerland, Paderewski, Witos and General Józef Haller drew up a pact which proposed a return to democracy under a Centre–Right government, and a move away from Beck's foreign policy towards renewing the alliance with France. An assortment of Centre parties backed the 'Morges Pact'. So, too, did General Władysław Sikorski. A clear-headed, incorruptible soldier, Sikorski had served with Piłsudski in the Legions and then held office as prime minister and minister of war in the early years of independence. But he had never been close to the Marshal, disapproving of his brusque and arbitrary style, and he regarded the policies of Piłsudski's successors with horror.

None of these upheavals and plans dislodged the régime. Śmigły-Rydz in his Marshal's uniform continued to preach the gospel of national unity. OZON filled the air with empty, noisy propaganda which now took on a distinctly anti-Semitic flavour. But OZON and Śmigły-Rydz himself overreached themselves by using language which suggested that they were preparing a coup to install a totalitarian régime, especially after the bloody peasant strikes of August 1937. Poland was by no means a cowed, prostrate society, and protests from the old Legionary associations, the PPS and several senior officers reached such a pitch that Śmigły-Rydz backed down, dismissed the OZON leaders and broke its connection with the Falanga.

By now, the menaces of Fascism, Communism and war were towering over Europe. In 1938, Hitler opened his campaign of demands against the Czechoslovak Republic. Stalin, in August that year, invited the Polish Communist leaders to Moscow, arrested and murdered most of them, and dissolved the party (KPP) on the cynical charge that it was infected with nationalism. All Poles could now see that the gathering international storm was bringing with it a threat to the very survival of the state, and the heat began to go out of domestic quarrels.

On the eve of war, a sort of calm returned to Poland. Śmigły-Rydz became more popular, as the international situation gave greater point to his appeals for patriotic unity. Economic recovery also played its part in this change of atmosphere. Kwiatkowski, the most gifted member of any government between the wars, had patiently set about breaking down monopolies, rescheduling Poland's foreign debts and designing a grand programme of state investment to prime the pump of industry. His Four-Year Plan set up an industrial development region in south-central Poland, and the later 1930s brought a steady rise in production and in real wages.

In October 1938, the Munich agreement allowed Hitler to annex the Sudetenland – the frontier regions of Czechoslovakia. Poland ought to have been horrified at this revelation of British and French weakness. Instead, Poland seized its share of plunder by invading the Cieszyn district of Czechoslovakia, with its large Polish population. For Józef Beck, this squalid act was a long-sought triumph. Most Poles rejoiced with him: their sympathy for Czechs was traditionally slight. But that very month Nazi Germany confronted Poland with its first demand for the 'return' of Danzig to the Reich and for territorial rights in the Polish Corridor.

The mist of euphoria over Cieszyn blew away. Suddenly, the true scale of the Nazi threat to Poland was plain to see. The Danzig demand was not only a challenge to Beck, but to the whole Pilsudskian approach to foreign policy. The line of conciliating Germany was obviously failing, and fast. If Danzig were abandoned, fresh Nazi pressure to revise the German frontier with Poland would certainly follow.

Beck and Śmigły-Rydz rejected Hitler's Note. But in preparing for war, they refused to contemplate any military pact with the Soviet Union against Germany. Their reasons were all too understandable. To meet a German attack, Soviet divisions would have to move forward into Polish territories claimed by the Soviet Union – and there could be no guarantee that they would ever move out again. History soon showed how true that was. But it was also true that Poland's decision to reject a Soviet alliance and to face Nazi Germany alone condemned the state to death. There was no way out of that dilemma, laid upon Poland six years before by Piłsudski's reluctance to join any European net of collective security treaties.

And yet, logically, there *was* a way out – a third option. Poland could have thrown in its lot with Hitler, joined the anti-Comintern Pact and eventually attacked the Soviet Union in alliance with Nazi Germany. Such a war would probably have ended with the defeat of both Poland and Germany. But Poles today will observe, with an irony that isn't entirely frivolous, that some nations which fought the war as Germany's allies – Hungary, for example – have ended up in a better economic and political condition than Poland, which fought the Nazis longer and at a proportionately higher cost in blood than any other country.

In any case, the 'German option' was never seriously considered in Warsaw in 1939. This was partly because Józef Beck clung to the false hope that Hitler would back off if his bluff were called over Danzig. But Poland's rulers also knew that such an alliance would reduce Poland to a helpless German vassal, and that the Polish people would never accept it.

Fatal events now followed rapidly. Germany occupied all Bohemia and Moravia in March 1939. Simultaneously, the Germans issued an ultimatum to Poland over Danzig, and Poland responded by moving troops up to the frontier.

Suddenly, and yet inevitably, the fate of Poland had become the most important question in the world, the hinge on whose swing peace or war would be decided. In France and above all in Britain, Hitler's extinction of Czechoslovakia in March had demolished what remained of the crumbling policy of appeasement. Public opinion insisted that the moment had come to make a stand, and the governments of the West could no longer resist it. Poland's significance was not so much strategic – Britain and France knew that there was little they could do to provide effective military aid – as political and moral.

On 31 March the British prime minister, Neville Chamberlain, announced that Britain would guarantee Polish independence in the event of attack. Beck flew to London, and the guarantee was made formal in April. Hitler retorted by renouncing his 1934 pact with Poland.

Within Poland, the opposition now offered its support to the government; Wincenty Witos and the other exiles hurried home. The Sanacja, however, still confident that the Polish army could resist an invasion, refused to broaden its base by sharing power with its opponents. Narrow-minded to the last, Beck and Śmigły-Rydz stuck to their old prejudices. The military talks held in Moscow that August by French, British and Soviet officers broke down over Poland's refusal to allow Soviet troops to cross its territory.

On 23 August, to the stupefaction of the world, Ribbentrop and Molotov signed the Nazi-Soviet Pact of Non-Aggression. A secret protocol to the pact provided for the partition of Poland and the Baltic States between Germany and the Soviet Union. Once again, the main dish at the feast of friendship between Poland's historic enemies proved to be Poland's independence.

The signing of the Nazi–Soviet Pact, 23 August 1939. Molotov is signing, for the Soviet Union. Behind him, on Stalin's right, stands Ribbentrop.

A few days later, Britain signed a more specific alliance, making it clear that a German attack would lead to war with Britain as well as with Poland. France was already committed.

On 1 September 1939, with no declaration of war, German troops crossed the Polish frontier. On 3 September, Britain and France declared war on Germany. Precisely a fortnight later, on 17 September, the Red Army entered Poland from the east.

4

Occupation: 1939–45

Poland is a country where brilliant ideas have been born, but seldom nursed up to full application. Nicolaus Copernicus, from Toruń, showed that the earth revolved round the sun; Michał Kalecki was a pioneer of modern socialist economics; Polish mathematicians from Poznań broke the secret of the German 'Enigma' coding machine. But it was not Poland that conquered the cosmos, ran a successful welfare state or won the 'secret war' of cryptography between 1939 and 1945.

Other countries put these ideas into practice. So it was with *Blitzkrieg*, the concept of waging offensive war with fast-moving columns of armour or motorised infantry, concentrating maximum force to punch through a minimum sector of enemy line. This theory came into the mind of a young French officer named Charles de Gaulle as he witnessed the rapid thrusts of the Polish–Soviet War, utterly unlike the broad-front offensives which had gained so little at such hideous cost on the Western Front a few years before. What if those cavalry armies could be replaced by tanks built for speed?

But it was British and German military thinkers who developed the idea of mobile warfare, years before de Gaulle finally put his thoughts on paper. And it was the Germans who first tested his theory, in the campaign against Poland in September 1939. Poland was attacked from three sides at once by Panzer divisions, and mobile units followed through the gaps they made. The German tanks outnumbered the Polish by at least ten to one, and – with an airforce five times as large as that of Poland – the Germans immediately seized command of the air.

It should have been an easy victory, but it was not. The Germans afterwards regarded it as a hard-fought campaign, and were disconcerted by the capacity of the Poles to keep fighting and regrouping in spite of such hopeless inferiority in weapons. The casualties Germany took were heavier than in the far longer campaign in France the following year.

But the result could not be in doubt. It was not just a matter of superiority in numbers and equipment. All the weaknesses of post-Piłsudski military thinking in Poland, strategic as well as tactical, were rapidly exposed. Before the war began, the Germans already half-encircled Poland, able to attack simultaneously from Slovakia in the south and from East Prussia in the north. Between these gaping jaws, any Polish attempt to hold the western frontier was bound to lead to the cutting-off of the main body of the Polish armies. This, however, was just what Śmigły-Rydz had planned to do in the event of war. It was an understandable decision: to abandon western Poland meant giving up

September 1939: the German attack on Poland. A girl and her sister, victim of a German bomb.

almost all the country's heavy industry. But it was a military mistake, now made worse by a political error. Śmigły-Rydz, ignoring the repeated and bitter lessons of history, assumed that France and Britain would immediately come to his aid.

Why he assumed this is not entirely clear. Most ordinary Poles made the same mistake. When France and Britain declared war on Germany on 3 September, their embassies in Warsaw were surrounded by cheering Poles certain that their country would now be saved. But Śmigły-Rydz should have been better informed. Earlier military conversations with the French had produced the idea that, if Poland could hold a German invasion for some two weeks, France would attack Germany from the west in a full-scale offensive. But this plan, never formalised or endorsed by the French or British governments, had been quietly dropped months before the war broke out. No preparations for such an onslaught were made in the west, and Polish military intelligence should have known this. The Germans clearly did: they thought it safe to risk stripping their western defences down to a mere thirty-four divisions in order to reinforce their Polish campaign. And Śmigły-Rydz also ignored Pilsudskian thinking in one fatal aspect. He took no effective precautions against a Soviet invasion from the east, although some of his senior officers correctly read the inner meaning of the Nazi–Soviet Pact and warned him of the danger.

Before the first week of war was out, Polish strategy was breaking up. The Panzer spearheads had pierced through the western defences, while other divisions driving down from the north were approaching Warsaw; armoured columns fanned out in the Polish rear and split one unit from another. With the Polish airforce hopelessly outnumbered, the dive-bombers of the *Luftwaffe* ranged freely over the landscape in these hot, clear days of late summer, plunging at will on cities, trains of refugees and columns of retreating Polish troops with their horse-drawn guns and carts.

Too late, Śmigły-Rydź ordered a retreat to a line of defences along the rivers Vistula and San. The jaws were now closing behind the main Polish force, which broke up into isolated groups fighting on with a steadiness and skill that amazed the Germans. A counter-attack on the Bzura river west of Warsaw threw the Germans back for a moment and killed thousands of the invaders, but by now the Polish supreme command was too disorganised to support this temporary success. The German armies reached and crossed the Vistula and San rivers before a Polish defence line could be established there, and on 10 September a fresh retreat was ordered to eastern Galicia, the south-eastern corner of Poland. It meant the abandonment of Warsaw, now under continuous air attack. The government and several foreign embassies had already left, driving towards the south-east by night to avoid the German bombers. All able-bodied men were ordered out of the city, and on 14 September the capital was surrounded.

Did Polish cavalry charge German tanks, as the old legend asserts? There were certainly episodes when they attacked German supply columns protected by light armoured cars, and won. And there were moments from another age. General Klemens Rudnicki remembers facing the officers and men of a cavalry squadron who refused the order to surrender and announced that they intended to die charging the enemy lines. 'I said that this is not the end of the war. It's only the beginning. And those who cannot accept defeat are not worthy of victory.'

But the spirit of those awful weeks was not so much romantic as dogged and enduring. The extraordinary thing about the Polish soldiers was their self-reliance: their capacity to reorganise into ever-smaller units, as all coherent command from above vanished, and to go on fighting. Part of the Polish navy had already escaped and reached British and French ports, ready to continue the war, and as resistance collapsed about a hundred Polish aircraft – all that remained – flew to Romania.

At 3.30 on the morning of 17 September 1939, the Polish ambassador in Moscow was summoned from his bed and handed a 'Note'. The Soviet Union announced that as the Polish state had ceased to exist (which was not true), steps had become necessary to protect the Ukrainian and Byelorussian minorities in the 'former' Polish territories. An hour later, Soviet troops crossed the frontier.

At first, the incredulous Poles imagined that the Red Army might be coming to their assistance. There was little resistance to the invasion, the eastern border being almost unprotected, but the truth became rapidly plain as the Soviet forces moved across eastern Poland to a demarcation line along the rivers Bug and San. A Fourth Partition of Poland was taking place. General Sosnkowski,

The September Campaign. Polish cavalry riding into action.

commanding the last coherent army group around Lwów, fought briefly on against both German and Soviet forces, but it was obvious that defeat was now imminent. At midnight the same day, President Ignacy Mościcki, with the gold of the state bank, crossed over into neutral Romania, followed an hour or so later by Śmigły-Rydz and the General Staff.

There was no surrender. In Poland, the fighting went on. The siege of Warsaw, its people starving and its buildings crumbling under bombs and artillery bombardment, cost tens of thousands of dead.

Zofia Kolarska remembers: 'We all lived in cellars, taking beds, mattresses and whatever we could with us. The army was there, so there were many horses: women would go up to the dead horses with sharp knifes and we'd cut off chunks of meat, and that helped us to live through those days.'

Warsaw's 'President' (mayor), the much-loved Stefan Starzyński, finally agreed to surrender on 27 September. Incredibly, the small Polish garrison on the Hel peninsula near Danzig, now hundreds of miles behind the lines, held out until 2 October, and the last shots of the campaign were fired at Kock, in central Poland, on 5 October.

For all their faults and errors in the past, the men who had governed Poland never contemplated an armistice. Poland had not ceased to exist and would not cease to fight simply because its armies had been defeated and its territory was occupied by the enemy. The problem was how to carry on the struggle; Romania, under extreme pressure from both Germany and the Soviet Union, had interned the Polish military and political leadership. However, the Romanians did not detain General Władysław Sikorski. As an old critic of the Sanacja regime, he had not held command in the September campaign and was allowed to leave Romania for France, where the Polish ambassador in Paris – on his own authority – charged him with raising a new Polish army out of refugees and Poles living in France.

From Romania, President Mościcki managed to send to Paris a message announcing his resignation. The group of Polish leaders who had already reached France accepted it, but rejected his ideas for a successor. They chose instead Władysław Raczkiewicz, a respected provincial governor who had not been tainted by too close an association with the Sanacja.

Under the guise of a 'correct' transfer of power, a discreet revolution was now overthrowing the Sanacja. President Raczkiewicz took the oath in the Paris embassy on 30 September, and at once appointed Sikorski as prime minister. Kazimierz Sosnkowski reached France a few days later, sank old animosities and joined the new government. Finally, the absent Śmigły-Rydz was induced to resign in November, and Sikorski became commander-in-chief as well as head of the government in exile.

France and Britain at once recognised the new administration, followed by the still-neutral United States. In some ways, this had all happened before. After the 1830 Rising, the Great Emigration had transferred Poland's cultural and political capital to Paris In the 1914–18 war, Roman Dmowski's National Committee had become a recognised government in waiting, also in Paris. Now again, with a deftness and confidence that only a nation accustomed to disaster and occupation could achieve, Poland had ensured its international survival.

Physical survival, for the Polish people at home, seemed less certain. The war had already cost the lives of 60,000 members of the armed forces and of many more civilians. Nearly half a million prisoners were in German hands and another 200,000 in Soviet camps. Much of Warsaw had been ruined, and bombing had scorched the heart out of towns and villages along the track of the armies. And yet, as the fighting ended, the sufferings of Poland in the Second World War had scarcely begun.

In the Soviet-occupied zone, the policy of the conquerors was at first erratic. Many Poles, then and now, see the secret protocol of the Nazi–Soviet pact and the 'stab in the back' of 17 September as the realisation of a coldly planned design, a natural expression of Russia's attitude to the existence of an independent Poland ever since the Russian state had been born. But in 1939 Stalin was probably less concerned with Poland itself than with Germany. Through the pact with Hitler, he had bought time and space. The Soviet occupation of eastern Poland at least kept the Germans 600 miles from Moscow; if Stalin had left all Poland to Hitler, the Nazi tanks would be only 400 miles from the Kremlin.

The new 'demarcation line' – which Stalin intended to make a permanent frontier – pushed 'the imperialist West' several hundred miles further away. This corrected Lenin's frontier compromise with Piłsudski at the Treaty of Riga eighteen years before, which the Soviet Union had always intended to revise when it was strong enough. No doubt Stalin in 1939 shared traditional Russian suspicion of Poland as a country dedicated to the break-up of Russian empires whether Tsarist or Soviet. But a stronger motive was his concern to end the partition of the Ukrainian and Byelorussian populations between the USSR and a foreign state. He wanted those unlucky peoples all to himself.

In the territories seized after 17 September, there were probably less than five million Poles out of over twelve million inhabitants, although they included cities like Lwów and Wilno which were strongly Polish and Polish-Jewish. The Soviet authorities carried out an immediate round of arrests and deportations, principally of Polish local leaders. Then there was a pause while the institutions of 'Sovietisation' were put in place. Rigged elections in November produced dummy assemblies of Ukrainians and Byelorussians who voted unanimously for their incorporation into the Soviet Union. There was some land reform, some nationalisation. Poles were everywhere removed from official posts.

By Soviet standards, this initial phase was deliberately mild. Stalin did not occupy all the Polish territory offered to him by the Nazi–Soviet Pact's secret protocol, but accepted instead 'influence' over Lithuania. Soviet troops entered Polish Lithuania and took Wilno on 18 September, but then restored the city and its region to the Lithuanian state. For a few months more, the Poles in Wilno were able to organise themselves and live in relative freedom. In Byelorussia and the Ukraine, religious education in schools was forbidden and monasteries commandeered, but religion itself – Uniate or Catholic – was not suppressed. However, the Soviet Union made it clear that the events of September implied not only the end of Polish rule in western Byelorussia and Ukraine but the final, irreversible abolition of Polish independence. Molotov announced that 'nothing is left of Poland, that hideous offspring of the Versailles Treaty'. On 28 September, the USSR and Nazi Germany signed a further 'Friendship and Frontier Agreement', whose secret clauses committed each power to suppress Polish agitation against the other, and to inform one another about 'suitable measures' for dealing with the Poles.

In late November 1939, the Soviet Union attacked Finland. Stalin intended a rapid campaign to push the Finnish frontier back from the approaches to Leningrad, but the 'Winter War' developed into a long, bloody struggle which disgusted the world and brought Britain and France to the verge of military intervention on the Finnish side. These setbacks may have prompted the Soviet Union to 'secure' its new western frontier.

In February 1940, there began the first of a series of huge and brutal deportations of Poles. Families in the occupied areas were driven from their homes and packed into unheated cattle-trucks, which headed slowly for Siberia and the Soviet far east while their occupants stifled, starved or froze to death. One survivor, Aleksandra Rymaszewska, recalls: 'We came to the long line of trains and the hordes and hordes of people being pushed into cattle trucks . . . there was nothing, just bunks from one wall to the other, a small barred window, the hole in the floor that was supposed to be our toilet. After a few days we were put in different trains which were on wider tracks, and these tracks, we knew, were leading into the depths of Russia.'

The deportations lasted until July 1940, and were followed by another round-up in June 1941. Between one and a half and two million Poles were herded into the trains, to be employed as slaves or forced labourers in mines and lumber camps near the Arctic Circle, or to be dumped in the steppes of Kazakhstan. No political distinctions were made, and Polish Communists from the abolished KPP (Communist Party of Poland) worked and perished alongside Catholic priests and university professors, farmers and railwaymen. Tens of thousands of Poles who had held official posts were 'tried' and consigned to long sentences in prisons or camps. No reliable figures exist on their fate, but it is estimated that anything between a third and a half of the deported Poles were dead by the time of Hitler's attack on the Soviet Union in June 1941. The 200,000 captured soldiers remained in Soviet custody, while the officers were segregated into separate camps. Some 10,000 of these Polish officers, held in camps in the Smolensk region, remained in intermittent touch with their families until about March 1940. Then all contact with them suddenly ceased.

After July 1940, another change came over Soviet policy towards the Poles under Soviet occupation. The three Baltic republics of Lithuania, Latvia and Estonia were invaded in June and in July annexed to the Soviet Union. But in Byelorussia and the Ukraine, the deportations were suspended, and cautious contact was made with some of the remaining Polish personalities in Lwów. The reason for this, fairly certainly, was Soviet alarm at the scale and ease of the Nazi victory over France and Britain in the west, beginning with the German offensive in May and ending with the surrender of France and the evacuation of the defeated British in June. Facing the possibility that Hitler would now turn his aggression eastward, the Soviet Union wavered between the existing policy of treating the Poles under Soviet control as a menace to security in a frontier region, and the need for allies where they could be found. A group of Polish officers, including Colonel Zygmunt Berling, was invited to discuss the possibility of raising a Polish division for the Red Army. Meanwhile Wanda Wasilewska, a Polish Communist who had survived in Lwów on her wits and through her connections with Stalin and his inner circle, was allowed to publish a magazine and to press for the restoration of a Polish Communist Party.

The treatment of the Poles by the Soviet Union between 1939 and 1941 is still an unfamiliar story to foreigners. News of what was going on came only scantily to the West at the time, and later in the war, when Britain and the United States became the allies of the USSR, discussion of the episode was judged tactless and was discouraged. The true story emerged only in fragments during the post-war years, and was understandably overshadowed by the more spectacular and better-publicised savageries of the Nazi occupation of Poland and the rest of Europe. Yet in its brutality and the sheer scale of its cold-blooded attempt to obliterate the Polish nation physically and culturally, this 21-month Soviet occupation far outdid all the crimes committed against Poland during the century-and-a-quarter of Russian occupation under the Tsars.

The recent memory of Soviet behaviour in Poland was the greatest single obstacle facing the new Communist authorities in Poland after the war. They had to conciliate a people for whom a Soviet-backed government seemed to threaten not only the abolition of private property and farms, and the suppression of the Catholic faith, but transportation to almost certain death in Siberian labour camps, probably to be followed by yet another cancellation of Polish independence.

The Germans controlled the heartland of Poland, with a population of nearly twenty-two million. They made no secret of their intentions. Hitler, who took the salute at a victory parade in Warsaw on 5 October 1939, spoke in

Adolf Hitler (on dais, lower right) takes the salute at a victory parade in Warsaw, 5 October 1939. Minutes before, his car had driven over a concealed bomb which the Polish resistance had been unable to detonate.

Danzig and Berlin of the 'artificial' and 'unviable' Polish state which was the foster-child of Western democracy and deserved its fate: 'to be swept off the face of the earth'.

A few days later, the whole of northern and western Poland, including Poznań, Danzig and its hinterland, and Polish Silesia, was annexed to the Reich. The rest of the German-controlled area became the so-called 'General Government': in effect a native reserve under martial law to be exploited for its resources and labour without consideration for the consequences. Its 'capital' was at Kraków, Warsaw being designated for eventual destruction and replacement by a small German colony. Hans Frank, a senior Nazi jurist with a princely lifestyle, became Governor-General and established his court at Kraków in the ancient Wawel Palace.

The Germans lost no time in showing the Poles what their occupation would mean. Behind the advancing front-line troops came the *Einsatzgruppen*, special execution squads drawn from the SS and the police, whose task was not only to crush resistance and opposition in the civilian population but to slaughter whole categories – the political and intellectual élite, the mentally sick, the leaders of Polish communities – as potential sources of racial or political infection.

Sometimes they shot, sometimes they merely arrested and terrorised. The first great atrocity of the occupation centred on the town of Bydgoszcz

In the regions of Western Poland annexed to the Reich, mass expulsion of Poles began

Reprisals. Polish civilians hanged by the Germans on an improvised gallows.

(Bromberg in German), where – the facts are still not established – a group of fanatical German civilians appear to have opened fire on retreating Polish troops during the September Campaign, leading to an outbreak of violence against Germans in which many lost their lives. An official German report in November 1939 wrote of some 5,400 German residents in Poland killed or missing in this and similar incidents elsewhere. In February 1940, the German press was instructed to revise this figure to 58,000. The *Einsatzgruppen* had already undertaken a reprisal for the Bromberg Massacre and had shot nearly 20,000 Poles.

In the regions annexed to the Reich, the Nazi intention was to carry through once and for all the colonisation policy which Prussian and German governments had failed to complete. The Polish inhabitants, numbering between eight and nine million, were to be removed and replaced by Germans. While this was being organised, these regions were subjected to a 'Germanisation' process: the Polish language were forbidden in public, special limited shopping hours were imposed on Poles, and all education over primary level and cultural activity were forbidden. In September 1940, a decree confiscated all Polish property in land or commerce. The Catholic Church was closely persecuted, and in October 1941 several hundred priests were arrested and sent to concentration camps, while only a handful of churches were permitted to remain open.

The colonisation programme began in December 1939 with a round-up of 90,000 Poles and Jews, mostly from the 'possessing classes', who were transported to the General Government – the Jews being sent to the newly established ghettos. The next category to suffer were the small farmers, often given less than an hour to leave their villages while SS men tore down the crucifixes and holy pictures from their walls. Most of them also went eastward to the General Government, though some were conscripted as forced labour for war industry in Germany. Meanwhile, as a part of the Nazi–Soviet understanding, the ethnic German groups living in the newly acquired territories of the USSR – the Baltic states, Volhynia, Bessarabia – were expelled 'home to the Reich' and resettled on the abandoned Polish farms.

For all its root-and-branch vigour, this colonisation project was not much more successful, even in the short-term, than its predecessors. Deportations were broken off in the spring of 1941 and never resumed. About half a million Poles had been removed, not much more than six per cent of the total in the annexed territories, while some 350,000 *Volksdeutschen* from the east arrived to replace them. At the end of the war, all were driven out of Poland for ever.

What was new about this episode of German repression was its almost unimaginable savagery and cruelty – an entirely new quality of method. Between 1939 and 1944, the Nazis murdered something like 330,000 Poles in these annexed regions alone. But the policies themselves were familiar to any Pole who had heard his father describe the Bismarck period: colonisation, expulsion, the simultaneous attack on the language and the Church. Equally familiar was the German assumption that the ruling class in Poland, and above all the intelligentsia, were incurable patriots, to be dealt with only by force. The Prussians had been saying this back in the 1880s. The Nazis found their own solution to the problem of the Polish intellectuals: systematic extermination.

In the General Government, with a population of over twelve million, a few weeks of weird calm followed the arrival of the Germans; theatres reopened, and the universities prepared for the new academic year. But things changed instantly when Hans Frank took office. Stefan Starzyński, President of Warsaw, was arrested; the professors of all higher education in Kraków were invited to a meeting, seized and sent to concentration camps where many of them were shot. Similar purges took place in all the cities, as the massacre of the intellectual class began. During the Nazi occupation, Poland lost half its doctors and more than half its lawyers, forty per cent of its university professors, half its engineers and eighteen per cent of its priests. Frank told a German police conference in Kraków: 'The Führer has told me that the leading groups in Polish society already in our hands are to be liquidated, and whoever appears to replace them is to be detained and after an appropriate interval exterminated . . . Gentlemen, we are not murderers. But as National Socialists, these times lay upon us all the duty to ensure that no further resistance emerges from the Polish people.'

The policy for the General Government was that this region, too, would eventually be Germanised. All education above primary and technical level was abolished; all museums and libraries were closed; cultural and artistic activities were forbidden; paintings and sculptures were removed to the Reich, and monuments to great figures in Polish history were demolished. A universal, indiscriminate reign of terror descended on the Polish population, while the Jews, many thousands of whom had already been tormented in public and shot out of hand, were herded into walled-off ghetto quarters in the principal towns. Factories and offices were placed under German direction, to serve the war effort, and wages were frozen. At the same time, a rapid inflation began, reducing the purchasing power of ordinary Poles to a fraction of its pre-war level. The food rationing system that was eventually introduced allowed 2,613 calories a day to a German, but a mere 669 to a Pole. This was a frankly genocidal policy. Like the Jews, but on a slower time scale, the Poles had been designated as an inferior, vermin-race to be eliminated from physical existence.

Especially after the German invasion of the Soviet Union in June 1941, the General Government was used as a reservoir of forced labour for the war industries and to replace German manpower called up for military service from the farms. By 1942, about a million Poles had been deported to work in Germany. Growing resistance to the mass round-ups, which required increasing numbers of police and troops and drove thousands of young men and women to seek refuge with the partisan bands in the forests, persuaded Hans Frank to question the whole policy. But he was overruled by the SS, now becoming an autonomous empire within the Reich which not only ran the concentration camps but possessed its own army – the Waffen-SS – and its own industrial economy. Village after village was burned and their inhabitants murdered for real or imagined resistance; as the historian Norman Davies has pointed out, the famous tragedy at Lidice in Czechoslovakia, where a village was destroyed and its inhabitants massacred, was repeated in some three hundred Polish villages during the Nazi occupation.

In November 1942, Heinrich Himmler, Reichsführer of the SS, ordered that the colonisation policy should now be applied to the General Government. In the district of Zamość, near Lublin, some 40,000 Poles were driven from their villages, to be replaced by German settlers from Bessarabia. Their children were torn from them. A farmer's daughter who was there, Wacława Kędzierska, saw how 'children up to the age of fourteen, even those as young as six weeks, were taken away. When their mothers didn't want to hand them over, the Germans hit the parents. And then they started to hit the children . . . a lot of the children were thrown into the mud, even into the cesspit. They killed them. They took them by their legs and hit them against the corner of the barrack.'

The children were screened for Aryan characteristics. Those suitable for germanisation were held in SS orphanages where many died of hunger or disease, and most were never seen again. The parents were either sent to concentration camps or deported for labour to the Reich.

The Zamość action was followed in early 1943 by a new series of manhunts in Warsaw and the main cities of the General Government. Streets were blocked, cinemas, streetcars or even churches surrounded, and all those caught within the cordon transported. This time their destination was the concentration camps. The SS had begun to exploit the unpaid labour of the camps, numbering many hundreds of thousands, by inviting German industry to settle in 'enterprise zones' around the camp peripheries. This was proving a great success, from the SS point of view, but the turn-over of labour was inconveniently rapid (the average life expectancy at Auschwitz, for those not at once sent to the gas chambers, was about twelve weeks) and needed constant replenishment.

On this occasion, one of the supreme officers of the SS, 'Gestapo' Müller, laid down a target of 35,000 prisoners for the round-ups in the Polish cities, but insisted that they must be fit for work, 'as otherwise and contrary to intentions the concentration camps will be overstrained'. In practice, chaos developed as German security forces grabbed everyone, fit or unfit, without papers or even with a German work permit, male or female, in order to fill Müller's quota. Those unfit for slave labour were picked out in the camps themselves. 'Overstrain' usually came to mean overloading the crematoria with their corpses.

For the Poles, life in the cities of the General Government slowly developed its own rules and expectations. Physical survival was the issue. There was no safety from the haphazard nature of Nazi terror. At any moment, one might be seized for a labour round-up, arrested as a hostage, or shot in the countless street executions – the inhabitants ordered to stay away from the windows; the victims, their mouths often stuffed with plaster-of-paris to stifle their screams, hustled up against the wall and machine-gunned to death.

These places instantly became shrines. General Bór-Komorowski, later the commander of the Warsaw Rising, describes in his memoirs how his wife Renia, 'with her baby in the pram, passed Senatorska Street where an execution had just taken place. The corpses had already been taken away, but blood was splashed all over the pavement and bits of brains were sticking to the walls. People were kneeling all around, and in a few seconds the whole place was covered with red and white flowers and burning candles. Flowers were put in every bullet-hole in the wall. My sister stopped to pray. German police appeared and she made off. When she looked back, they were shouting and beating people up – all in vain, for after a moment the crowd was back again and new flowers and new candles had appeared.'[1]

To stay alive required not only luck but law-breaking, and most of the population was involved in black-marketeering, rackets in stolen German

1. Tadeusz Bór-Komorowski, *The Secret Army*, Battery Press, New York, 1984, p 156.

supplies, theft from German-run factories and offices, bribery and the forgery of every kind of document. The peasants were besieged by town dwellers seeking food in exchange for jewellery, gold or furniture. Władysław Baran, a small farmer, recalls: 'People started to come to me from Warsaw, on bicycles. They could carry fifty kilos on a cycle; they weren't well dressed, their cycles were falling apart, and they pushed them on foot from Warsaw. Each took a few kilos of wholemeal flour or potatoes; they were a picture of poverty . . .'

The only Germans in close contact with the city Poles were the German carpet-baggers and fortune-hunters who flocked to the General Government. They sold precious supplies and identity papers, but they were always dangerous and unreliable. An intense solidarity developed among Poles, who devised elaborate alarm systems and code-words to warn each other of nearby Germans or of a *łapanka* (round-up) in the next street. The exception was the odious class of Jew-hunters, who made a living by spotting and blackmailing Jews who had escaped from the ghettos and were trying to pass themselves off as Gentiles. The Resistance imposed a death penalty for this crime, but the trade thrived throughout the occupation.

The Poles remain proud that – alone in Nazi-occupied Europe – they produced no 'Quislings', no régime to collaborate with the Germans. However, this was partly the result of German policy, oriented towards the genocide of the Polish nation rather than towards establishing any client state. And a few minor Polish figures, among them the elderly politician Władysław Studnicki, did make approaches to Berlin suggesting that a collaborationist government might be set up in exchange for ending the mass deportations and executions. The Germans ignored them, and Studnicki was arrested.

Resistance began to be organised even before the final defeat of the Polish armies. The day before Warsaw fell, the city authorities gave General Tokarzewski the task of organising a Polish military force throughout the country. He established a coalition of pre-war opposition parties – the PPS, the Peasant Party, the Nationalists (National Democrats) and the small Democratic Party – under the title of the Service for Poland's Victory (SZP), and set off on a tour of the occupied areas. Spontaneous resistance groups had formed already, as soldiers avoided surrender and vanished into the forest with their weapons; the most famous of these bands was commanded by Major 'Hubal' (Dobrzański), who conducted his own partisan war on horseback among the villages of the Kielce region until the Germans killed him in April 1940.

Tokarzewski was able to track down many of these groups and link them up into the skeleton of a nationwide armed resistance. But he at once ran into severe trouble – at the hands not of Germans but of Poles.

The problem was political. At Angers, where General Sikorski had pitched his headquarters in France, there was no intention of allowing any power centre to appear in Poland which was independent of the authority of the government. In October 1939, Sikorski ordered the dissolution of the SZP, and replaced it with an organisation of his own: the Union of Armed Struggle (ZWZ). At this stage, contact with Poland was only possible by couriers, who made slow and dangerous journeys through the Balkans or across the Baltic to neutral Sweden. No proper radio link had been established. In spite of this, Sikorski at first attempted to run the resistance directly from Angers, putting it under the command of General Sosnkowski. He demoted Tokarzewski and ordered him to move to Lwów (he was arrested by Soviet patrols on the way), and appointed his deputy, the resourceful Colonel Stefan Rowecki, as effective resistance commander within Poland.

These were the months of 'phoney war', before the Nazi onslaught on France in May 1940. The Poles at Angers shared the illusion that Germany might be rapidly defeated in the west, and therefore suspected that any independent resistance leadership might soon challenge their authority by setting itself up as the government of a liberated Poland. Sikorski's harsh treatment of Tokarzewski, absurd in hindsight, sprang from his fears that the SZP included too many old Pilsudskians, and might form the embryo of a revived Sanacja.

The fall of France in June 1940 led to a break in contact with Poland, while Sikorski's government reorganised itself in London. In June 1941, Hitler attacked the Soviet Union and all the territories of pre-war Poland soon fell under the control of the advancing German armies. On 30 July, under British pressure, but with deep misgivings and reluctance, Sikorski's government signed a pact of alliance with the Soviet Union.

Against the background of these tremendous events, the Polish resistance painfully worked out a permanent structure. The Government Delegate in Warsaw, responsible to London, had authority over four departments. These were a political council (PKP), the *Delegatura* (administration), the armed forces which in 1942 united as the Home Army (AK), and the Directorate of Underground Struggle, which ran the welfare, relief and education services of the 'underground state'.

One of the few intelligent actions ever undertaken by Heinrich Himmler was to circulate to his security commanders a monograph on the 1863 Rising in Poland. The parallels were striking. As in 1863, the Polish strategy was to establish a working under-

The Home Army. A young officer of the resistance.

Images of peace. Three Home Army partisans made welcome by their friends.

ground state, equipped with universities, schools, law courts and the rudiments of a parliament. A force of armed partisans scattered throughout the land in small groups was led by a clandestine command group in Warsaw, and relied upon a far larger force of part-time auxiliaries leading 'normal' lives who were also soldiers of the Home Army. The aim of military resistance was to prepare for an insurrection on a national scale, which would come into the open and liberate Poland as foreign assistance approached.

The AK was, and remained, far the largest resistance force in Poland. At its height, in 1944, it numbered some 200,000 men and women, and its allies in the countryside, the Peasant Battalions, were nearly as numerous. But it was inpossible to find arms for this sea of passionate volunteers, and the AK seems never to have possessed more than 32,000 guns. Some arms and supplies were dropped by Allied aircraft, but Poland was at the extreme edge of their range and only a few hundred tons arrived. This meant that the traditional 'national insurrection' would never become practical, remaining a dream which the AK leaders were unable to forsake.

Lack of arms also restricted the AK for most of its existence to harrying rather than confronting the enemy, to attacking railways and roads, to sabotage, to the rescue of prisoners and the assassination of individual SS and police officers. The AK efficiently harboured Allied prisoners-of-war on the run, and set up a spectacularly successful intelligence service which provided the Western Allies with details and even large fragments of new German weapons: the V-1 pilotless aircraft and the V-2 rocket. For all its shortage of weapons, the Home Army's sheer size and spread across the country held down large German forces, killing some 150,000 in the course of the occupation, and the AK became a continuous menace to the German lines of communication to the Eastern Front. But the penalty for resistance of any kind was death, and the losses of the AK, in battle, by execution or in the camps, were tragic. Among the dead were Professor Jan Piekalkiewicz, the Government Delegate until 1943, and General Stefan Rowecki himself, captured in the same year and shot in a concentration camp in 1944.

The 'underground state', reviving the 1863 tradition, became widespread and effective. Illegal schools educated about a million children, while the universities of Warsaw, Kraków, Lwów and Wilno all operated in clandestinity.

The secrecy was all too necessary. Bogna Domańska, a resistance worker, was involved with a secret youth education centre in a poor district of Warsaw. 'These young people were learning professions, learning to read and write and all that. It was all conducted very well. The young people went willingly. One beautiful day, cars drove up. All the young people were turned out and twenty-seven previous pupils of this training school were hanged at the back . . . a rope on which there hung twenty-seven young men.'

A network of courts, working in a society in which illegal behaviour was not only necessary to stay alive but the condition of resistance itself, tried to deal with the worst cases of banditry, blackmail and anti-social racketeering. A large and varied press sprang up in the underground, publishing over a thousand

The Underground State. Secret schooling from primary to university level was maintained. The penalty for teacher and pupils was death.

books and pamphlets – some of them regularly printed – and numerous clan-destine newspapers, periodicals and bulletins. Mrs Domańska helped to produce a fake version of the official daily paper published by the Germans; her version contained the real, uncensored news. 'Our boys on bicycles rode around and gave them out. The whole of Warsaw was reading them. All the news from Britain, from America, from Europe, from the Polish resistance. One old man was standing and reading. And then he began to cry a bit, and he folded the paper, put it in his pocket and said: "Thank you." Just like that – into the air.'

Lack of food and medicines, and the shortage of clothes and especially shoes (many families wore wooden clogs in winter and went barefoot in summer), led to a collapse of public health; deaths from tuberculosis, for example, rose almost fourfold in Warsaw between 1939 and 1941. Self-help committees, tolerated by the Germans but backed by the resistance, ran soup kitchens and relief centres. Cultural life survived as best it could. The Germans took over all cinemas – the resistance mounted a rather unsuccessful movie boycott – but underground theatres flourished in many towns. One of these, the Rhapsodic Theatre in Kraków, featured a young actor named Karol Wojtyła, the future Pope John Paul II.

During the occupation, the Catholic Church itself underwent a transforma-tion, both in its social attitudes and in its relationship to the population. This was partly a consequence of persecu-tion – several thousand priests died at Nazi hands – and partly of isolation. Little help or support came from the Vatican, where the new Pope Pius XII, elected in March 1939, pursued a line of compromise with Germany and National Socialism which deeply shocked Polish opinion. At the same time, the Primate, Cardinal Hlond, who was abroad, decided not to return to Poland. The Church was deprived of its leader at the moment of desperate national crisis, but Hlond represented the least attractive features of the pre-war Church; its highly conservative attitudes, as owner of large estates and ally of the propertied classes, and its anti-Semitism. (In 1936, Hlond had pro-claimed in a pastoral letter that 'the Jews fight against the Catholic Church and constitute the vanguard

Father Maximilian Kolbe, declared a saint in 1982. In Auschwitz he volunteered to be starved to death in a punishment cell, taking the place of a Pole with many children.

of atheism, Bolshevism and revolution; the Jews are committing frauds and dealing in white slavery'.)

On its own, and exposed to the full onslaught of Nazi terror, especially in the annexed territories of the west – 752 priests out of 2,500 in the region around Poznań were murdered – the Church shared the sufferings of ordinary people. They in turn sought refuge from the horrors of their lives in religion, once again functioning as the inmost fortress of Polish identity. The resistance leadership was not always at one with Church policies. It condemned the way that Bishop Adamski in Upper Silesia encouraged some cooperation with the Germans, while welcoming the tougher stand of Archbishop Adam Sapieha in Kraków, whose diocese helped and protected thousands. But the foundations of a less arrogant and more enduring 'church of the people' were being laid. The appropriate symbol of this change was to be Father Maximilian Kolbe, who offered himself for death at Auschwitz as a substitute for a Polish father of a family and was canonised in 1982 – all the more appropriate because Father Kolbe had edited a distinctly anti-Semitic Church paper before the war.

Two main political problems faced the AK and its leadership. The first was that it failed to unite the whole resistance under its command. On the right, a breakaway group of National Democrats set up the National Armed Forces (NSZ), which rejected Sikorski's pact with the Soviet Union and fought its

The communist partisans. Four soldiers of the People's Army, in a village near Zamość.

own war of terrorism not only against Germans but against Jews, and sometimes against the AK itself. On the left, a Communist resistance appeared in 1942, after Stalin had permitted the restoration of a Polish Communist Party under the title of Polish Workers' Party (PPR). But PPR attempts to draw the Government Delegate and the AK into a common military and political front were rejected. The numbers of the Communist resistance were not impressive, less than a tenth of the combined strength of the AK and the Peasant Battalions. But as it became clear by late 1943 that the Soviet armies, rather than the West, would liberate Poland, the absence of any relationship between the 'London' resistance and the PPR, backed by the Soviet Union, became dangerous and eventually fateful.

The second problem, closely related, was the surge of radical feeling in wartime Poland. In this, the Poles were sharing the longing of all European resistance movements for a cleaner world after the war, for social equality and full employment. In Poland – in contrast to Italy or France – memories of 1920 and 1939 were too fresh to turn this emotion into support for Communism. But there was an absolute determination never to return to the traditions of the Sanacja, and to construct a radical democracy which would deal once and for all with the curses of rural poverty, landlordism and industrial weakness.

This set problems for the London government and the resistance leadership, composed, as in part they were, of dissident survivors of the pre-war régimes. The new AK commander after the arrest of Rowecki, General Tadeusz Bór-Komorowski, persuaded the political authorities to issue a series of draft programmes for social reform, including the break-up of all landholdings over fifty hectares. Fear of Communism, and the wish to outbid any reform programme which the approaching Soviet armies might bring with them, were only some of the motives. Bór-Komorowski was convinced that his own forces would welcome such post-war reforms. But these concessions were not enough to produce agreement with the Polish Communists and their People's Army (AL), whose negotiator was Władysław Gomułka.

There was in fact no great difference between the reforms proposed by the PPR and those advanced by the 'London' resistance. The contacts stalled over the eastern frontiers. Here the Government Delegate, backed by London, absolutely refused to budge, insisting that the Communists recognise the pre-war frontier established by the Treaty of Riga and demanding a PPR promise that the Communists would actually take up arms against the Soviet Union if Stalin insisted on restoring the frontier he had gained in September 1939. The talks naturally collapsed, and the PPR went ahead with its own policy, eventually setting up a National Council of the Homeland (KRN) in December 1943. The Home Army correctly saw in this the germ of a Communist-led provisional government, and denounced the PPR for 'treason'.

✳　✳　✳

In the midst of these events, the greatest tragedy of the twentieth century was taking place on Polish soil. The 'Final Solution of the Jewish Problem', the systematic annihilation of the Jews of Europe, took place partly in the Baltic states and Nazi-dominated Russia, where it was carried out by the firing-squads of the *Einsatzgruppen*. But the central horror, the extermination of millions of human beings by industrial methods, was carried out in the gas chambers of concentration camps built on the territory of the General Government.

Intermittent massacres of Jews had marked the first months of Nazi occupation. There followed a series of decrees which stripped Jews of all human and economic rights, reduced their rations to starvation level and – in the course of 1940 – herded them into walled-off ghettos within the larger cities and towns. The penalty for leaving the ghettos or for sheltering Jews was death. The Jewish Councils (*Judenräte*), set up by the Germans, struggled to protect the ghetto populations by a series of ever-retreating compromises with the German authorities, but their task was hopeless. By 1941, over 100,000 Polish Jews had died or been murdered. Nightmarish conditions existed in typhus-ridden ghettos like that of Warsaw, where skeletal children prowled the streets and the corpses of those who had died of hunger or disease lay about the pavements.

The exact 'when' – and even the 'why' – of Hitler's secret order to carry out the methodical murder of European Jewry is not known. The order seems to have been given in late 1941, and was only confirmed by the infamous Wannsee Conference in Berlin on 20 January 1942.

For all the screaming rhetoric of 'extermination' and 'wiping-out', Nazi policy towards the Jews was impromptu and erratic. The first idea, forced emigration, was frustrated by the 'closed-door' attitude of the West, especially of Britain in Palestine, and then by the outbreak of war. The next plan seems to have been the deportation of Europe's Jews to Asian territories conquered from the Soviet Union, where they would be separated by sex to prevent breeding and then worked to death. The massacres by the *Einsatzgruppen*, who killed over a million Jews behind the advancing German armies, were seen as a mere clearing of the ground for what was to follow.

It has been argued that the halting of the German armies before Moscow in December 1941 determined the final form that the 'Solution' took. There was now no prospect of a rapid conquest of vast and empty Soviet territories; the war in the east would be long and hard. Meanwhile, the conditions in the ghettos and camps where Polish and other European Jews were being dumped were growing so appalling that the orderly German mind was alarmed. The time, space and resources for a 'working to death' policy were no longer available. An end had to be put to the 'Jewish problem', quickly and on the spot.

The first experiments in gassing were carried out at Chełmno in 1941. Early in the following year, extermination camps with gas chambers were constructed at Treblinka, Sobibór and Bełżec, in the General Government, and in the winter of 1942–3 the concentration camp at Auschwitz, in Silesia, was extended to take a battery of immense gas chambers and crematoria which could – and did – slaughter and consume up to 15,000 people within twenty-four hours. Not only the Jews but the gypsy nation was condemned to genocide, accompanied by hundreds of thousands of others from almost every country in Europe. Auschwitz alone accounted for nearly 3 million dead. About 2.8 million Polish Jews perished in the extermination camps, with another million Jews brought to the gas chambers by train from all over the continent. Over 5 million Jews of all nationalities died in occupied Poland, in the camps or outside them.

In July 1942, the Germans began to deport the population of the Warsaw Ghetto to the gas chambers at Treblinka. Against the prevailing mood of hopeless fatalism, a Jewish Fighting Organisation was set up, and managed to make contact with the Home Army outside. Bunkers and petrol bombs were prepared, and when the SS entered the almost empty ghetto for the final round-up on 19 April 1943, the Jewish resistance went into battle. It was a fight which the ghetto warriors knew they must lose; the odds were crushingly against them, and the Home Army and the Communist underground were able to do little to help. But this was a fight not for victory but for honour, and for the future of the Jewish people. The handful of men and women held out against tanks and artillery for almost a month, while the smoke of burning buildings and the stink of burning bodies drifted across Warsaw. Before he committed suicide with his comrades, Mordechai Anielewicz, the leader of the Ghetto Rising, said: 'I have seen Jewish self-defence in all its glory.'

Out of 3.35 million Polish Jews, about 340,000 were alive by the end of the war, most of them refugees in the Soviet Union. Those who managed to hide in Poland until liberation had grim stories to tell which still haunt Polish–Jewish relations. Poles like to say that any Jew who survived owed his life to a Pole – a statement which is not so much untruthful as incomplete. On the credit side, there were many Poles prepared to hide Jews, although they risked the execution of themselves and their families. A special department of the resistance existed to help Jews, and the organisation Żegota, founded to rescue Jewish fellow citizens, did its heroic best and paid a high price for it. The AK command sent desperate messages to London describing the systematic murder of the Jewish people, and these messages were relayed to the world by the Polish government in exile – a world which remained disbelieving and indifferent.

All this is true. On the other hand, the experiences of Jewish fugitives from the ghettos taught them that they were never safe. 'I wasn't afraid of the Germans,' recalls one Jewish woman. 'I was afraid of the Poles.' There were the marauding blackmailers, walking the streets in search of a Jewish face. There were the Poles, and they were numerous, who saw no reason to get involved with the fate of a people they had never liked, and who even felt glad that the Jews were being destroyed – though shocked at the methods, which they feared might next be applied to themselves. At the extreme, there were a few partisan units – usually of the NSZ – who shot Jews when they found them in the woods.

Children in the Warsaw Ghetto, 1940

The Łódź Ghetto: printing work by Jewish inmates

Destruction of the Warsaw Ghetto: May 1943. General Jürgen Stroop, commander of the Nazi forces, watches Jews leaping to their death from burning houses.

There are some – like the film-maker Claude Lanzmann, director of *Shoah* – who charge the Poles with direct complicity in the murder of the Jews, arguing that Hitler placed the gas chambers in Poland because he could rely on Polish anti-Semitism to raise no protest. This is historically wrong, but also a misunderstanding of Polish attitudes. Polish anti-Semitism – which is still widespread – was an archaic, principally religious, distrust, located in a mental world remote from the 'scientific' and systematic racism of the Nazis. The peasantry, especially, regarded the Jews as the people who had murdered Christ; those who hid Jews often did so on the grounds that the 'debt' had been paid by what was now being done to the Jewish population. A Jew knocking on a cottage door could have no idea of the consequences. He might be thrown out, or denounced to the Germans, or concealed in the hope of 'Jewish gold'. Or – one example is the family who hid the boy who grew up to be another film-maker, Roman Polanski – the peasants might take him to their hearts because to shelter a Jew from murderers struck them as precisely the sort of mercy that Christ had spoken of.

In July 1943, the hinge of the war began to turn. At the biggest tank battle in history, Hitler's offensive near Kursk was brought to a standstill and then driven back. The Red Army began to move westward, in a slow advance which was to end in Berlin almost two years later. In January 1944, the first Soviet troops crossed the line which had been the old Polish frontier in 1939.

Much had happened to the Poles, both to the London government and its resistance within the country. In April 1943, after the discovery of the bodies of thousands of Polish officers in the Katyń forest, near Smolensk, the Polish government had accused the Soviet Union of their murder, and Stalin had broken off relations with Sikorski. A month later, he had begun to recruit a Polish army under Soviet command. In July, Sikorski had been killed in an air crash at Gibraltar. After his death, his combined powers were divided between two of his senior colleagues in London: Stanisław Mikołajczyk, the Peasant Party leader, who became prime minister, and General Sosnkowski, who took command of Poland's armed forces.

In Poland, Rowecki had been arrested and was succeeded as AK commander by Bór-Komorowski, a cavalry officer of conservative outlook. Meanwhile, the Communists and their allies were preparing for the arrival of the Red Army, and setting up what looked like the foundations for a pro-Soviet government.

The 'London' resistance clung on to the hope – or illusion – that Poland might be liberated from the west, or at least by Anglo-American and Polish forces arriving at the same time as the Red Army. In late 1943, however, the Warsaw leadership faced the growing possibility that this would not happen. If Poland were to be occupied by the Soviet Union alone, what should the resistance do to maintain and assert Poland's independence, and to prevent the reduction of Poland to a Soviet protectorate?

Instructions arrived from London that the whole structure – the AK, the Government Delegate and all the rest – should stay concealed as the Soviet armies rolled over Poland and await further orders. Bór-Komorowski and his colleagues found this absurd and dishonourable. Instead, they planned an active policy. As the Soviet forces drew near, one AK unit after another would launch an insurrection against the disintegrating Germans, liberate its region, and meet the Red Army as 'host' in a manifestly free Polish state whose government would soon return from London.

This was 'Operation Tempest'. Its weaknesses sprang from the ignorance of the underground leaders about the balance of power and priorities in the anti-Hitler coalition. In the first place, 'Tempest' assumed that the Soviet forces could be made to respect the pre-war frontiers. In fact, they had no intention of doing so, considering the lands acquired in September 1939 as integral regions of the USSR, while the British and Americans had shown that they would not risk a breach with Stalin by insisting that Poland should regain its old borders. Secondly, 'Tempest' was based on the belief that Stalin would accept the *fait accompli* of an anti-Communist government in Poland with Western support. Again, this overlooked the Teheran meeting in November/ December 1943, at which Roosevelt and Churchill had extracted no guarantee from Stalin that he would recognise a post-war Polish government that refused to accept the new Soviet frontier along the 'Curzon Line' – roughly, the partition line between Germany and the Soviet Union in 1939.

So 'Tempest' ran its doomed course. In February 1944, the AK in Volhynia launched a local rising and joined forces with the advancing Soviet troops. At first, the Soviet officers were affable and cooperative, though they declined to make any political statements about frontiers. However, in April the new 'allies' were defeated by a German counter-attack, and many of the Polish survivors were forced to enlist in the Soviet-commanded Polish army under General Berling. In July 1944, AK units helped the Red Army to drive the Germans out of Wilno, but a few days later their officers were arrested and their men either interned or drafted into the Berling army. Later in July, 6,000 AK troops joined Soviet forces in a stiff battle for Lwów. The outcome was much the same; the AK commander was told that Lwów was a Soviet city and his men were given the choice of joining the Red Army or the Berling forces. When the pattern was repeated yet again near Lublin, within the Polish borders as the Soviet Union understood them, it was plain that 'Tempest' had failed. In military terms, the Home Army had fought well and gained glory. Politically, the attempt to make the Soviet commanders recognise its authority as the army of Poland's legal government was completely ineffective.

On 22 July, the authority of the London government over Poland had been formally challenged. The Soviet-backed Polish Committee of National Liberation issued its *July Manifesto* in Moscow, proclaiming a programme of democratic reforms and friendship with the Soviet Union. A few days later, it moved to newly liberated Lublin, and was recognised by the USSR as the legitimate authority in Poland. Meanwhile, the forward troops of Marshal Rokossowsky's First Byelorussian Army reached the Vistula on 25 July. The guns of the approaching Red Army could be heard in Warsaw, where the Germans began a frantic evacuation. It seemed obvious that Soviet forces would be in Warsaw within a few days.

Bór-Komorowski and his officers decided for a rising in Warsaw. Indeed, given the wild excitement boiling up in the capital, they might not have been able to prevent one. All their calculations – about enemy strength, about relief by the Red Army, about Allied support, about the political effects of the rising – proved quite wrong. There began on 1 August 1944 the biggest, the most heroic, and by far the bloodiest, urban insurrection that Europe has ever seen. It ended in disaster – a disaster in which not one of its survivors has ever regretted taking part.

5

Friends and Neighbours: 1939–45

In 1940, Winston Churchill broadcast to the Polish nation. He spoke from a Britain under siege, carrying on the war against Hitler alone – but not quite alone, for in the streets of London, between the German air raids, there could be seen soldiers in foreign uniforms, some of them wearing the 'Poland' shoulder-flash.

He said: 'This war will be long and hard, but the end is sure. The end will reward all toil, all disappointment, all suffering, in those who faithfully serve the cause of European and world freedom.'

No nation served that cause more faithfully than the Poles. They fought Hitler from the first day of war to the last, on land, at sea and in the air. Polish troops fought in Poland itself, in Russia and North Africa, in Norway, Italy, France and the Low Countries. They were in at the kill in Germany, and Polish troops helped to conquer Berlin. The Polish navy was in action, on the surface and in submarines, through the Battle of the Atlantic, in the North Sea and the English Channel. Poland's airmen took part in the Battle of Britain, in the bombing offensive against Germany, and in the support of the armies over every front. One in five of the entire population of Poland perished in the conflict. They gave new meaning to the old slogan of the Polish exiles who fought in every revolution for democracy throughout Europe in the nineteenth century: 'For your freedom and ours!' But in the end it was true to say that, while no nation suffered so much, none gained so little.

The end of the war turned out a poor reward for 'all toil, all disappointment'. Poland in 1939 was an independent sovereign state. It was no longer a parliamentary democracy and the colonels' régime of the Sanacja after Piłsudski's death was disliked by most of the population, but these were private problems which the Poles intended to solve within the family. In 1945, a ruined and decimated Poland had regained its formal independence, but was tied closely to the foreign policies of the Soviet Union and controlled by Polish Communists whose ideology was alien to the great majority of Poles. The

Polish airmen fought in the Battle of Britain, in the summer of 1940, shooting down a sixth of all German aircraft destroyed. This is the Polish 303 squadron (*Tadeusz Kościuszko*), marking up their 178th kill. The fighter is a Spitfire.

Allies had withdrawn recognition from the legal government to which most Poles had given allegiance throughout the German occupation, and had forced upon the nation the loss of its eastern territories, granting in exchange the German provinces as far west as the rivers Oder and Neisse. A ruthless civil conflict was being waged between pro-Communist forces, aided by the Red Army, and the remnants of the wartime Home Army resistance in the hills and forests.

This was hardly the 'independence' that the British guarantee to Poland in 1939 had sworn to restore. Tens of thousands of Polish soldiers in the West, who had for six years told themselves that every pace in their march through so many foreign countries was a step on the way home, now chose to stay abroad as exiles.

Many things might have been different, but only in detail. The outlines of what was to happen to Poland became inevitable on 22 June 1941, when Hitler attacked the Soviet Union. This had two results, both inescapable. The first was to ensure the eventual defeat of Germany, which had broken the fundamental precept of German strategy: to avoid a war on two fronts. The second was to bring Russian power permanently into the heart of Europe, something which statesmen had been trying to prevent for over a hundred years. Everything else followed. There was no chance that the armies of the

West, weaker and led with less resolution than the Red Army, could liberate Poland before the Soviet Union. There was no chance that Britain and the United States would risk the collapse of the anti-Hitler coalition in the middle of the war by defying Stalin over the future of Poland – and even if they had done so, no chance that their defiance would have been effective. Finally, although Stalin seems to have been at first flexible about the nature of the internal régime he preferred for Poland, there was no chance that he would permit the Polish state to regain the freedom of action it had possessed before the war.

In 1940, none of this was apparent. The Soviet Union was Hitler's ally, supplying him with trainloads of grain and oil. The United States was neutral, though hostile to Germany. In France, the British and French armies waited cautiously for the inevitable German offensive to begin. Their prime ministers, Neville Chamberlain and Edouard Daladier, still clung to the hope that the war might not last long, and could end in a negotiated peace.

"HI! YOU CAN'T DO THAT THERE 'ERE"

The British, ignorant of history, were baffled by the enduring suspicion of Russia among the Poles in London, even after Stalin joined the war against Hitler in June 1941. The cartoonist is David Low.

With great difficulty, some 43,000 Polish officers and men, determined to carry on the war, had made their way to France from Romania and Hungary. Another 40,000 men were recruited from the large Polish community in France, mostly from the coal-mining regions of the north. Sikorski's army saw action in April 1940, when the Germans invaded Norway and Denmark; a Polish brigade landed with the Allied force near Narvik, only to be evacuated again a few weeks later.

On 10 May the German armies attacked in the west. Holland surrendered after five days, Belgium was rapidly overrun, and General von Rundstedt achieved complete surprise as his Panzer divisions thrust through the Ardennes, outflanked the Maginot Line defences and drove deep into France. Within ten days, the British had been cut off and were preparing to evacuate across the Channel through Dunkirk. The French in the north-east were in chaotic retreat.

The Poles were stationed further to the south. By the time they went into action, in early June, the campaign was lost. Though the Poles fought hard, they were driven into retreat as the French divisions around them fell to pieces. Some 13,000 men were forced back against the Swiss frontier; they beat off German attacks, but – in a hopeless situation – decided to cross the border and seek refuge in neutral Switzerland. Other units retreated across France until they reached the Atlantic coast, where some were able to board ship for Britain. Out of his army of 80,000, Sikorski was left with about 25,000, counting the air force and the navy. Between a quarter and a fifth were officers; at the end of the September Campaign in 1939 many ordinary soldiers had chosen to stay in Poland rather than cross the borders into exile. The broken remains of the Polish regiments were now sent to Scotland, where they prepared to defend the east coast against the expected German invasion.

Winston Churchill had become the British prime minister and formed an all-party government on the day that the German offensive began. Now he assured Sikorski of his full support, ordering the heads of his armed forces to give the Poles every assistance. The Polish government reassembled in London, setting up its General Staff in the Rubens Hotel.

In August 1940, the Battle of Britain opened, as the Germans began the air offensive against southern England and London which was intended to break the Royal Air Force and clear the way for a sea-borne invasion across the Channel. Eighty-one Polish pilots fought in the RAF, and two Polish fighter squadrons – 302 Poznań and 303 Tadeusz Kościuszko – took part in the battle. The Polish fighter pilots became a legend in wartime Britain for their ferocity, skill and recklessness, and accounted for one in six of all German aircraft shot down in the four months of the Battle. But it was more than thirty years later that Britain revealed another, secret Polish contribution to the Battle of Britain and to eventual Allied victory. By 1940, the British had broken the code of the German 'Enigma' enciphering machine and were able to read Nazi radio traffic. This was only made possible by a pre-war feat of Polish military intelligence, aided by a group of brilliant young mathematicians: they had worked out the 'Enigma' system, built a replica, and passed all its results to the French and the British.

As the threat of German invasion receded, the Poles in Britain were given a badly needed pause. In Scotland, the army trained and exercised, striking up a warm friendship with the Scottish people. General Sosnkowski regained contact with the underground in Poland, and from February 1941 couriers and agents were parachuted into the German-occupied areas. The only land fighting was in North Africa, where in December 1940 the British attacked and destroyed a far larger Italian army. The Polish Carpathian Brigade, composed of troops who had escaped from Romania, was nearby in Palestine, but did not take part in the offensive for the bizarre reason that Sikorski had forgotten to declare war on Italy. This was hastily remedied.

The European war became a world war on 22 June 1941, when German armies stormed across the demarcation line in Poland and attacked the Soviet Union. Churchill at once offered Stalin unconditional support. This put Sikorski in a delicate position, dependent as he was on British hospitality. He issued a statement rejoicing at the outbreak of war between Poland's enemies and suggesting that any Polish–Soviet alliance should be conditional on Soviet recognition of the 1939 frontiers and the release of Poles in captivity within the USSR. Combined British and Soviet pressure, however, showed Sikorski that he would have to shelve the frontier problem, and on 30 July a Polish–Soviet agreement was signed in London. It was too much for several members of the Polish government, including Sosnkowski, who assumed that the Soviet Union would be rapidly crushed by Hitler and saw no reason to make concessions to Stalin. They resigned.

The agreement promised mutual support in the war, arranged for the formation of a Polish army under the London government on Soviet soil, and declared that Poles captive in the Soviet Union should receive 'amnesty' (although they had committed no crime save that of being Polish). On frontiers, the pact merely stated that territorial changes under the Nazi–Soviet pact were no longer valid. To comfort Sikorski, the British issued a declaration that they did not recognise changes in Poland's borders after August 1939.

Whatever its political shortcomings from the Polish point of view, the Polish–Soviet agreement was utterly justified in human terms. Slowly and reluctantly, the gates of the Siberian and Asian prison camps swung open, and hundreds of thousands of Poles – soldiers, women, officials, priests, even orphaned children – began to make their way towards the centres where the new Polish army was being gathered. Many had already died; many were not released. But the rest set out on the journey by rail, sledge, river raft, or on foot. In the chaos of wartime, the Soviet authorities gave them little assistance or food, and thousands perished on the way. Aleksandra Jarmulska was in an

Arctic labour camp when the news came of the Polish–Soviet agreement. 'We slept in a communal hut just on wooden planks, and there was no cruelty: we were just told that we can't escape from there; we would be eaten by polar bears or die in the snows if we did, but if we worked and earned some money, we could survive.' When they were released, Aleksandra and her companions made a raft for their river journey to find their army. 'The river started freezing at the banks, and sometimes the raft couldn't get through and we just had to cut pieces of the supports away to negotiate ourselves along. And sometimes the raft would stick in the shallows, and then whoever was on it had to get into the river to push.'

The army commander chosen by Sikorski, General Władysław Anders, had spent the last two years in the Lubyanka prison in Moscow. Energetic and aggressive, Anders was intensely anti-Russian, and was personally convinced that the Soviet Union was losing the war against Hitler. He set up his headquarters at Buzuluk, between the Volga and the Ural mountains. By December 1941, he had 40,000 Polish soldiers, and 70,000 by March 1942. This was hard to correlate with Polish records which showed that some 180,000 men had been taken prisoner by Soviet forces in 1939. Stranger still was the absence of officers. Only a few hundred arrived in the early months, although some 15,000 had been made Soviet prisoners-of-war.

On 30 November, Sikorski himself arrived in the Soviet Union, welcomed on the snowy airfield by Vyacheslav Molotov, the man whose signature on the Nazi–Soviet pact had condemned Poland to extinction. On 3 December, he

'The soldiers who were assigned to the job of burying them were like the ghosts of an army.' At Buzuluk, on the edge of Siberia, sick and hungry Polish troops bury another comrade.

and Anders met Stalin and were guests at a banquet the following day. There were arguments about the slow pace of the releases of Poles, about the missing officers, about inadequate rations and about the Polish frontiers. On all these problems Stalin was evasive. But before the newsreel cameras, Stalin and Sikorski signed a joint declaration proclaiming their intention to fight Germany to the end. Sikorski went on to Buzuluk, where he inspected the troops, confirmed to his satisfaction their impatience to get back into battle against the Germans, and saw the mass of Polish civilians and families around the camps being slowly fed and nursed back to health.

Many of those who had reached the Anders army were too far gone to recover. Aleksandra Jarmulska, who had made the journey from the Arctic by raft and train, found starvation even in the army camps. The civilians were still being denied Soviet food ration cards. 'One morning, I just woke up and couldn't wake my mother. And then I realised she had died in her sleep . . . There were so many people dying there at that time and the soldiers who were assigned to the job of burying them were like the ghosts of an army. They just couldn't cope with it.'

Scenes like these, coupled with his impressions of the Soviet leaders, left Sikorski with no illusions about Soviet–Polish relations in the past and their problems for the future. But he remained convinced that there was no alternative to the pact with Stalin if Poland were to revive, victorious and independent, after the war.

But the problems grew worse, not better. The Polish forces under Anders were moved eastward to new camps near the Caspian Sea. Their rations were cut by the Soviet authorities, and disease broke out. Early in 1942, Anders refused a Soviet request to send a division to the front on the plausible grounds that his men were under-armed and unfit. This refusal, later made much of by Soviet propaganda as evidence that the Poles were reluctant to fight the 'Hitlerites', covered a serious disagreement now emerging between Sikorski and Anders.

Sikorski continued to stand by his agreement with Stalin that the Polish forces in the Soviet Union would fight on the Eastern Front alongside the Red Army. But Anders, whose distrust of Russians had grown even stronger, now pressed Sikorski to allow his forces to be evacuated to Iran, which was under British control.

At first, Sikorski would not hear of this. He allowed Anders to evacuate those he could not feed because of the ration shortage. But he had three powerful reasons for keeping Polish troops in the Soviet Union. He would retain some leverage over Stalin, the army would continue to act as magnet and refuge for hundreds of thousands of Poles still missing, and – above all – a free Polish army under his command would help to liberate Poland from the east, frustrating any Soviet attempt to bring Poland under Soviet domination. Unfortunately, Stalin understood this last reason perfectly well.

Stalin decided that this alien presence on his own soil was more trouble than it was worth; the German thrust at Moscow had been beaten off in December 1941, and his military situation was no longer desperate. He began to encourage Anders in his plans to leave. In London, Churchill – now desperate in turn for troops to stem the German offensive against Egypt, which began under General Rommel in June 1942 – also started pushing the Polish government to let Anders come out of Russia. Sikorski was in no position to defy this combined pressure, and in August 1942 ships carrying Polish troops set out across the Caspian Sea for the Iranian shore.

In all, Anders was able to lead some 115,000 soldiers and civilians out of the Soviet Union. In the safety of Iran, they were at last given sufficient food and clothing by the British, and the troops were issued with new weapons. At the last moment Anders had beaten off a Soviet objection to the departure of soldiers and their families who had Polish citizenship but not Polish 'nationality' – which meant Jews. They came too. But over a million Poles remained in the Soviet Union. With the army gone, the Polish embassy in Moscow had little leverage to use in persuading Stalin to release them. The evacuation to Iran was seen by many Poles as a divine mercy, a flight from Babylonian captivity. For Sikorski, however, it was his worst diplomatic defeat, a calamity for his plans.

Deprived of a presence on the Eastern Front, the weakness of Sikorski's position became steadily more painful. In December 1942, he flew to the United States and urged Roosevelt to think seriously about an invasion of the Balkans. He hoped that an Anglo-American force could reach Poland through Jugoslavia and Hungary, and lay the foundations of a free Central European Federation before the Red Army arrived. Roosevelt gave him only vague answers. A few weeks later, in January 1943, the Soviet Union informed the Polish government in London that all Poles who had been living in the territories seized in 1939 were now Soviet citizens. This not only deprived the Polish embassy in Moscow of its right to help Poles left in the Soviet Union; it revealed beyond all doubt that Stalin intended to keep those territories after the war.

But all Sikorski's efforts to preserve at least a working relationship with the Soviet Union were about to be smashed apart. On 13 April 1943, German radio announced the discovery of mass graves near the village of Katyń, in the district of Smolensk. Katyń was Soviet territory, but it had been occupied by the Nazis since the summer of 1941. In the graves lay the bodies of Polish officers, their hands tied behind their backs, their skulls shattered by pistol-shots from behind. The first Nazi broadcast claimed there were 10,000 of them. In fact, some 4,300 bodies were finally dug up.

The Germans proclaimed that the Polish officers had been 'murdered by the Bolsheviks'. At first, the Poles hesitated. They instinctively rejected murder charges made by mass murderers like the Nazis. They could see the deadly

The Katyń Massacre. The bodies of two Polish officer-prisoners, exhumed by the Germans in April 1943.

diplomatic trap into which Nazi propaganda intended to push them. They found it hard to believe that even the Russians could have committed a crime so revolting.

But the evidence was too strong. Papers found on the bodies, their condition and the degree of vegetation growth above them, left little room for doubt. These were the officers from Kozielsk, one of the three Soviet camps for officer-prisoners established in 1939, and they had been shot between April and early June 1940. Now the Poles recalled all their enquiries about the missing 15,000 officers in 1941 and 1942, whose letters had stopped so suddenly in the spring of 1940. They remembered Stalin's queer, evasive answers to Sikorski and to Anders: 'They escaped to Manchuria', or just, 'Things sometimes happen . . .'

Two days later, Radio Moscow announced that the Germans had committed the atrocity in 1941, after capturing Smolensk. Nearly fifty years later, this is still the Soviet version of events. Almost nothing supports it; all the evidence accumulated since points even more directly at Soviet guilt. Few Poles, in Poland or abroad, believe anything different.

There had been about 5,000 officers in the Kozielsk 'special camp'. No trace has ever been found of the 4,000 officers in Starobielsk camp or of the 6,500 prisoners at Ostashkov. Both camps were 'wound up' in April 1940. After that, there is only silence and darkness. One account, circulating years later in the gulags, said that the Poles were locked inside barges which were deliberately sunk in the White Sea.

Why? Nobody knows that either, outside the Kremlin. It looks like an act of selective genocide against a part of the Polish national élite, closely parallel to Hitler's order to exterminate the Polish intellectual class. For Stalin, this would have been a small affair compared to some of his other slaughters. Some think it was simply an error by the NKVD (predecessor of the KGB), who misunderstood an order to 'liquidate' the special camps.

The Polish government, in spite of Churchill's warnings to Sikorski, demanded a Katyń enquiry by the International Red Cross. For the first time, an open split had appeared in the anti-Hitler coalition. German propaganda rejoiced over its triumph. On 24 April, the Soviet Union broke off diplomatic relations with the Polish government in London, accusing it of a 'treacherous blow to the USSR' and of trying to 'please Hitler's tyranny'.

Stalin now moved rapidly to set up a new and menacing Polish policy of his own. In May, the nucleus of a Polish army under Soviet command was formed, led by Colonel – soon General – Zygmunt Berling. Its political guidance came from the Union of Polish Patriots (ZPP), a grouping of pro-Soviet Poles headed by Wanda Wasilewska. It was not long before volunteers began to pour into the Berling army's camps. Most of them were Poles who had not been able to reach the Anders army in time; they had no affection for the Soviet Union, but here, at least, was a chance both to return home and to fight the Nazis. They had to swear an oath to the Soviet Union as well as to Poland, but the Polish flag was flown, the national anthem sung, and there was even a priest to say Mass. By July 1943, they already numbered over 14,000. By early 1944 Berling and his second-in-command, General Karol Świerczewski, who had fought as the illustrious 'General Walter' in the Spanish Civil War, had nearly 44,000 men behind them.

In the aftermath of the Katyń affair, while the British still reproached the Poles for provoking a breach in the alliance, Sikorski flew to the Middle

Stalin's rival Polish army. Colonel (later General) Zygmunt Berling and Wanda Wasilewska, from the Union of Polish Patriots, singing the Polish national anthem at an early parade of the new force in May 1943.

General Władysław Sikorski, prime minister and commander-in-chief of the Polish government in exile. On 4 July 1943, the day after this parade in Gibraltar, he died when his aircraft crashed just after take-off.

East. He met General Anders and visited his troops, now in Iraq and about to be formed into the Second Polish Corps to take part in the invasion of Italy. He set off home, and made a landing at Gibraltar. The next day on 4 July 1943, his aircraft took off from the Gibraltar airfield, at once lost height, and crashed into the sea. All but the Czech pilot died.

Władysław Sikorski's body was brought back to Britain and buried in the Polish military cemetary at Newark, deep in the English countryside. A British enquiry found no traces of sabotage in the aircraft wreck, concluding that a rudder had probably failed. But in their grief the Poles fell prey to many suspicions: that Soviet agents or Sikorski's political rivals or even Churchill had engineered his death. No serious evidence for any of these theories has emerged.

The death of Sikorski was both tragic and disastrous. Upright, austere, not without arrogance, Sikorski possessed a heroic authority which had held the exile factions together; only he would have been capable of forcing through a policy of alliance with the Soviet Union which broke with the Pilsudskian tradition of hostility to Russia and went against the deep emotional reactions of Poles to the events of 1939. Even after Katyń, he had been planning to overcome the breach with Stalin. Now the Polish leadership divided. General Kazimierz Sosnkowski, the restlessly suspicious officer who mistrusted both the Russian and Anglo-American intentions for Poland, took over Sikorski's post as commander-in-chief. The office of prime minister went to Stanisław Mikołajczyk, leader of the Peasant Party, a stubborn but radical politician who was determined to carry forward the ideas of his dead predecessor.

Sosnkowski and Mikołajczyk, never close, now become bitter adversaries. There were periods when the two leaders of Poland refused even to speak to one another, and diverted their energies into blocking each other's intentions. On the whole, though, Mikołajczyk prevailed. In the east, the Red Army was now on the offensive, heading towards Poland. Mikołajczyk knew that some relationship with the Soviet Union must be rebuilt. If he did not try to achieve that, he would be abdicating all responsibility for his country.

At the end of November 1943, Churchill, Roosevelt and Stalin met at Teheran. Their central purpose was to reach agreement on how to carry forward the war. Stalin and Roosevelt rejected Churchill's argument for an invasion of the Balkans, which might have forestalled the Soviet liberation and occupation of at least part of eastern Europe, and it was agreed instead that the Americans and the British would land in northern France and fight their way towards Germany.

The Teheran Conference, November 1943. Churchill, Roosevelt and Stalin decide in secret that the Polish state will be moved to the west after the war, losing its eastern regions to the Soviet Union and acquiring the eastern provinces of Germany.

Near the end of the conference, there was a discussion on the future of eastern Europe. The Big Three accepted that there would be predominant Soviet influence in Bulgaria, Romania, Hungary, the annexed Baltic states and Jugoslavia. Poland was more complicated. Stalin repeated his promise that he would establish a 'strong and independent' Poland, a promise which in his own way he kept: Polish fears that he intended to absorb the whole of Poland as a new republic of the Soviet Union were groundless. But the three men at Teheran decided, in secret and without consulting Mikołajczyk, that the Polish state would be moved bodily several hundred miles to the west. The Soviet Union would absorb the old eastern territories, in which Poles were a minority, and set its frontier along the 1920 Curzon Line. In the west, Poland would take over almost the whole of Germany east of the rivers Oder and Neisse: Silesia with its mineral wealth and industries and the great city of Breslau, Pomerania with a long stretch of Baltic coast including Danzig, and the southern part of East Prussia.

Churchill thought he could persuade the Polish government in exile to accept an outline of these terms. After all, they offered Poland a strong state which would be ethnically much more united – once the Germans had been expelled from their lost provinces – and economically stronger. Stalin had his doubts, and reserved the right to set up a government which would consent to these terms if the London Poles refused. Stalin was right. Mikołajczyk's government rebelled. They could hardly reject the offer of expansion to the west – an ambition harboured by many Poles before the war – but would not recognise the new Western Territories as 'compensation' for lands lost in the east. The Curzon Line was the sticking-point. There now followed months of wrangling over the frontier between the London Poles and an increasingly exasperated British government. The Poles suggested in February 1944 that they could renounce some of the old eastern lands, but absolutely refused to give up the ancient Polish centres of Lwów and Wilno. Churchill and his foreign secretary Anthony Eden, obliged to spend precious hours and days arguing over 'obscure' place-names in eastern Europe, came to consider the London Poles as unrealistic and unreasonable.

There was a failure of imagination here. The British could not understand why the Poles seemed unable to divorce the two issues of independence and frontiers, which appeared to the pragmatic Churchill quite separate.

The problem was history: the history of the Partitions. Every loss of territory inflicted by Poland's neighbours had led at once to a reduction of Poland's independence, and to an internal weakening of the Polish state. The Polish government in London and the Delegation and Home Army command in Warsaw were unanimous: a surrender of territory to Russia would mean that the future Poland would be a Soviet puppet, and 'compensation' elsewhere was irrelevant.

Mikołajczyk, however, refused to give up the struggle. He was determined to find a way of renewing relations with the Soviet Union which would be acceptable to his more obstinate colleagues in the Polish government, who now began to suspect him of 'pro-Soviet' weakness. In June 1944, he met Roosevelt once more, in the very days that the Allies were landing on the Normandy beaches. He was welcomed like a great statesman – Roosevelt had his eye on the Polish vote in the approaching election. The President, good-natured but evasive, told his guest that he would see that Poland kept the city of Lwów and much of Galicia after the war, but doubted whether Stalin could be persuaded to give up Wilno. This was a gross deceit on the part of Roosevelt, who at Teheran had agreed in secret talks that Poland's frontier would be the Curzon Line – granting Lwów and eastern Galicia to the Soviet Union.

In Poland itself, events were beginning to slip out of Mikołajczyk's control. The Red Army was closing on Warsaw, accompanied by the Berling army which had grown in size and prowess since its first hard-fought battle at Lenino in September 1943. 'Operation Tempest', the attempt by the Home Army to liberate regions of Poland before the Soviet troops arrived, was failing. The Communist-dominated Committee of National Liberation (PKWN) installed itself at Lublin in late July; if Mikołajczyk was to prevent

The professional smile. President Roosevelt greets Stanisław Mikołajczyk, Polish prime minister in exile, in the White House in June 1944. Roosevelt did not tell his guest that he had secretly assured Stalin that the Soviet Union could absorb Poland's eastern territories.

the PKWN becoming the provisional government of Poland, he had little time left.

Churchill urged him to find some way of merging the London government with the PKWN, accepting a Communist element in the future Polish regime as the price for retaining some influence over events. On 29 July, Mikołajczyk and his foreign minister, Tadeusz Romer, flew to Moscow for a visit that lasted a fortnight. It was the last hope for the London government.

Two days after Mikołajczyk's arrival, the Warsaw Rising began. Taken by surprise and suspicious of its motives, Stalin reproached Mikołajczyk for not informing him in advance – although Soviet broadcasts to Warsaw had been calling for an insurrection for days before it broke out. He refused to consider any other eastern frontier than the Curzon Line, which put both Lwów and Wilno on the Soviet side of the border, and urged the Polish prime minister to talk to the PKWN. A meeting was arranged, and Mikołajczyk found himself facing some of the unknown men and women who were about to take power in his country: Wanda Wasilewska, Bolesław Bierut, a loyal supporter of Stalin and a Communist, and Edward Osóbka-Morawski, an obscure member of the Polish Socialist Party. They offered him a coalition government in which they would have fourteen seats in the Cabinet and London would have only four, although Mikołajczyk would become prime minister. Mikołajczyk, angry and agonised over Soviet reluctance to help the Warsaw Rising, turned them down and returned to London on 10 August.

By now, Polish soldiers on all fronts were becoming aware of the outlines of the Teheran decisions, and of a proposed change of frontiers. For many of them, these changes meant that they would never see their homes again, unless they chose to become Soviet citizens after the war. The men of Berling's army, recruited from those imprisoned or deported in 1939, came almost entirely from the eastern territories. But so, for the same reasons, did the Polish Second Corps under General Anders, now fighting in Italy. And a large part of the Polish forces in Britain, who crossed the Channel to enter the Normandy battles in August 1944, were also easterners who had been with the regiments that took refuge in Romania and Hungary in 1939 or had been evacuated from the Soviet Union in 1942.

There was bitter talk, in the officers' messes and in the ranks. But the Poles, loyal to their alliance even when they saw that they were losing their country, fought on. In May 1944, the Second Corps – at an appalling cost in dead and wounded – succeeded where the British and Americans had failed and stormed the Italian monastery of Monte Cassino. In France, the Polish First Armoured Division helped to inflict on the Germans the disastrous defeat at Falaise; under General Maczek, the divison drove on through the Low Countries and liberated the Dutch city of Breda in October. A Polish paratroop brigade commanded by General Sosabowski took part in the airborne landings at Arnhem in September 1944, a noble but avoidable failure.

Given a choice, they would all have preferred to be in Warsaw, fighting and dying with their own people. The Rising, intended to last only a few days before the Soviet forces arrived, went on for two months of desperate street fighting which cost about 200,000 lives and left most of the capital an uninhabited wilderness of ruins.

General Bór-Komorowski and his commanders had some 30,000 men and women in their forces, mostly from the Home Army but including formations from the NSZ and the Communist People's Army. They had no heavy weapons and just over 700 automatic weapons, including machine-pistols. For an action lasting less than a week, against the rearguard of a departing enemy, this might have been enough.

But everything went wrong, not always through the mistakes of the Rising's leaders. In the first days, in glorious festivals of patriotic rejoicing, much of the city was liberated. Meanwhile, however, the German retreat had stopped, and armoured divisions moved across the Vistula to inflict a sharp defeat on the Soviet forces approaching the city. The Red Army fell back, but even when it had reorganised itself, made no further move to come to Warsaw's rescue. The Soviet aircraft which had been seen over the city every day now suddenly vanished. German reinforcements arrived, closed a ring around Warsaw, and – with the help of units from General Vlasov's renegade Russian army – began to fight their way back street by street.

The temporary setback before Warsaw does not explain the fact that the Soviet forces now sat passively in their trenches, week after week, while the Germans crushed the Rising. Stalin cabled Mikołajczyk that the Rising was a 'reckless adventure' which he would not assist. On 12 August, Roosevelt and Churchill asked him to permit Western aircraft dropping supplies to Warsaw to land on Soviet airfields. Stalin refused. Only on 12 September did he allow American bombers to land at Poltava in the Ukraine, and order some Soviet airdrops to the insurgents. By then, Warsaw was hidden by smoke and the insurgents had been driven back into a small perimeter; most containers of arms and supplies fell into German hands. Stalin dismissed the Rising as a 'mindless brawl mounted by adventurers'. But in fact he could read all too clearly the minds of those who had launched it, and knew that the Rising was intended to confront him with the accomplished fact of a free capital city controlled by the representatives of a non-Communist government. He had no intention of helping this design to succeed.

So the Poles in Warsaw fought and died at their barricades and cursed the Russians for doing nothing, while the German bombers – unchallenged – steadily reduced the town to rubble. A few days after the start of the Rising, the Germans counter-attacked with tanks and artillery and cut the liberated area into several pieces. As they advanced, they methodically drove civilians into the courtyards, machine-gunned them and then set fire to the buildings. The siege of the Old Town lasted until 1 September, when the surviving defenders escaped through the sewers to another bastion of resistance in the modern centre of Warsaw.

The British and Americans had not been warned of the Rising any more than the Soviet Union. Six days before it broke out, General Bór-Komorowski appealed for the Polish Paratroop Brigade to be dropped into the city. Nobody had given serious thought to the reinforcement problems of a prolonged insurrection, and this idea was completely impractical; there was no way that an armada of slow-moving gliders and towing aircraft could reach Warsaw, even if they were not shot down on the way. But the Allies made efforts to supply the Rising, even without the use of Soviet airfields. Polish, British and South African squadrons flew missions from Brindisi in Italy, a 1,700-mile return flight. Their losses in men and aircraft were suicidal, and – counting the later American mission – only 44 out of 149 parachuted containers reached the insurgents.

On 10 September, the Soviet forces to the east of the Vistula at last mounted an attack and reached the bank of the river in the Warsaw suburb of Praga. Among them were Polish troops of the Berling army, who could now see the burning city across the water and hear the noise of battle. Some Polish units managed to cross the Vistula, but the Germans now held the other shore in strength, and they were forced to give up their bridgeheads with heavy losses. The army group commanded by Marshal Rokossovsky, to which the Poles belonged, made no attempt at a full-scale river crossing.

District by district, the last pockets held by the Rising began to fall. The Germans drove unarmed Polish civilians before their troops as they advanced, to screen them from fire. The execution squads, some from the SS, some composed of drunken Russian deserters, slaughtered their way from house to house. Home Army hospitals, when captured, were burned with patients, doctors and nurses still inside. Hungry, filthy, exhausted and almost without ammunition, the defenders fell back from cellar to cellar, women and children attacking German tanks with home-made petrol-bombs, the dead buried in gardens and bomb craters.

The final surrender did not come until 2 October 1944. The Home Army survivors were granted the status of combatants and made prisoners-of-war; the entire remaining civilian population was marched out of the city to internment camps. Hitler ordered the complete razing of Warsaw, so that no settlement would ever arise there again, and demolition squads set to work with flame-throwers and dynamite among the silent, gutted streets. When they had finished, ninety-three per cent of the city's buildings were destroyed or beyond repair.

The Warsaw Rising of 1944 is one of the supreme events of Polish history. It brought to an awful climax the romantic tradition of armed uprising which stretched back to 1794. It convinced most of the generation who took part in it that in modern conditions that tradition no longer had a place: after another

The Warsaw Rising; 1 August–2 October 1944. Insurgents after escaping from the Old Town through the sewers.

The Warsaw Rising. Another Old Town survivor.

such rising, there would be no Poland left. But the Warsaw Rising was also a time of freedom, a 63-day revelation of how Poles could act and feel and behave to one another, which left a hot residue of pride to keep the nation warm through the bleak years that followed.

The Rising was not just a military action, but a community of the people with their soldiers, a community with its own songs and newspapers, its radio and theatres, its own film unit and cinemas. Even children took a full part. All who took part remember with love the *łączniczki*, the girls who ran with messages for the insurgents and died in their hundreds and the *Szare Szeregi* (Grey Ranks), the boys and girls of the Scout movement who fought to the end. Like many Polish upheavals, the Rising also left a moral legacy behind it. Many older citizens of Warsaw today still try to measure their own behaviour by the devotion, purity and generosity which they remember from the summer of 1944.

The best historian of the Warsaw Rising, Jan Ciechanowski, concludes that its political motives and its military motives could never have been reconciled. 'In view of the total absence of liaison with the Russians, and the lack of reliable data concerning their deployment and intentions, the Home Army leaders were militarily unjustified in embarking on an insurrection against the Germans.' The predicament of Bór-Komorowski was this: 'to fight against the Germans successfully he had to cooperate with the Russians militarily, yet he was unable to do so wholeheartedly because he wished to oppose them politically . . .'[1]

The failure of the Rising was a fatal and decisive defeat both for the Home Army and for the Polish government in London. With its leadership dead or imprisoned, and the capital destroyed, much of the fighting spirit went out of the Home Army. Some units ceased active operations, allowing many of their men to bury their weapons and return home. A few prepared for a new armed struggle against Soviet forces and the Communist authorities. In the liberated areas, where the PKWN now announced conscription, many thousands of ex-Home Army soldiers allowed themselves to be drawn into the Berling army, which numbered 290,000 by the end of 1944.

Stalin's decision in September to give the Rising some assistance, though too little and too late, inspired Churchill to make one last effort to solve what he called, in moments of despair, 'the Polish imbroglio'. In London, General Sosnkowski had been dismissed from the post of commander-in-chief after an outburst in which he accused Britain of betraying Poland; Churchill hoped that Mikołajczyk, free of his implacably anti-Russian rival, might now find it possible to bargain with Stalin. In October 1944, Churchill and Eden flew to Moscow, and Mikołajczyk followed them on 12 October.

1. Jan Ciechanowski, *The Warsaw Rising of 1944*, Cambridge University Press, Cambridge, 1974, p. 260, p. 270.

LEFT: The Warsaw Rising. Young insurgents in the ruins of the French Embassy on Frascati Street. The photograph has been damaged by fire.

BELOW: The Warsaw Rising: defeat. General Tadeusz Bór-Komorowski, commander of the Home Army, (left, in civilian clothes), surrenders to SS General Erich von dem Bach-Zelewski, commander of the German forces in Warsaw, on 2 October after sixty-three days of fighting.

There took place in Moscow a tragic, Shakespearian confrontation. It was a collision between Churchill and Mikołajczyk, two men who shared the same political values of liberty and democracy, whose stubborn temperaments were similar, and who at heart regarded one another with real affection. Stalin and Molotov scarcely took part.

Mikołajczyk brought with him his Cabinet's final offer: an all-party government for post-war Poland in which the Communists would have a fifth of the ministries, and a redrawing of the eastern frontier which would leave Wilno and Lwów, with the nearby Galician oilfields, in Poland. Stalin turned this down. When Mikołajczyk retorted that Roosevelt had told him that Lwów should stay Polish, Molotov revealed to him that the President had agreed to the Curzon Line at Teheran, ten months earlier.

Deeply shaken, Mikołajczyk now met Churchill and Eden in private. Churchill reproached him: if he had only agreed to the Curzon Line frontier earlier in the year, Stalin would not have set up a rival 'government' in the form of the Lublin Committee – the PKWN. Mikołajczyk bitterly reminded him of Britain's pledges to Poland. Churchill shouted at him that he wanted to start a third world war. 'You're a callous people who want to wreck Europe. I shall leave you to your own troubles. You have only your miserable, petty, selfish interests in mind!'

He threatened to withdraw recognition of the London government, and added that Mikołajczyk ought to be in a lunatic asylum. Beside himself with rage and misery, Mikołajczyk demanded permission to be parachuted into

The Lublin Committee (Polish Committee of National Liberation) in about August 1944. Bolesław Bierut (hands on the table) is in the chair. Behind him is the Polish white eagle but without the crown which was the traditional religious symbol of Mary, Queen of Poland. On his right, Edward Osóbka-Morawski, later prime minister in the Provisional Government. General Berling is at the far left of the picture.

Poland, so that he could perish in battle with the Home Army. 'I prefer to die fighting for the independence of my country, rather than to be hanged later by the Russians in full view of your British ambassador!'

At this Churchill marched out of the room. Both men were close to tears. After some moments, Churchill returned and put his arm round the Pole's shoulders. But they had reached the end of a line, and they knew it. A last suggestion by Mikołajczyk that Poland could give up Wilno if Lwów could be saved was put to the Kremlin. Stalin, no doubt aware of this highly satisfactory quarrel through well-placed microphones, placidly refused.

Stanisław Mikołajczyk went back to London. There he told his colleagues candidly that there was no longer any room for manoeuvre. If they wanted to have any share of the future government, they would have to swallow the Soviet terms and the Curzon Line. He urged them to do so, reminding them of the rich new territories promised to Poland in the west. But it was too much for most of the London Poles, and on 24 November Mikołajczyk resigned.

This was the end of the Polish exile government as a force in international politics. From now on, world statesmen acted as if it no longer existed. In December, the PKWN proclaimed itself the provisional government of Poland, with Osóbka-Morawski as prime minister, Bolesław Bierut as head of state and Władysław Gomułka as a deputy premier. It was recognised by the Soviet Union a few days later.

On 12 January 1945, the Soviet armies on the Vistula resumed the offensive. The German defences broke, and the Red Army drove rapidly across central and western Poland towards the German frontier. The men of the Berling army entered Warsaw on 17 January, stepping in horrified silence through a desert of frozen rubble. Behind them, well wrapped up against the savage frost, came a group of men whom most Poles had never heard of – the new government. After more than five years of Nazi occupation, liberation had come at last, but wearing a uniform woven of irony.

6

Stalinist Poland: 1945–56

In early February 1945, Churchill, Roosevelt and Stalin met at Yalta in the Crimea. They planned the final phase of the war and the joint administration of occupied Germany in the interval before the peace conference. But no peace conference has ever taken place to make a formal settlement of the Second World War, and in its absence the agreements reached by the Big Three at Yalta have been treated as the charter for the division of Europe into 'zones of influence'. At Yalta, many now believe, Britain and the United States betrayed all the principles for which the war had been fought by handing over Europe east of the river Elbe to Joseph Stalin.

Yalta does not really deserve this bad name. In the first place, there was little Churchill and Roosevelt could do to prevent Soviet domination of the areas liberated by the Red Army, short of threatening a fresh war. Secondly, Yalta for the most part only ratified decisions taken earlier, especially at Teheran. As far as Poland was concerned, the West did attempt – in a callous, casual way – to ensure that Poland would not become a Communised puppet of the Soviet Union, and that the political will of the Polish people would be freely expressed. The worst that can be said about Churchill and Roosevelt on this occasion is that they willingly deceived themselves about Stalin's intention to keep his promises.

The three leaders agreed that Poland would be run by a provisional government including 'all democratic and anti-Nazi elements', until free elections could be held. This temporary government was to include Poles from the London camp. On frontiers, Yalta again confirmed the Curzon Line in the east, but there was no precise agreement on how much of Germany would be added to Poland in the west.

Stanisław Mikołajczyk decided to accept the Yalta blueprint. It was a frightening gamble. The London government in exile had instantly denounced Yalta as a new Partition. In March, sixteen leaders of the resistance in Poland were invited to a 'meeting' with Marshal Zhukov, kidnapped and imprisoned in the Lubyanka in Moscow to await trial for – among other grotesque charges – collaborating with the Germans. In the Polish forests and villages, remnants of partisan bands were beginning to clash with Soviet security forces. But Mikołajczyk felt that if the Soviet assurances at Yalta meant anything at all, he stood a chance of rallying the Peasant Party within Poland and leading a non-Communist block of parties to victory in the elections.

On 2 May, Berlin fell to Soviet and Polish troops. On 8 May, the war in Europe ended. On 5 July, Britain and the United States recognised the new provisional government as the legal authority in Poland. Out of twenty-five members, sixteen came from the Soviet-sponsored 'Lublin Committee', including Osóbka-Morawski, now prime minister, and Bierut as head of state. But much of the real strength lay with Władysław Gomułka; he was a deputy premier but also, far more importantly, secretary of the Polish Workers' Party (PPR), the Communists.

The other deputy premier was Mikołajczyk, who also became minister of agriculture. Huge crowds welcomed Mikołajczyk when he flew back to Warsaw, and, with Bierut scowling anxiously in the background, he made a brave speech promising to heal all wounds and restore 'a truly free, independent and sovereign Polish Republic'.

Poland in the summer of 1945 was a land in which everyone was on the move. The cities were mostly in ruins, except for Kraków which became for a while the intellectual centre of the nation. From the east came much of the

Polish soldiers of the Berling Army in captured Berlin, May 1945

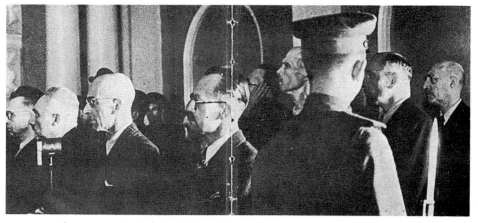

June 1945: the Moscow trial of the sixteen kidnapped leaders of the Polish wartime underground, Leopold Okulicki, commander of the Home Army, is at the extreme left.

Polish population of the lost lands beyond the Curzon Line, making their way by train, cart or on foot towards new homes in the west. From Britain and Germany came returning soldiers and tattered, emaciated thousands freed from the concentration camps, factories and farms of the Third Reich. From what had been Pomerania, Silesia and East Prussia, about three million Germans had already fled. Now, the first of over three million who remained were being driven out of their homes, most of them to land up in the British zone of Germany; the cities of Breslau and Danzig, both smashed to rubble in the last months of war, became Wrocław and Gdańsk. The surviving railway lines were clogged with Soviet trains crawling eastwards, carrying not only an incredible assortment of personal booty but the machinery and stock of German factories in the new Western Territories which were by right Polish property. It was three years before the great 'resettlements' came to rest.

The war had cost Poland the death of a fifth of its population, and the destruction of over a third of the national wealth. As if that blood-letting had not been enough, Poles were killing each other as remnants of the resistance fought on against the

Stanisław Mikołajczyk, returning to Poland in 1945 as deputy prime minister in the Provisional Government, promises crowds at Warsaw airport that he will fight for true independence

new régime. And yet these first post-war years were also a time of irrepressible energy, even of optimism. Much of the energy was spontaneous, as the Poles threw themselves into the business of building what was almost a new country. The Western Territories, taken from the Germans, were at first a 'Wild West' where the incoming Polish settlers seized what had been left behind, pulled ploughs themselves where there were no horses and organised their own communities long before official authority became effective. Workers took over factories and started production on their own, without waiting for a manager to arrive. The people of Warsaw went back to the ruins and piled bricks together to make shelters; the legend tells that the first shop to open was a boutique for ladies' hats.

The English novelist Storm Jameson visited Warsaw in September 1945. She saw 'narrow lanes tracing the lines of vanished streets between the scorched shells of houses, each vomiting its dust-choked torrent of rubble. With only spades and bare hands, men and a few women working headlong to clear them. The faintly sweetish stench of the bodies rotting under the rubble still clung to it . . .'

And yet, she felt, 'what sprang from these stones was not sadness, not defeat. It was an inextinguishable energy. The man or woman who had cobbled together a room without light, heat or water on the upper floor of a tottering building, reached by fragments of a staircase jutting precariously from the

Boy Scouts help to clear the rubble of Warsaw

shaky wall, would not have set a pot of geraniums on the fire-blackened sill unless he had decided fiercely not only to live, but to live gaily . . . A narrow room at street level, cleared of rubble to be used, with mad disregard of the wall about to fall and crush it, as a shop, was selling a few saucerless cups, a single pair of worn shoes – and flowers.'[1]

After all the half-measures of the years before 1939, a sweeping and radical land reform was carried through. The estates were broken up and distributed to the peasants; only in the Western Territories did the government keep the big Prussian estates intact, to be used as state farms. It is one of the ironies of Polish history that it was Communist-inspired policy that turned most of Poland into a patchwork of little private strip-fields, owned by peasants whose fierce independence and primitive methods have hampered the planned economy ever since. Basic industries were nationalised, and by 1946 the state sector controlled over ninety per cent of industrial production.

Poland in 1945 was ready, even impatient, for swift and revolutionary social change. The radical mood which had arisen during the Nazi occupation still prevailed; not only workers and peasants but the surviving intellectuals wanted to create a new, strong, socially just and egalitarian nation, to overcome all the weaknesses which had contributed to the loss of independence in 1939. In another country, this mood would have given a Communist Party its historic opportunity to take the leadership of this hunger for change. But in Poland, where the Communists had been escorted to power by Soviet bayonets, it was a different matter.

As party leader, Władysław Gomułka saw this very clearly. He was unlike most of his colleagues in the PPR leadership in two ways: he was a worker rather than an intellectual, and he had spent the war in the underground in Poland rather than in the Soviet Union. His two predecessors, both parachuted in from Moscow, had died in the war: Marceli Nowotko was murdered in a still-mysterious feud in 1942, and his successor Paweł Finder had been arrested by the Gestapo the following year. Gomułka had led the PPR side in the unsuccessful negotiations for a common military and political platform with the Home Army. As the new secretary of the PPR, he had taken an independent line, helped by an accidental but convenient breakdown in radio contact with Moscow when he took office.

Gomułka was a harsh intolerant personality with a violent temper. His grim, bony skull, eyes peering at the world through steel-rimmed spectacles, encouraged his opponents to regard him as a pitiless Marxist fanatic. But although he was a convinced Communist, he was never a 'Comintern man' who took orders unquestioningly from the Great Socialist Motherland. The fact that he was in prison at the time probably saved him from the fate of his

1. Storm Jameson, *Journey from the North* (Vol. 2), Collins & Harvill, London, 1970, pp. 150–51.

comrades in the old KPP, who were summoned to Moscow and for the most part murdered in 1938.

This was a crime which Gomułka never forgot. He accepted the need for close alliance between Poland and the Soviet Union, and the Soviet military and political support without which – given the strength of the non-Communist parties in the first years – the Communists would neither have acquired the main share of power nor kept it for more than a few weeks. But he intended to find a 'Polish Road to Socialism' which would avoid the mistakes of the Soviet Union and find gradual acceptance in a Catholic nation whose patriotic tradition was anti-Russian.

In this uphill task, he faced three main problems. The first was Soviet behaviour within Poland, where Soviet 'advisers' had taken command of the security police and where Russian soldiers were running wild, looting and frequently killing. The second was his own party. The PPR membership had risen from 30,000 at the beginning of 1945 to some 300,000 by April, swamping the party with careerists, half-baked revolutionaries and mere brigands who in some places were threatening to collectivise the land and even announcing that Poland was to become a republic of the Soviet Union.

The third problem, which became dangerous the moment that Mikołajczyk returned to Poland, was the huge revival of non-Communist politics, headed by the Peasant Party. Gomułka might wish to give a democratic appearance as he moved cautiously along his 'Polish Road' but, unless he could smash or cripple these political rivals before the 'free elections' prescribed by Yalta, the PPR would be swept away.

Gomułka made some progress. He ensured that the new government behaved with ostentatious respect towards the Church, and Bierut, as head of state, walked with Catholic bishops in religious processions. The Soviet Union made a faint show of goodwill by imposing only light sentences on the kidnapped resistance leaders in Moscow. More important for Poland's stability was the final Big Three meeting at Potsdam in July 1945, at which Stalin – against British and American doubts – insisted on the demarcation of Poland's new western border along the rivers Oder and Neisse, including the city of Stettin (Szczecin) on the west bank of the Oder estuary. Final recognition of the Oder–Neisse frontier was deferred to a future peace conference. As for Gomułka's problems with the PPR, the bubble burst soon after Mikołajczyk's return; party membership collapsed to about 65,000 in the summer of 1945 as masses of Poles defected to the Peasant Party and the other reviving groups.

But the bloodshed went on. Although Bór-Komorowski's successor as head of the Home Army, General Leopold Okulicki, had dissolved the AK in January, some Home Army units and many NSZ bands carried on the struggle, raiding towns and villages to murder PPR members and ambushing Soviet convoys on the roads. In return, Polish security troops aided by Soviet

The Western Territories. A Polish settler in lands taken from Germany ploughs the battlefield.

regulars carried out their own repressions and atrocities. An amnesty in August 1945 brought 42,000 men and women out of the underground, but Okulicki's successor, Colonel Jan Rzepecki, then organised a new Freedom and Independence Resistance (WiN), in touch with the exile government in London, and fought on. A separate problem was a desperate and determined army of Ukrainian partisans in the foothills of the Carpathians, whose final success before dissolving and escaping to the West was to ambush and kill General Karol Świerczewski ('General Walter' of the Spanish Civil War) in March 1947.

The fighting – almost a Polish Civil war – cost tens of thousands of lives and poisoned political life with hatred, as Gomułka and Bierut accused Mikołajczyk and his allies of secret contact with the underground. It petered out only in early 1947, when another amnesty brought most of the surviving guerrillas out of the forests. The Ukrainian population of south-eastern Poland suffered savage punishment. Their villages were destroyed; some Ukrainian groups were resettled in the Western Territories and the rest deported to summary execution or labour camps in the Soviet Union.

In June 1946, there was a first trial of strength between the political parties of the new Poland. The Communists needed public evidence that the 'programme of the left' had popular support; ingeniously, they proposed a referendum on three questions to which they knew that most Poles – whatever their politics – would be inclined to answer 'Yes'. The referendum asked the electors whether they approved of the abolition of the Senate (the upper house of parliament), of land reform and the nationalisation of basic industries, and of the new frontiers on the Oder–Neisse line.

The Civil War. The bodies of three security men, killed by anti-Communist partisans in a forest near Łódź.

These questions put Mikołajczyk in a trap – as they were meant to. His party had supported all three changes. Yet he could not miss this chance to show the world the strength of the PSL. Rather unconvincingly, he launched a campaign for a 'Yes' to the last two points but a 'No' to the abolition of the Senate. The PPR, supported by most of the Polish Socialist Party (PPS), toured the country calling for 'Three Times Yes'.

The question on the Senate had become a vote of confidence in the government's domination by the Communists, and the campaign was a chaos of abuse and intimidation. The polling took place on 30 June. Ten days later, the government announced the results: on the vital first question, sixty-eight per cent had voted 'Yes' and only thirty-two per cent 'No'. Jerzy Morawski, then one of the younger Communist leaders, today admits with bitter candour: 'I found out afterwards that the results had been faked. In reality, the situation was probably just the reverse: two-thirds had voted for what Mikołajczyk was asking.'

For the inner circle of the PPR (the Communists), who knew the real totals, the referendum was an ugly shock. Morawski recalls: 'It was a warning which showed how strong the influence of Mikołajczyk's opposition was in Poland. It showed how much effort to pressurise, destroy, intimidate and discredit Mikołajczyk's opposition was still needed in order to win the elections.'

It was an effort which Gomułka and Bierut now proceeded to make. The Yalta 'free' elections did not take place until January 1947, but the six months that followed the 'Three Times Yes' referendum brought an onslaught of official terror against the Peasant Party. Meetings of the PSL were broken up by mobs, party buildings were destroyed, PSL members were threatened with the loss of their jobs, and there was a string of arrests, kidnappings and murders.

In the midst of this violence, a horrific incident took place at Kielce in July 1946, when a building sheltering Jews on their way from the USSR to Palestine was attacked and forty of them were killed. At the time, everybody blamed everyone else for the 'Kielce Pogrom'. Mikołajczyk claimed it was a Communist police provocation, while others saw it as a spontaneous explosion of the anti-Semitism which was, undeniably, a part of the hysterical mood of Poland in the first years after the war. The Communists said the pogrom was the work of right-wing nationalists. The right-wingers and several Catholic bishops retorted by pointing out that many of the Communist leaders who had spent the war in the Soviet Union were Jews, especially in the secret police: a propaganda point which has festered in Polish consciousness ever since.

In the teeth of the storm, Mikołajczyk fought an erratic campaign. He appealed for international supervision of the elections, but Britain and the United States, now preoccupied with their confrontation with the Soviet

Warsaw 1947: a shop in the ruins. Above it is the 'Three Times Yes' slogan of the June 1946 referendum. The girl is a Scot, the wife of a Polish soldier returned from the West.

Jewish survivors of the Holocaust at a Polish frontier station, on their way to Austria and – if possible – Palestine

Union in occupied Germany, paid no attention. For a time, the key to his victory seemed to lie with the PPS, the Polish socialists, now in tragic disorder. One faction in the PPS wanted an open struggle against the Communists; even the pliable Osóbka-Morawski, the prime minister, was now rebelling against Gomułka's domineering style. Others, some from a genuine belief that the left must hold together and put through a socialist programme, some because they were fellow travellers planted in the PPS by the Communists or by Soviet intelligence, stood by the government and looked forward to an eventual fusion with the PPR. But when the Polish socialists approached the Peasant Party and asked them to join the 'democratic bloc', hoping to keep Communist influence in the next government to a minimum, Mikołajczyk turned them down, refusing a secret offer of a quarter of the Sejm seats which would have made a mockery of the elections before they were even held.

Another body-blow to Mikołajczyk followed in September. Under President Truman, the United States was growing increasingly nervous about Soviet intentions in Europe. The Communist parties in France and Italy were powerful and militant; the western zones of Germany were sinking into a mire of hunger and hopelessness which looked like a breeding-ground for revolution. Conditions might soon be ripe for Stalin to advance his ideology and power to the Atlantic, if he so wished. In this situation, American aims rapidly changed from the hope of keeping Europe united to a policy of drawing a fire-break across the continent which Communism could not surmount.

The first requirement of the new policy was to show the Germans that the United States was not a hostile occupying power but a potential friend, sympathetic even to their sense of national loss. On 6 September 1946, Secretary of State James F. Byrnes made a decisive speech in Stuttgart. In this speech, aimed at the German people, Byrnes said that the Oder–Neisse frontier had been drawn 'unilaterally' by Stalin, that the United States had not recognised it, and – Byrnes hinted – that Germany might regain some of the lost territories.

The impact of the Stuttgart speech in Poland was catastrophic. To anti-Communist Poles, above all, it was the final betrayal of Poland: the West, which had helped Stalin rob them of their old eastern frontiers, now wished to deprive them of their western territories as well. Gomułka's outrage was genuine too, but the Stuttgart speech was also a gift from heaven to use against his opponents who still believed in Western protection. Mikołajczyk, in Denmark at a conference, summoned the press and denounced Byrnes. But all mention of his words was censored from the Polish papers, and the PSL was accused of committing national treachery by silently supporting 'American imperialism' in its attack on Poland's territorial integrity.

The elections took place on 19 January 1947. By now, thousands of PSL activists were in prison, including 142 candidates, while all the telephones at the PSL headquarters in Warsaw were cut off. A fifth of the electoral districts, those where the PSL was especially strong, was disqualified. There was

The new men of power. Left to right: Bolesław Bierut; Vyacheslav Molotov; the Soviet foreign minister; Józef Cyrankiewicz, the Socialist survivor of Auschwitz who was prime minister of Poland for twenty-two years.

blatant and widespread fraud in the polling stations. The 'democratic bloc' announced that it had won over eighty per cent of the votes, giving it 394 seats in the Sejm against only 28 for Mikołajczyk. Such was the outcome of Stalin's guarantee at Yalta of free elections in Poland. Britain and the United States composed notes of protest. The Soviet Union rejected them.

Mikołajczyk was now powerless. The Peasant Party began to disintegrate, and that autumn, warned that he was about to be arrested, Mikołajczyk was smuggled to the coast in an American embassy car and put aboard a ship for the West. He was received kindly in Britain by Churchill, less kindly by the remnants of the Polish government in exile, and died in America nineteen years later.

In Warsaw, the victorious 'democratic bloc' entrenched its power. The wavering Osóbka-Morawski was dismissed and replaced as prime minister by another socialist, the enigmatic Józef Cyrankiewicz. A man of high culture and courage who had organised resistance within Auschwitz, Cyrankiewicz had emerged from the camp convinced that the PPS must at all costs defend its independence and identity against Communist encroachment. But for reasons which are still a puzzle, he suddenly changed his mind and became the most forceful leader of the PPS minority prepared to work closely with Gomułka and the PPR and to support a merger of Communists and Socialists into a single movement. Cyrankiewicz became in many ways more intimate with Stalin than Gomułka was, and it may be that his secret intention was to save at least an element of the old PPS by making it a useful Soviet instrument of control over Gomułka and his independent 'Polish Road' colleagues. Anyone who remained prime minister of Poland for the incredible span of twenty-two years, as Cyrankiewicz did, clearly must have had powerful sponsors.

The new government brought into office a group of energetic, self-confident Communists who had spent the war in the Soviet Union and did not share Gomułka's doubts about Stalin's infallibility. Hilary Minc took over the economy, Jakub Berman guided matters of ideology and security from the offices of the prime minister, and the merciless Stanisław Radkiewicz became minister of public security. Gomułka, who remained the leader of the PPR, confined his state jobs to deputy prime minister and minister for the Western Territories. Over the protests of Mikołajczyk and his surviving handful of opposition deputies, the Sejm agreed to the so-called 'Little Constitution' of February 1947, an enabling act which reduced the Sejm to a rubber stamp by permitting the Cabinet to govern by decree when parliament was not sitting.

Although he did not know it, the 1947 election 'victory' marked the beginning of the end for Gomułka. In the two years since the liberation, his 'Polish Road' policy of defending Poland's limited independence within the Soviet zone of Europe had made some progress. Against his record stood the bloodshed of the civil war, now ending, and the outrage done to Poland's democratic feelings by his brutal hounding of the Peasant Party. Gomułka in

1947 knew that Polish Communism still had little genuine support, and still required Soviet armed force in the background to stay in power. But there were achievements, all the same.

He had refused to follow Soviet models, and had applied a Marxist programme of reforms tempered to Polish conditions. Both the nationalising of basic industries and the distribution of land to the peasants had been popular; Gomułka had beaten off pressures to collectivise the land in imitation of the Soviet *kolkhozes* – which had been the real dread of the Polish peasantry. The personal energy he applied to settling and developing the Western Territories, and the Byrnes speech crisis, had given him a chance to display his patriotism in public. With some success, Gomułka had tried to bring the plunderings and maraudings by Soviet troops under control, and he had almost stopped the Soviet removals of ex-German-factory equipment to the USSR. A start had been made with the creation of new heavy industries designed to give employment in regions in rural over-population, like the steel mill at Nowa Huta near Kraków.

With the elections over, the opposition shattered and the last partisans leaving the forests to surrender, Gomułka might have expected an interval of calm in which he could consolidate his position and push ahead with his own version of a 'socialist transformation' of Poland. Nothing of the kind happened. Instead, his authority now rapidly weakened and then collapsed. In part, this was because he had few personal supporters. 'Muscovites' like Bierut and Berman now dominated the PPR, while Cyrankiewicz and the other PPS socialists in government were making their peace with Moscow behind his back. The main reason for Gomułka's fall, however, was the onset of the Cold War and Stalin's change of policy towards eastern Europe.

There is much to suggest that Stalin had not worked out any master-plan for the part of Europe that he controlled. There is little evidence that he always intended to 'Sovietise' it, to reduce the states of eastern Europe to obedient clones of the USSR. There is nothing to prove that he meant to move Soviet power forward to the Atlantic, by inciting the Western Communist parties to subversion and revolution. In fact, he took steps to prevent the Italian and French Communist parties from using their huge support in the first post-war years to take power in their own countries. Stalin's attitude was defensive, and he was unwilling – while America still had a monopoly of atomic weapons – to take action which might wreck what remained of Big Three cooperation in the world.

Among Stalin's few principles was an acute distrust of foreign Communists, whom he suspected of the crime of independent thought. Nationalists he found easier to manipulate. Thus in Romania, Bulgaria, Hungary and Poland he established hybrid 'peoples' democracies', régimes usually imposed by force but in which the power of local Communists was diluted through coalition governments with 'bourgeois' parties. Only Albania and Jugoslavia, countries which had liberated themselves without much Soviet help, at once carried through full-blooded Communist revolutions, much to Stalin's annoyance. Both countries, Jugoslavia first, and Albania some years later, were to break with the Soviet Union and defy its claim to control the world Communist movement.

Nobody can say how long these queer compromise governments might have lasted. But in 1947, the wartime anti-Hitler coalition finally tore apart. The Stuttgart speech had been a warning; in March 1947 President Truman's 'doctrine' declared an American policy of 'containing Communism' all over the globe. He was soon supported by the British, and the Four-Power administration of conquered Germany began to break down. The Cold War which now opened was founded on two misperceptions. Truman and the West thought, wrongly, that Stalin was preparing to communise the whole of Europe by subversion and war. Stalin thought, equally wrongly, that the West was preparing to drive Soviet power out of Europe and probably out of the Soviet Union as well by subversion and war, backed by a revived German *Wehrmacht*.

Stalin now followed Truman in walling off his own part of Europe. In the summer of 1947, he forced Poland and Czechoslovakia – which was still under a western, democratic form of government – to reject American aid offered in the form of the Marshall Plan; this was an especially hard blow to the Poles, who urgently needed the money for reconstruction after the war and who had managed to keep up a fairly friendly relationship with the United States. Stalin's next step was to tighten direct Soviet control over eastern Europe, moving to replace the 'peoples' democracies' with a uniform Communist system close to that of the Soviet Union. That September, he established the Communist Information Bureau (Cominform), an international body to enforce discipline and unanimity on the world Communist movement.

In the Cominform, Gomułka saw the return of precisely that dogmatic Soviet control of foreign Communist parties which had paralysed them before the war, and which he had been determined to avoid. The inaugural meeting of the Cominform took place at Szklarska Poręba, in Poland, late in September 1947. Although he was formally the host, Gomułka gave no welcome to the new organisation, and when the Cominform proposed a resolution calling for full collectivisation of the land, Gomułka alone vigorously opposed it.

A few months before, he had repeated his promises to the Polish peasantry that the land would never be collectivised. Now he became the first Communist leader in the post-war world to defy Stalin directly. Gomułka was alone not only at the conference but in his own party; Bierut, Berman and the others regarded his disobedience as close to blasphemy.

Early in 1948, there began the quarrel between Tito and Stalin which finally exploded in June, when Jugoslavia rejected Soviet tutelage, proclaimed its right to follow an independent route to Communism, and was expelled from the

Cominform. In a cacophony of hysterical abuse against the 'Fascist traitor' Tito, other east European Communists frantically proclaimed their loyalty to Stalin, while camps and prisons began to fill with alleged 'Titoist' victims. Gomułka stood firm, and as late as June 1948 told the PPR to avoid dogmatic solutions and to respect Polish patriotism and independence.

Gomułka soon met his fate. In September the PPR dismissed him as secretary of the party and replaced him with Bierut. In strange, rambling speeches, Gomułka sometimes justified himself, sometimes begged forgiveness for his errors; his purpose seems to have been to leave a political testament behind him without splitting the party and exposing his followers to vengeance as 'Titoists' and 'anti-party' plotters. He was gradually pushed into obscurity, and finally arrested in 1951.

The day after his fall, the party declared that the land would be collectivised. A purge of his supporters began which reduced party membership by 50,000 in four months, and was to last for another three years. And on 15 December 1948, the pro-Soviet rump of the Polish Socialist Party (PPS) finally united with the PPR to form the Polish United Workers' Party (PZPR), which still officially holds 'the leading role' in Polish society today. Socialists opposed to the merger had been expelled over the previous year. Two small puppet parties remained, the United Peasant Party (ZSL), a pro-Communist peasant movement, and the Democratic Party, supposedly a formation of white-collar workers and private craftsmen. But as Bolesław Bierut and Józef Cyrankiewicz shook hands at the fusion congress, while the audience dutifully shouted 'Down with Gomułka!' and 'Down with nationalism!', Poland had in effect become a one-party state.

For the next six years, Poland experienced the terror, misery and absurdity of Stalinism. With the UB (secret police) snapping at its heels, the whole nation was mobilised into a breakneck drive to create a Soviet model state on the Vistula. All independent opinion was stamped out while a totalitarian party dictatorship set about destroying and then rebuilding Polish institutions on the Soviet pattern. With this went a torrent of servile propaganda glorifying Stalin, trumpeting mendacious nonsense about happy workers vying to achieve astronomical production targets, and urging the population to be 'vigilant' against the 'aggressive plans' of the 'imperialist' West. 'Stalin is the best ally, the great Friend of Poland,' ran a contemporary school textbook. 'The genius of Comrade Stalin sees through all the plans of the warmongers.'

At the core of government policy was the Six-Year Plan, launched by Hilary Minc in 1950. The Three-Year Plan (1947–50) of the Gomułka period had been a rational affair drawn up by professional economists; its aim was to improve living standards and to encourage light consumer industry and the private sector. Under Minc, the whole economy was concentrated upon the rush to establish heavy industry, and only production figures counted. The private sector was abolished almost completely, nearly half the national income was

PRZYJAŹŃ, PRZYKŁAD, POMOC Z.S.R.R.
GWARANCJĄ WYKONANIA PLANU 6-LETNIEGO

The Stalinist style. The words on the poster read: 'The Friendship, the Example, the Aid of the Soviet Union are the Guarantee of the Fulfilment of the Six-Year Plan'.

invested in grandiose long-term industrial projects, and the Polish standard of living fell rapidly. To impress Stalin, Minc used the outbreak of the Korean War in 1950 as an excuse to raise the targets of the Six-Year Plan by nearly half. The workers were reduced to a form of serfdom: the old trade unions were replaced by a Sovietic structure which acted as the party's transmission belt in raising production, and new laws tied employees to their jobs.

While Minc's central planners drove Poland to the edge of ruin, the UB subjected the Poles to waves of paranoid, irrational terror. Veterans of the Home Army and the armies in the West were thrown out of their jobs and frequently imprisoned. The same fate threatened members of the Party who had fought in the Spanish Civil War or in the Communist resistance within Poland where, it was suspected, they had been infected with 'nationalism'. Prisoners were regularly tortured, and there were many death sentences.

Kazimierz Leski had been an officer in the Home Army. He still finds it difficult to repeat aloud what his fellow countrymen did to him in Bierut's prisons. 'The investigation was carried out, as one might say, with gloves off. That's when my hearing was badly damaged, and my teeth were knocked out. Apart from that, one had to sleep on concrete and also . . . various other things like crushing the joints in one's hands or beating one's shins. Later, there was the so-called "Winter Sports", which was perhaps the most painful. One was interrogated all day and then at night put in a cell, a completely empty cell with the window taken out, and it took place in winter, so it was freezing outside and freezing in the cell as well. The person was made to stand naked in front of that window and one had to stand all night like that, because one couldn't move or there would instantly be further punishment.'

All over eastern Europe, Soviet 'advisers' were now ordering the preparation of show trials designed, if possible, to implicate Communist leaders suspected of a trace of independence. Poland's response was the Tatar trial of August 1951, at which nine former Home Army officers were accused on absurd evidence of conspiracy. The star witness was Marian Spychalski, a former associate of Gomułka's, who was induced by torture to declare that Gomułka had been party to a plot to undermine the loyalty of the Polish army.

While Polish schoolchildren were sent to the fields and beaches to hunt for Colorado beetles, supposedly dropped by American agents, the Party moved against the two stoutest institutions of Polish life: the private peasantry and the Catholic Church. The grand collectivisation campaign was in fact a fiasco: by 1955, only 9.2 per cent of the land had been transformed into *kolkhozes*. But the whole rural economy was disrupted and brutalised as a futile campaign raged to destroy the larger peasant farmers (known by the Soviet term *kulaks*) and to squeeze food out of the villages to the expanding urban population. Compulsory deliveries of grain were imposed in 1951, and extended to meat, potatoes and milk the following year.

For the first time in history, a Polish régime persecuted the Catholic Church. Its charities were taken over by the state, and there were widespread arrests of priests and even bishops. A pro-government organisation of lay Catholics, Pax, was established under none other than Bolesław Piasecki, the pre-war Falanga thug who had contrived to save his skin by a deal with Soviet intelligence. In September 1953, the UB finally dared to arrest the Primate of Poland, the indomitable Cardinal Stefan Wyszyński, who was confined to a monastery.

And yet, at the outset, the Stalinist onslaught was not without genuine supporters. Something about this cavalry charge to overcome Poland's backwardness and catch up with the developed world in a single leap appealed to the impetuous Polish tradition. There were writers and intellectuals caught up in the excitement, prepared to lay aside old 'bourgeois' values for the sake of the vision ahead. Looking back, Polish intellectuals of that age-group have tried to explain the mood of moral abdication. The novelist and film-maker Tadeusz Konwicki says: 'I belong to the generation that lost the war. That is to say, the generation of young Home Army soldiers whose dreams and aspirations when they went into the underground movement or joined the partisans were not fulfilled . . . The war we had been through was horrific; we had seen the annihilation of the material world and then the annihilation of the moral world.'

The writer Andrzej Szczypiorski expands this thought. 'Artists have to believe in something, otherwise they cannot be artists. Having, not without reason, lost their faith in democratic principles and in humanist civilisation that had effectively failed to oppose Hitler's tyranny, the intellectuals began feverishly to search for a new faith. They found it in the doctrine of collective living, scientific forecasting of the future . . . The decline of the world of values that had bred Hitlerism was undeniable. The spiritual vacuum in the Polish graveyard could not last indefinitely. Stalinism filled that vacuum.'[2]

But all ended in disillusion. Literature and the arts were confined to the infantile 'socialist realist' manner of the Soviet Union; the vivid inheritance of Polish painting and graphic arts was reduced to solemn canvases of bulging peasant muscles and stern-jawed workers.

The workers and the peasants, who paid the price for these dreams, resisted in their own sullen way. In the factories, standards of work and personal honesty collapsed; in the villages, the farmers saw no point in planting crops or raising pigs which would be taken from them for less than their production costs. The inevitable logic of this was that the régime had to rely increasingly on police coercion to achieve any of its targets. The UB, now a huge state within the state, was instructed by Lavrenti Beria, the head of Soviet security, to set up a 'Tenth Department' in January 1952 whose task was to spy on the party leadership itself. Only two leaders were exempt: Bierut himself and Marshal Konstantin Rokossovsky, a Soviet commander of Polish origins who had been appointed in 1949 to be minister of defence and commander-in-chief of the Polish armed forces.

A trainload of presents was despatched to Moscow for Stalin's seventieth birthday. New buildings were designed in the heavily decorated, pseudo-classical style of the Soviet 1930s and in the centre of Warsaw rose the mountainous Palace of Culture, Stalin's 'gift to the Polish people', soaring from a Palladian base through medieval crenellations to a very Russian onion spire. And yet, within the apple of cringing loyalty to Stalin, worms of dissent were beginning to writhe.

Polish Stalinism was not all that it seemed. Bad as it was, the scale of terror never reached that of other east European states in the 1950s. The slow pace of collectivisation in the Polish countryside, which – as the Party knew – would have required something like a civil war to enforce universally, contrasted sharply with the almost total abolition of private farming in Hungary, Czechoslovakia and East Germany. Above all, there was no real Polish parallel to the show trials elsewhere, to the judicial murders of Patrascanu in Romania, of Kostov in Bulgaria, of Rajk in Hungary, or of Slánský and his associates in Czechoslovakia. There, Stalin's local henchmen had insisted on the 'exposure' and public martyrdom of the party leaders themselves. In Poland, after the

2. Andrzej Szczypiorski, *The Polish Ordeal*, Croom Helm, London, 1982, pp. 55–6.

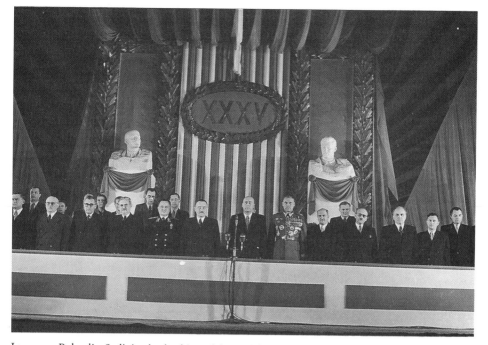

In 1952, Poland's Stalinist leadership celebrates the thirty-fifth anniversary of the Bolshevik Revolution. Bierut is on the left of the microphone; Cyrankiewicz on the right. Next to Cyrankiewicz is Marshal Konstantin Rokossovsky, a Russian of Polish descent imposed on Poland as minister of defence.

Tatar trial, the next step in the terror process was not taken. Gomułka and Spychalski were the obvious victims. But, although they were interrogated in prison and work was begun on preparing a trial with the usual false 'confessions', they never came to court. Stalin died in March 1953. The following year, without any public announcement, Gomułka was quietly released.

Nobody knows for sure why Bierut held his hand. Soviet pressure for a Gomułka trial was acute. Possibly he thought Gomułka too tough to break, and feared that at a trial he would declare that Bierut and the rest of the leadership had supported his 'traitorous' policies before 1948. Outwardly, Bolesław Bierut – with his impassive, foxy face and his little toothbrush moustache – seemed cold and conformist, a figure trained only to obey. But, deep in his complex personality, Bierut also resented Soviet interference and remembered the fate of the KPP leaders in the 1930s. To murder another generation of Polish Communist leaders would generate an unappeasable blood-feud within the party.

From the outside, Stalinism in Poland looked like an ideology of extremes. In practice, it was a rickety structure of half-measures. This combination of brutality and compromise left future Communist régimes in Poland with appalling problems. It was not just that the working class was alienated, that all the ingrained anti-Communist and anti-Russian prejudices of the population had been reinforced, or that the economy had been distorted and had fallen under the management of ignorant party loyalists. The half-measures created their own difficulties too. The peasantry had not been destroyed, but it had been so bullied and mishandled that it acquired a hatred of the authorities which was never overcome. The Church had survived, but it had been sufficiently persecuted to win even greater affection among the patriotic masses. Finally, the fact that the party itself was not terrorised in Poland to the extent that it was in – say – Hungary or Czechoslovakia had paradoxical consequences.

Supporters of Gomułka and the 'Polish Road to Socialism' lived on, demoted and humiliated but at least not hanged, to dream of fighting another day. More important was the formation of almost immovable power cliques, especially at provincial level, where the permanent party bureaucracy grew to feel immune and to learn ways of evading or shelving orders from Warsaw. This 'middle apparatus' was able to block some of the madder Stalinist instructions. But when, a few years later, the party line changed and the local apparatchiks were instructed to behave in a more liberal way and apply reforms, they were able to block these new orders as well. The failure of Stalinism to enforce discipline and obedience on its own officials hampers the party to this day.

When Stalin died in March 1953, little changed in Poland. But Bierut was privately relieved. It meant that he need no longer fear pressure for a grand show trial. These trials had acquired an anti-Zionist element in other countries of the Soviet bloc, and Stalin had expired at the climax of a fresh attack of anti-Jewish paranoia. Bierut was now spared the danger that he might have to sacrifice some of his Jewish colleagues – Berman, Minc, and most of the UB leadership – as the Czechoslovak Communists had sacrificed Rudolf Slánský in November 1952.

Elsewhere in eastern Europe, Stalin's death was followed by the first explosions of popular protest since 1948. There were strikes and riots at Plzeň in Czechoslovakia, in May 1953, and then the far larger working-class revolt in the German Democratic Republic in June. But Poland, for once, remained calm. Coaxed by Malenkov, Stalin's immediate successor, Bierut began an almost imperceptible relaxation late that year, which relieved some of the pressure on the peasants. But the great industrialisation drive went on, as tens of thousands of young men left the land to live in the crowded hut-camps or bleak new towns around the scaffolding of new steelworks and shipyards.

Cautiously at first, the Polish intellectuals began to recover confidence. Though censorship remained tight, critical articles began to appear in the press. Some of the most fanatical Stalinist writers now lost their faith, and began to work for change within the party and – above all – for a breach in the wall of suffocating isolation which had separated Poland from the culture of the West.

This process was powerfully helped in late 1954 when Lieutenant-Colonel Józef Światło, a senior member of the UB Tenth Department who had defected the year before, began to broadcast his memoirs over Radio Free Europe. Week by week, Światło fascinated and horrified the Polish public with revelations of torture and blackmail, and of the extent to which Soviet officials interfered in Polish affairs, vetting and correcting the list of the delegates to PZPR congresses as a matter of course and dictating the operations of the UB. Effectively and deliberately, Światło harped on the unjust fate of Gomułka and his colleagues, and presented them as patriots who had been sacrificed because they defended the independence of the nation.

At the end of that year, the unity of the régime was beginning to crack. The intellectuals were in full cry, challenging dogmatism in all the sciences and hinting at a form of Marxist socialism in which the press was free and the government did not lie. Within the party, although behind closed doors, Bierut faced open criticism. He made concessions, liberating Gomułka and sacking Radkiewicz, minister of public security. But, with the Cold War's first phase abating into a thaw, the impatience for change only grew stronger. Contending party groups took shape: neo-Stalinists demanding the trial of Berman as a Jewish scapegoat, and a more influential liberalising group in which old supporters of Gomułka now reappeared.

In the summer of 1955, the World Youth Festival was held in Warsaw. It brought an invasion of young people from the outside world, a relief force storming in with their music, their new clothes, their accounts of how life was in the West. The Festival broke a permanent hole in Poland's isolation and convinced the young Polish generation that the nightmare of Stalinism was ending, and must never be allowed to return.

Poland was coming to the boil. The régime floundered, now trying to reapply discipline and conformity, now permitting fresh outbursts of criticism which became steadily more radical. The battle for reform within the PZPR leadership was already intense when, in February 1956, Khrushchev delivered his secret speech to the Twentieth Congress of the Soviet Communist Party at which he denounced the crimes of Stalin.

Bierut, in Moscow for the Congress, took his cue and died – from natural causes. It was a sign of the times that reforming Communists in Warsaw not only circulated the secret speech throughout the party but handed its text to Western journalists, who spread it across the front pages of the world. Battle was instantly joined for the succession to Bierut. Nikita Khrushchev arrived from Moscow, suggesting that a purge of Jews from the PZPR leadership might restore the Party's popularity – a proposal that horrified the numerous Communists 'of Jewish origin' on all wings of the Party. Instead, the PZPR chose as first secretary Edward Ochab, a solid, honest and shrewd politician well aware of the need for change.

Then, in June 1956, the workers of Poznań rebelled. On 28 June, workers from the Cegielski engineering plant marched through the streets to protest against the refusal of the authorities to reduce their work norms and raise wages. But the march became a raging demonstration of over 100,000 people as the city's population rushed to join it. Rioting started; the security police and the army opened fire. Nearly eighty demonstrators were killed, a prison was attacked, and hundreds were wounded.

At first, the Warsaw leadership reacted violently. Józef Cyrankiewicz, the prime minister, made a broadcast blaming the Poznań outbreak on imperialist agents, and threatening that 'the hand raised against the people's power will be cut off'. Then, suddenly, the line changed, and the official media began to speak of 'justified' workers' grievances. In the teeth of Soviet protests and warnings, the PZPR central committee met in July and decided on 'democratisation'. Real wages would rise, the Sejm would be given more responsibility, industrial investment would be cut, and workers consulted in the management of their factories.

But in the wake of Poznań, the party itself was beginning to dissolve as thousands of Poles – industrial workers above all – threw back their cards. By now, the reformist leaders were in touch with Władysław Gomułka. Even some of the Stalinists backed the idea that he should be restored to central committee membership, as the last hope of staving off a general insurrection against party rule. Gomułka, however, held out for real power. He demanded the office of first secretary and the removal of his enemies from the PZPR politburo.

June 1956. The city of Poznań in revolt.

Lacking a majority in the central committee, Gomułka's supporters turned to the factories. Workers' councils were set up in all the larger plants, powerful arenas for revolutionary debate which organised public mass rallies calling for the return of Gomułka. Poland was reaching a point of no return; if the remnants of the old Stalinist clique hung on to power, the party would solve its differences by violence on the streets.

In early October 1956, the leadership caved in and called another central committee session, the famous Eighth Plenum. The meeting began on 19 October. Poland was in ferment, the population staying by the radio or grabbing the newspapers as they arrived at the kiosks. Gomułka was at the Plenum, although he had not yet been re-elected to the central committee. So, too, was a party of uninvited guests. Nikita Khrushchev and most of the Soviet leadership – Vyacheslav Molotov, Anastas Mikoyan, Lazar Kaganovich and some dozen generals – had flown in that morning.

The next twenty-four hours brought Poland to the brink of catastrophe. Soviet troops massed on the borders, and Soviet armour stationed within Poland moved out of its bases and began to converge on Warsaw. The PZPR called the workers to defend their factories. The Polish Internal Security Corps blocked the road from Poznań to Warsaw against the Soviet advance.

Meanwhile, Khrushchev and his team argued furiously with Gomułka and the politburo. Essentially, he had come to protest; an historic change in

Soviet armoured units move to surround Warsaw, October 1956, pictured by a hidden camera

Poland's leadership was taking place, and he had not been consulted in advance. He raged at Gomułka, then, suddenly, gave way. Partly, no doubt, he saw that the cost of crushing Gomułka would be a Polish–Soviet war. But when he had released his wrath, he took a closer look at the man before him. Gomułka was an obstinate patriot. But he was not a 'bourgeois Polish nationalist'. Under Gomułka, Poland would go its own way within the Soviet alliance, but he would never allow the party to lose its 'leading role'. Gomułka was not the Communist that Khrushchev would have chosen, but a Communist he certainly was.

The confrontation went on all night. The Poles assured Khrushchev that attacks on the Soviet Union in the Polish press would be restrained, and that Soviet troops could remain on Polish territory. Khrushchev, feeling that he had saved what could be saved, summoned his exhausted team and flew home to Moscow. The way for Władysław Gomułka's return to the leadership of Poland, after eight years of disgrace and confinement, was open.

October 1956. The Polish United Workers' Party defies Soviet threats and brings Władysław Gomułka back to power. Gomułka (in spectacles) is flanked on his left by Cyrankiewicz. On his right are, first, Adam Rapacki, who became foreign minister, and Artur Starewicz, who was to be Gomułka's adviser on propaganda and the press.

7

The Gomułka Years: 1956–70

Post-war Polish history has run in cycles, each lasting between ten and fourteen years. The cycle begins with the arrival of a new party leadership, promising more democracy, economic changes which will bring benefit directly to every Polish family, a grand extension of human liberty. Gradually the new authorities drift off course. Power becomes the monopoly of a clique out of touch with the needs and hopes of the Polish people. The economy begins to forget the consumer and wastes itself in grandiose, often futile investment projects. The industrial workers, praised to the skies at the outset of the cycle, see their living standards fall and their rights trampled upon until they can take no more: they rebel, and the governing clique collapses. A new team arrives, once again promising a free press, respect for human rights and sausage for all, and the next cycle begins.

Władysław Gomułka came back to power as the first of these cycles ended. But he was to preside over the second cycle, and to end up as its victim. The writer Andrzej Szczypiorski observed that 'when he became leader of the party, he enjoyed universal respect and trust, and his authority was unquestioned. On his departure fourteen years later, he was followed by the curses of all Poles . . .'[1]

In October 1956, as Khrushchev and his delegation flew back to Moscow, Gomułka became the hero of the nation. The day they left, before he was elected first secretary of the party, Gomułka addressed the Eighth Plenum in a speech broadcast directly to the nation. He honoured the Poznań workers, 'protesting against the evil that has become so widespread in our social system'. He denounced the collective farms. He attacked the memory of Stalin and his 'cult of the personality', and promised: 'We have finished with this system, we shall finish with it once and for all.' He emphasised his loyalty to the Soviet Union, but declared that there was no single model of socialism which must be

1. Andrzej Szczypiorski, *The Polish Ordeal*, Croom Helm, London, 1982, p. 69.

Gomułka as national hero: addressing the vast crowd outside the Palace of Culture in Warsaw on 24 October 1956

imitated and followed – resurrecting his old slogan of an independent 'Polish Road' towards a Communist society.

A surge of universal joy greeted this speech throughout Poland. Hanka Bratkowska, a journalist and a party member, was typical of a young generation who believed that Gomułka was committed to a new, democratic form of Communism. 'We felt close to this programme, incredibly close, because compared to the Stalinist years it was a revelation. It was a socialism close to our own programme, and our dreams, and therefore also to those of mankind . . . An older colleague warned us: "He is an autocrat!" But we made light of this. Quite simply, we supported the programme, and not the character traits of this man.'

Four days later, on 24 October, over half a million people gathered to hear him in the enormous square beneath the Palace of Culture. When he appeared, they did not sing official party anthems but burst spontaneously into the old Polish greeting song for birthdays and celebrations: 'A hundred years, may he live a hundred years . . .' Nothing like this dedication of a people to its leader had been seen since the funeral of Piłsudski. And Gomułka's political position was secure: in contrast to 1947, he now had a PZPR politburo dominated by his own supporters. His 'personal union' with the masses seemed invincible.

But in fact the great Warsaw rally alarmed Gomułka. Looking down at those swaying, ecstatic hordes chanting his name, he saw spontaneity – something any orthodox Communist mistrusted – and he saw all the reckless, combative wildness of Polish nationalism revived and uncontrolled. At the end of the rally, a part of the crowd headed for the Soviet Embassy and were dissuaded only narrowly from attacking it.

The day before, an enormous demonstration in Budapest had marched to the monument of General Józef Bem, the Pole who had fought for Hungarian liberty in 1848. The régime answered with bullets, and, as Gomułka spoke, a national armed insurrection was breaking out in Hungary. The crowds in Warsaw chanted 'Katyń, Katyń!' at the Soviet embassy, but they carried Hungarian flags as well.

In the days that followed, Gomułka strained all his new authority to hold back Polish passions and prevent an anti-Russian rising which would drown all eastern Europe in blood. There were collections in every Polish town for supplies of food and blood to be flown to Budapest, and the Polish leadership sent a message of solidarity to the new Hungarian government under Imre Nagy, even backing its demand for the withdrawal of Soviet troops.

At first, the Soviet Union seemed to accept the new situation in Hungary. But on 4 November, with world opinion diverted by the Anglo-French invasion of Egypt at the peak of the 'Suez crisis', the Soviet tanks drove back into Budapest and the death-struggle of the Hungarian uprising began. Suddenly the Poles saw before them again the abyss of war from which they

Po Prostu (In Truth), the student paper which became the voice of radical democratic reform. The headline reads: 'The Polish October'. Published during the brief triumph of the Hungarian Revolution, this number carries at the right verses by the Hungarian poet Attila Jozsef.

'It is harder to live for Poland than to die for her.' Cardinal Stefan Wyszyński, Primate of Poland, a few days after his return to Warsaw in October 1956.

had crawled only eleven years before. Cardinal Wyszyński, released from confinement a few days previously, seized this mood in his first sermon. 'A man dies once and is quickly covered with glory, but he lives in difficulty, in hardship, pain and suffering for long years – and that is a greater heroism.'

Slowly, Poland began to cool. There were outbreaks and demonstrations, even attacks on Soviet buildings. But the danger of a fresh insurrection was over. On 14 November, Gomułka and Cyrankiewicz left for Moscow, where they negotiated the terms of their new relationship with the Soviet Union. Polish national sovereignty would be respected. Poles living or imprisoned in the USSR would be allowed to come home at last. The Soviet officers in the Polish forces, including Marshal Rokossovsky himself, and the 'advisers' in the secret police would also go home.

This was something Hanka Bratkowska could see with her own eyes. 'Next to the Polytechnic, there is a huge building known in Warsaw as the Pekin. It was entirely occupied by Soviet advisers. Now, in broad daylight, they were busily packing their chairs, bundles, pots and pans and everything else into a heap and on to trucks. We stood by and watched what seemed to us the visual, theatrical result of what Gomułka had achieved . . .'

Khrushchev agreed to cancel all Polish debts and to compensate Poland for years of extorting raw materials at derisory prices. When the train came back, crowds along the line and in Warsaw greeted Gomułka with flowers and songs.

These were the happy months; the 'Polish October' lasted for nearly a year. On the land, the collectives simply dissolved themselves without waiting for orders and the peasants took back their land. In the factories, the workers took control and operated a democratic self-management. Censorship vanished, and there was an outpouring of free journalism, good writing, avant-garde painting, film-making of a quality which soon fascinated the world, and an inrush of Western books, art and visitors. From student clubs and cellar cafés, which sprang up in their dozens as small private business was allowed to revive, came a roar of jazz. From apartment blocks came the sound of Radio Free Europe, broadcasting from Munich: radio jamming had been abolished. In colleges, universities and research institutes the classics of Marxist-Leninism were locked away in glass-fronted bookcases as their compulsory study was cancelled. The works of Stalin found their way to the stalls of the flea-markets, where they lay stacked beside heaps of old UB uniforms, for most of the secret police had been disbanded.

On his return, Cardinal Wyszyński at once negotiated a new relationship with the Communist state. Government relaxed its control over Church appointments, religious education returned to the state schools, Catholic chaplains were appointed to prisons and hospitals and new, authentic Catholic lay organisations complete with their own newspapers were licensed to break the monopoly of Bolesław Piasecki's *Pax*. In return, the Church promised not to undermine the state or to sponsor political parties of its own. This compact, which has formed the real foundation of the Polish social compromise ever since, was unique in eastern Europe, but the Vatican, uneasy at such an armistice with 'atheist Bolshevism', at first treated its terms with chilly reproach.

From the start, however, there were contradictions within the 'Polish October' which soon became evident. The first was the contrast between the reforming party intellectuals and the population as a whole. For many Poles, the collapse of Stalinism offered a chance to return to the past. The Catholic Church had regained its old authority and many of its privileges. Now, as organisations great and small met to throw out old leaders and elect new committees, graves began to open all over Poland. The official party youth organisation was dissolved, and the Boy Scout movement – in Poland, always seen as a legion of the patriotic young – reappeared in old uniforms which had been hidden by the previous generation. The puppet United Peasant Party (ZSL) began to acquire life of its own, as veterans of Mikołajczyk's old party took over its local committees. Survivors of the Home Army and the Peasant Battalions entered the official ex-combatants' association (Fighters for Freedom and Democracy, shortened to ZBoWiD in the Polish acronym) and threw out its leadership.

The young party intellectuals in the vanguard of what they called 'the Polish revolution' had a different vision. Some of them, like the 27-year-old philosopher Leszek Kołakowski, had been zealous Stalinists a few years earlier. Now, with the passion of converts, they urged an open, pluralistic form of Marxist socialism, a workers' democracy which would break completely away from the Soviet model and construct a society somewhere between that of Jugoslavia and Western social democracy. The new Poland would not be a revival of traditional, 'bourgeois' Poland, although they respected those traditions, but an entirely new experiment in left-wing politics.

Western socialists welcomed their ideas with joy, seeing a possible 'third way' between compromise with capitalism and the deformed Communism of the Soviet Union. But Gomułka – and here was the second contradiction of 'October' – did not welcome them at all. The mass membership of the PZPR was disintegrating; its activists were turning all their energy into rooting out

Workers' councils in the factories put their faith in Gomułka, seen here visiting the Żerań car plant at Warsaw. On his right is Lechosław Goździk, the Żerań workers' leader whose oratory helped to bring Gomułka back to power. Later, when he was no longer needed, Goździk was pushed out of his job and into obscurity.

every old Stalinist, every trace of Stalinist practices. Gomułka, who had relied on the 'revisionist' intellectuals to bring him to power, was now determined to reassert party authority.

Gomułka knew that a situation in which he was acclaimed as a national liberator by people who spat at the name of the PZPR, the party he led, could not endure. The party must gradually be brought back into a 'leading role' – the monopoly of political power. Communism as he understood it could not be reconciled with the heretical, 'liberal' ideas of his younger followers. Poland needed order and constructive work, not an anarchic hunt for scapegoats which would undermine all discipline.

Looking back at those months with the advantage of thirty years of hindsight, Leszek Kołakowski – now a Fellow of All Souls at Oxford – feels that the mood of unity was an illusion. 'This feeling of common cause, which united both the Party and its leadership and society, could last only for a short period. The comedies of national unity are short-lived, and it couldn't have been otherwise.'

Gomułka's first test came with the parliamentary elections of January 1957. In October, he made one of the promises which were to be repeated at the outset of each succeeding cycle: there would be a separation of powers, leaving the government to govern while the party confined itself to laying down general guidelines. Although it had been made clear that no opposition parties would be tolerated outside the coalition 'Front of National Unity', firmly under PZPR control, there were high hopes that the Sejm might once more become a centre of genuine debate and initiative. There was a single list of candidates in each constituency, but the new system gave the voter the chance to choose between one candidate and another by crossing off names – or even to cross off the entire list.

As the election approached, Gomułka began to fear that too many concessions had been made. In theory, it was possible that the electors could use their negative power in such a way that no Communist candidates would be returned to the Sejm at all. His anxiety was far-fetched. With such a complex system, it would have required a sophisticated anti-Communist campaign to show people how to use their crossing-out rights to produce that result – and no such campaign existed. But the Catholic Church, from the pulpits, now urged the Poles to give the régime a vote of confidence. And, on the eve of polling day, Gomułka himself appealed to the voters not to use their right of veto. 'Crossing out our party's candidate means crossing out the independence of our country, crossing out Poland from the map of European states.'

The result was an enormous vote of confidence in Gomułka. All but one of the list candidates were returned, although non-party figures on the list won a distinctly higher vote than party members. But the inner meaning of Gomułka's appeal disquieted many Poles. He had not put his supreme emphasis on what the party could do for Poland. Instead, he had warned that if

Poland did not remain under Communist control, it would be invaded and occupied by the Soviet Union. This crude definition of Poland's *raison d'état* left no real choice for the future. Whatever line the party took, however badly it ruled, it could return to this final argument: either you leave us in power, or Poland will lose its independence.

After the elections, there followed five years in which the impetus of the 'Polish October' slowly ran down and stopped. In the economy, they spoke of the 'Little Stabilisation', which seemed to suit what was happening everywhere in Poland. The vogue word of the early sixties was *rozczarowanie* – disenchantment.

The writer Tadeusz Konwicki comments that 'the second period of Gomułka's rule started with a putting-to-sleep; a putting-to-sleep of society and of our culture. It has to be remembered that this was a period of dreadful boredom, horrific boredom, in Poland, a period of interminable conferences, plenary sessions, speeches of – I don't know – four or six hours by Gomułka himself who monotonously read reports.'

All through 1957, Gomułka was busy pushing out of influence the young Communist radicals who still believed in a 'Polish Revolution'. Their last fortress was the student magazine *Po Prostu (Speaking Truthfully)*, a source of brilliant, sometimes constructive and sometimes impudent criticism. The board of the party daily *Trybuna Ludu*, which had also become a radical reforming platform, was sacked early in the year. *Po Prostu* was warned and harassed; its editor was removed and then in October 1957 it was closed down. The Warsaw Polytechnic students demonstrated, but were clubbed down by the police, touching off four nights of bitter but aimless rioting in the centre of the city. Repression had returned, and systematic press censorship gradually crept back in its wake.

The PZPR itself was slowly rebuilt. Gomułka, anxious to present himself as a man of the centre, declared war on the two extremes: 'dogmatism' (the remaining Stalinists) and 'revisionism' (the democratic radicals). He linked them, quite illogically, as aspects of a single affliction: 'revisionist tuberculosis can only strengthen the dogmatist influenza'. At the end of 1957, a purge of the party began which removed about a fifth of its members, mostly from the 'revisionist' wing. In 1959, a PZPR congress was held, at which Gomułka's most powerful reforming supporters in 1956 were removed from the leadership. Jerzy Morawski was dropped from the politburo, and the original, humane Władysław Bieńkowski ceased to be minister of education – both men who had served Gomułka loyally since the days of the Nazi occupation.

The 'centre' which remained was not remarkable for talent. Gomułka came to depend heavily on Zenon Kliszko, an arrogant busybody who tended to supply his master only with the news he thought he would like to hear, and on Marian Spychalski, now a melancholy and reserved figure who became minister of defence with the title of Marshal and then Chairman of the Council of State – the equivalent of president. But none of these purges and changes succeeded in imposing unity on the Polish Communists who – as they always had – continued to form factions and jostle for power, some groups intriguing out of political conviction, others merely pursuing personal ambition.

As the years passed, Gomułka himself increasingly lost touch with public opinion and with the reality of what was happening within the PZPR. An incurable workaholic, he was an easy victim for those who censored or slanted his supply of information for their own ends. His violent temper also discouraged colleagues from criticising him or telling him unwelcome facts. At politburo meetings, Gomułka was often the only man who had actually read the enormous, highly technical documents laid before each member. Comments or questions were crushed with an acid rebuke, and vital decisions were taken without debate.

In Bierut's time, everything had been judged by political standards. Now, although the leadership included few people who had any real understanding of economics, the party talked almost exclusively about industry, productivity and statistics of economic performance. Judged by this new standard, the performance was thoroughly depressing. In the months after the 'October', Gomułka had been urged to introduce a drastic economic reform, a socialist 'new model' which would decentralise management and let the market pressures of supply and demand determine production and prices. These voices were ignored, and in 1958 Gomułka returned to the old strategy of rapid, forced industrial investment.

Some of these long-term decisions, like the investment in new mineral resources – copper, sulphur, brown coal – were to pay off years after Gomułka had left the scene. But in the medium term, the results were disastrous. Both productivity and real wages fell in the following five years. Worst of all was the drop in agricultural production, supposed to rise by thirty per cent by 1965. In part, this was due to over-confidence encouraged by the United States, which – eager to show its support for Gomułka's independent line – offered Poland huge loans to purchase American grain. The party almost ceased investing in private agriculture; farm production fell heavily and food shortages became a chronic problem again. In the factories, the workers' councils of 1956 were undermined, and management fell back into the grasp of unqualified party nominees, backed by a repressive trade union system concerned only to enforce discipline and obedience.

Relations between state and Church grew tense again, after the false dawn of 1956. There could be no question of returning to the Stalinist attempt to terrorise the Church into submission. But the party, determined to reassert its 'leading role' in society, embarked on a disastrous policy of trying to drive back the frontiers of church influence. In July 1959, the police raided the monastery of Jasna Góra at Częstochowa, the national shrine of Poland where the icon of the Black Madonna is kept, and seized unlicensed printing equipment. A campaign began to limit religious education, which was gradually evicted again from state schools. But the most ominous incident took place in April 1960 at Nowa Huta, where the authorities' refusal to allow the building of a church provoked mass demonstrations and a violent riot. This event, in a supposedly 'socialist city' built around the steelworks, showed for the first time that the party could not count on the loyalty of the new working class, which had transferred its religious and patriotic passions intact from the peasant countryside to the cities.

The Church was not intimidated. Instead, Cardinal Wyszyński set about preparations for the millenium of Polish Christianity and the foundation of the Polish state in 1966 – the commemoration of the baptism of Mieszko I a thousand years before. It was assumed that state and Church could hold joint celebrations.

In 1965, the Polish bishops attending the Second Vatican Council decided to include the West German bishops in their list of guests to the following year's millenium ceremonies. This was a moment at which relations between Poland and the Bonn government were at their worst. The West Germans, supported with a cynical lack of conviction by Britain and the United States, were not only refusing to accept the existence of the East German state but were also laying claim to the 'frontiers of 1937' – in other words, to the Western Territories of Poland east of the Oder–Neisse line which Germany had lost in 1945. In return, Polish official propaganda harped incessantly on the horrors of the Nazi occupation, proclaimed that the rearmed West German army intended to lead NATO into an aggressive war to win fresh *Lebensraum* in the East, and abused the Bonn government as a neo-Nazi clique slavering to repeat the crimes of the Teutonic Knights, Bismarck and Adolf Hitler.

The invitation letter of the Polish bishops combined true Christian charity with astonishing political imprudence. In its final sentences, it begged the West German episcopate to forgive and to accept forgiveness. For a moment, all Poles – Catholic or Communist – were stupified. Was Poland to forgive the crimes of the Nazis and – inconceivably – to beg the pardon of the nation which had murdered a fifth of the entire population? Could the expulsion of Germans from lands which Poles regarded as historically Polish be equated with five years of systematic genocide, torture and starvation? Gomułka seized his chance, and assailed the Church in a concerted media campaign. Wyszyński was denied a passport to travel to Rome, while the Pope was refused an invitation from the state to attend the millenium.

But the campaign misfired. As the government attacked the Polish bishops, public opinion – swallowing its resentment and doubt – moved sharply back to the side of the Church. Other quarrels developed, and the millenium ceremonies the following year ended in bad-tempered confusion, with Church and state holding separate programmes of celebration.

The German problem obsessed Gomułka, and dominated Polish foreign policy. In public, only one German question was admitted: the refusal of West Germany and the NATO states (except for France) to recognise the Oder–Neisse frontier and the 'threat' posed to European peace by West German rearmament. In reality, though, there was a second, even more menacing, aspect to it. This was the nightmarish possibility that the Soviet Union would do a deal with the Bonn government, conceding the reunification of Germany in return for some form of neutrality and placing Poland once again between the Soviet Union and a huge, hostile German state greedy to reoccupy its lost territories – the pattern which had led up to the Partitions and to the Nazi–Soviet pact of 1939.

In March 1952, Stalin had sent a celebrated 'Note' to the West in which he raised this possibility, suggesting that if all foreign forces were withdrawn, Germany could be united as a neutral state. Not only the United States, Britain and France, but the new West German state firmly rejected the offer. In 1964, however, Stalin's idea returned. At a meeting at Lańsk, in north-eastern Poland, in January 1964, Khrushchev told Gomułka that he intended to seek a radical rapprochement with Bonn. Although Gomułka frantically resisted this plan, Khrushchev's erratic son-in-law, Alexei Adzhubey, visited the Federal Republic that summer and threw out hints that Stalin's offer – reunification in exchange for neutrality – might be presented again in a more acceptable form. The peril, if it was ever a real one, ended suddenly on 15 October, when Khrushchev was deposed in Moscow.

Gomułka's policy was a double one. Its first aim was to maintain the division of Germany, which meant working for a general European security settlement to recognise the post-war frontiers of the continent – including West German recognition of the existence of the German Democratic Republic. To prepare the way for such a settlement, the Poles in October 1957 advanced the 'Rapacki Plan', named after the honourable and well-respected Adam Rapacki who served Gomułka as foreign minister. The plan called for the establishment of a nuclear-free zone in central Europe, including Poland, Czechoslovakia and both German states. It won some interest in the West, but foundered on West Germany's refusal to contemplate the practical recognition of East Germany which the plan implied. Polish diplomacy, however, continued to build tentative bridges between East and West, and the European Security Conference which finally met at Helsinki in 1975 owed much to Polish initiatives.

The second track of Gomułka's German policy was to persuade West Germany to recognise the Oder–Neisse line. This required some courage. Fear of West German 'revanchism' was the only argument for Poland's reliance on the Soviet Union which had much genuine support among ordinary Poles; to solve this problem would also remove the soundest justification for the Soviet alliance. However, the Polish government hinted to Bonn in 1957 that normal diplomatic relations might be possible without a prior agreement on the Oder–Neisse frontier.

When Bonn turned this down, Gomułka took a tougher line and insisted that recognition of the frontier must be a precondition for any formal relationship. These provinces were now completely Polish in population, all but a tiny remnant of their German inhabitants having been expelled in the two years following the end of the war. Gomułka began to lay more emphasis on the historical argument that these were 'Regained Territories', an integral part of the ancient Polish Kingdom, although in fact most of them had been under German control for some six centuries.

Years of apparent stalemate followed. East Germany had recognised the Oder–Neisse frontier in 1950, but relations between Gomułka's unorthodox Poland and the stiffly dogmatic régime of Walter Ulbricht remained cool. West Germany stayed the target of violently hostile Polish propaganda, but contacts quietly developed, especially economic ones, and in 1963 the two states exchanged trade missions which were in fact diplomatic missions in discreet disguise. In the later sixties, the West German position began to soften as the Social Democrat leader Willy Brandt, first as foreign minister and then as Chancellor, opened up his *Ostpolitik* of contact and reconciliation with the states of central and eastern Europe. Wisely, Gomułka made no premature concessions, but waited for the moment when Bonn would be ready to accept his conditions.

The Cold War in Europe had reached its final and most dangerous peak in the Berlin Crisis of 1958–61. Then, after the building of the Berlin Wall in August 1961 and the understanding between the United States and the Soviet Union that followed the terrifying Cuba missile confrontation in 1962, the tension began to fall away. In this new period of détente, the Poles took an energetic part, encouraging contact between the smaller nations of divided Europe and even trying – without much success – to mediate in the Vietnam war which began to cloud East–West relations after 1965.

At home, however, there was no détente. Gomułka's rule grew steadily more oppressive. Warsaw's best cultural periodicals were suppressed in 1962, independent discussion clubs were closed, and in 1964 the poet Antoni Słonimski organised a petition against censorship and the suffocation of culture, the 'Letter of the Thirty-Four'. This was only the beginning of a long guerrilla struggle between Gomułka and the intellectuals, conducted by more petitions and open letters which were answered by expulsions from the party and dismissals from public posts. Among those thrown out of the party was Leszek Kołakowski, now a professor at Warsaw University, who delivered a biting attack on the stagnation of the régime at a meeting called to commemorate the tenth anniversary of October 1956. There was much harsher treatment for two other junior Warsaw academics, Jacek Kuroń and Karol Modzelewski, who in 1965 distributed an 'open letter' claiming that 'state socialism' was as alienating and exploitative as capitalism, and calling for a workers' democracy which followed closely the ideas

Gomułka with his most obedient henchman, Zenon Kliszko, in 1963. Gomułka's autocratic manner had already lost him much support.

of Trotsky. They were both sentenced to three-and-a-half years in prison.

At the same time, there began to appear a new, nationalist current of opposition to Gomułka within the party. Not only the emotions of 1956 but Gomułka's prolonged propaganda campaign against West Germany had encouraged a fervent official patriotism, constantly ferreting through history to produce more garish examples of Polish heroism, more tales of bravery and suffering in the Nazi occupation, and more – often dubious – evidence to back Poland's claim that the Western Territories were in fact 'Regained Territories'.

Gradually, as disillusion with Gomułka's grey, austere style began to grow, this current was turned against him. General Mieczysław Moczar, a wartime commander of Communist partisans, had become the head of the revived security police (UB) in 1959. In a party where serious Marxist debate had almost died out, being replaced by a cynical and increasingly corrupt pragmatism, Moczar now played the patriotic card. He built a power base in the Veterans' Association (ZBoWiD) making great show of awarding decorations and pensions to neglected soldiers of the Home Army or the Polish forces in the West. Moczar won over a section of the intellectuals, acting as patron to a series of books and films which glorified Poland's military past and the insurrections.

By the later 1960s, the 'disillusion' catchword·had been replaced by 'stagnation'. In a bleak landscape, Moczar seemed to offer colour, pride and excitement. And he offered even more, for it soon became clear that he and his followers were intriguing their way towards power.

The 'Partisans' as Moczar's group was known, presented themselves as true Polish patriots, with the credentials of men who had fought in Poland against the Nazi occupation while other Communists had enjoyed a safe refuge in Moscow. Their platform had essentially three planks. The first was a shrill, traditional chauvinism, coupled with calls for a restoration of strong authority under a real 'leader'. The second, used discreetly, was an appeal to anti-Russian resentment; Moczar let it be known that he would like the truth about Katyń to be told. The third was anti-Semitism.

Moczar's tame journalists worked hard to revive the old prejudice which associated Jews with Russian Communism and with disloyalty to the cause of Polish independence. At this time, fewer than 30,000 Jews lived in Poland. But the Partisans hinted at a new 'national' Communism purged of Soviet and Jewish 'contamination', drawing attention to the Jewish origin both of some of the reforming intellectuals and of survivors of the 'Muscovite' group who had passed the war in the Soviet Union.

In June 1967, the second Arab–Israeli war broke out, ending in rapid and dazzling victory for Israel. As the Soviet Union supported the Arab cause, many Poles greeted this outcome with delight. Gomułka, suspicious of the Partisans but uncertain how to deal with them, gave way to one of his intemperate outbursts in which he accused a 'Zionist fifth column' within Poland of celebrating Israel's triumph. Instantly, Moczar's mouthpieces with the support of the security police proclaimed a violent 'anti-Zionist' campaign of slander and denunciation. Books appeared alleging that Polish Jews had collaborated with the Nazis and were now conspiring with the West Germans against Polish independence. Everywhere, Jews in party or official positions were harassed, intimidated and dismissed.

One example can stand for many. Blima B., a woman of Jewish family, was an engineer in Łódź. One night, she received a phone call – in a pseudo-Yiddish accent – telling her that she should get out and go to Israel 'because Moshe Dayan wants you there'. A few days later, she was sacked from her job; her boss suggested she emigrate to Israel. Again she refused. When she returned home, she found in her letterbox a leaflet warning that 'the problem of Judaism must be totally solved in Poland . . . The Jews themselves must be convinced that their presence in Poland is an anachronism and has no more point.

Next day, Blima B. went to clear her office desk. There she heard two typists gossiping. 'What is Zionism anyway?' one asked. The other replied: 'I read in the papers that in America and Israel the rabbis are putting a curse on Poles who are supposed to be persecuting Stalinist Jews. That's what Zionism is!'

Blima B. recalls: 'After hearing that conversaton, I realised that there was no longer a place for me in Poland'.[2]

Most Poles took no part in this witch-hunt, seeing it as a self-destructive power struggle among their rulers. But the outside world was appalled. The survivors of the Holocaust were being persecuted. The United States, especially, concluded that the Polish nation was revealing that primitive anti-Semitism formed an inherent part of the national character. It was a disaster for Poland's international good name, as the sympathy created in 1956 drained away.

The effect of the campaign was to strengthen vastly the grip of Moczar's security police on the nation. Fear and resentment mounted, especially among intellectuals, and by early 1968 the tension was ready to be detonated.

The occasion was a production in Warsaw of the poetic drama *Forefathers' Eve*, by Adam Mickiewicz. Written in the early nineteenth century, this beloved and mysterious play sanctifies the national struggle against the Tsar, a work about morality, religion and the nation which no Pole can witness without feeling that he or she is being given a key to the present. In January 1968, all the audience's pent-up emotion burst out in passionate applause at passages taunting Russian power.

Gustaw Holoubek, one of Poland's most famous actors, played the leading part. 'People received this performance with unprecedented enthusiasm. In my whole career in the theatre, which was thirty years long even then, I don't

2. Quoted in Christian Jelen, *La Purge*, Fayard, Paris, 1972, p. 150.

'As we say in the theatre – a bomb went off!' Gustaw Holoubek playing the lead in the production of *Forefathers' Eve*, whose banning by the authorities on 31 January 1968 set off protest demonstrations.

remember such an audience reaction. As we say in the theatre – a bomb went off!' In panic, the authorities closed the production down on 31 January.

A student demonstration was broken up by police. But Warsaw University continued to simmer. On 8 March, a mass meeting was held; bus-loads of thugs and police reservists poured across the campus to attack the students, and street rioting broke out, lasting sporadically for several weeks and spreading to most Polish universities. The Catholic Church spoke out against police brutality, and was bravely supported by the independent Catholic members of the Sejm. Only the workers, in spite of appeals from students and intellectuals, refused to be drawn into the struggle.

Chaos descended on Poland. The Moczar faction, seeing a chance of power, redoubled its hysterical onslaught on Jews, liberals and imagined traitors; by

March 1968: student demonstrations in Warsaw

the end of 1968, two-thirds of Poland's remaining Jews had been forced into emigration. Over a thousand students were arrested, and the security police instigated a full-scale purge of all higher education. Only a few Poles in authority found the courage to stand up to this madness. Adam Rapacki refused to enter his own ministry – where officials were now being asked to prove the racial origin of their grandparents – and was replaced at the end of the year. Mieczysław Rakowski, editor of the party weekly *Polityka*, gave no space to the anti-Semitic slanders and sent some of his better-known Jewish employees into temporary refuge abroad.

Nobody seemed to be in control. Gomułka clearly was not. In neighbouring Czechoslovakia, the 'Prague Spring' of 1968 was beginning, and the Warsaw students had carried banners proclaiming that 'Poland is waiting for its Dubček'. Infuriated, Gomułka tried to condemn the 'revisionist' liberals and intellectuals while discouraging the attacks on 'Jewish cosmopolitans' (his own wife was of Jewish origin). Nobody paid attention, and by mid-1968 it was beginning to look as if Gomułka would soon be overthrown by his rivals.

In the Soviet Union, however, there was alarm at the turn events were taking in Poland. Leonid Brezhnev and his colleagues were well aware of what Mieczysław Moczar stood for. They had registered his manipulation of anti-Russian feelings, and they had no wish to see a revival of militant Polish nationalism. In Romania, President Nicolae Ceausescu was already pursuing an independent, chauvinistic line; Moczar or one of his allies might well repeat that pattern of ultra-patriotic police dictatorship. More pressing still, the crisis over Czechoslovakia was coming to a head.

Here, at least, Gomułka was reliable. The man who had spoken out for civil liberties and a democratic model of socialism in 1956 now had no hesitation in condemning Alexander Dubček's policies as 'counter-revolution'. The man who had defied Soviet armed force in the name of national independence now urged the rather reluctant Soviet leadership to take military action against Czechoslovakia, and when the Warsaw Pact army of intervention poured over the Czech and Slovak frontiers on the night of 20–21 August 1968, Polish troops and tanks went with it. In Poland, only a minority registered their shame and horror at the sight of Polish soldiers acting as occupiers of a friendly country. Most Poles, falling back on traditional dislike of the Czechs, were curiously indifferent.

Through his loyalty over Czechoslovakia, Gomułka made himself indispensable to Brezhnev. That November, when the Fifth Congress of the PZPR gathered in Warsaw, he received his reward. Without Soviet support and pressure behind the scenes, Gomułka might well have been chased out of the leadership by his Partisan rivals. But Brezhnev arrived and stayed protectively until the end of the congress. Moczar was kept out of the politburo, and many of his supporters failed to be elected to the central committee. Another powerful challenger, the ex-miner Edward Gierek who had built up a strong fiefdom for himself as party secretary in the industrial region of Upper Silesia, pressed forward as a compromise candidate but could not muster enough backing.

Gomułka was re-elected as first secretary. In October 1956, he had won control of Poland because he refused to submit to Soviet interference. In November 1968, he retained power only because Soviet influence intervened to save him.

The 'March events' of 1968 and the upheavals which followed brought about fundamental changes in Poland. Gomułka, though back in the saddle, had now lost almost all real support inside and outside the party. More significant was the change in the nature of opposition. Up to 1968, intellectual protest had put its faith in a renewal of the principles of 1956, in the capacity of the party and the system to reform itself and lead the nation towards democracy under the right leadership. The mainstream of opposition had been liberal, in the sense that it sought to find a sceptical, humanist path between the dogmatic blocks of Catholicism and Communism. Many of its leading lights had been assimilated Jews, often from a Marxist background.

In March 1968, this tradition died under the police clubs. The intellectuals and students found themselves isolated, without active support either from the workers or from the Catholic mass of the population. One consequence was the end of the assumption, dating back to the Romantic period of revolution in the early nineteenth century, that the function of intellectuals was to formulate and lead the protests of the nation in times of peril. Another result was that intellectuals abandoned hope that the party could regenerate itself. They were forced to look elsewhere for inspiration. And when intellectual opposition revived again, nearly ten years later, it took a very different form: more conservative, more influenced by history, above all looking to the Catholic Church for moral guidance and protection. Forsaking old claims, this new opposition saw its duty as assisting and servicing working-class protest rather than attempting to lead it.

In his last two years of power, Gomułka made a desperate attempt to drag the Polish economy out of stagnation. A reform programme was drawn up, a project to modernise and revive the economy without any of the corresponding political reforms which such changes required to win popular support. Bolesław Jaszczuk, put in charge of the programme, concentrated investment on a few key sectors – electronics, machine tools, chemicals – which might attract Western investment and bring modern technology into Poland. To pay for this, money for other sectors of society – agriculture, housing, social services – was frozen or reduced. Meanwhile Jaszczuk introduced incentive schemes to raise wages in successful enterprises, and threatened factories that did not pay their way with closure.

The problem with all such schemes for introducing 'market' forces into a centralised socialist economy is that the workers have to pay the initial price.

After generations of secure employment in plants concerned with meeting production targets rather than with the question of whether anyone wanted their products, workers suddenly face the prospect of reduced earnings and even of losing their jobs altogether. In this Polish 'reform from above', there was no question of compensating workers by offering them a share in management or a voice to express their grievances freely.

Nobody bothered to explain to the workers at the grassroots why the old system of subsidised prices and wages would have to go. As a result, they simply felt that they were being swindled. Henryk Frankiewicz worked in the Gdańsk shipyards and remembers well the feelings of his mates. 'Gomułka had made more and more appearances, always grumbling and complaining about the growth in the cost of building housing and how the state had to subsidise it – that sort of thing, all the time. And that began to annoy people, they began to get angry. What was he complaining about? After all, we were working just as we usually did, giving it everything we had and in return the state subsidised us. We, the working class, we couldn't accept what he was saying . . .'

Under the surface, the exasperation of the working class began to accumulate dangerously. It was made worse by the government's neglect of the private farmers. Meat production, especially, began to drop off. It was a recurrent plague of the post-war Polish economy that purchasing power and supply constantly lost touch with each other: too much money chased too few goods, food above all, which would then vanish from the shops. To the complaints of the workers in 1969–70 were now added the long meat queues in which their families were obliged to stand.

On previous occasions, the authorities had found a crude answer to this problem. They had simply imposed without warning a massive increase in prices at the shops. The counters would then fill up again with food and goods, for the elementary reason that fewer people could afford them. Jaszczuk prepared to use this well-tried device once more.

A few weeks before he did so, Chancellor Willy Brandt arrived in Warsaw. On 7 December 1970, he and Józef Cyrankiewicz, the Polish prime minister, signed the Warsaw Treaty which recognised the Oder–Neisse line as Poland's frontier, abandoned West Germany's claim to the Reich borders of 1937, and agreed to the opening of full diplomatic relations. By settling the last important frontier dispute in Europe, the treaty opened the way to the détente process of the 1970s and made possible the European Security Conference a few years later. It led to a string of further treaties between the Bonn government and other states in central and eastern Europe, including the 1972 Basic Treaty between the two German states, and indirectly to the Four-Power agreement which was to stabilise the Berlin problem. It unlocked for Poland the door to the rich industrial economy and money markets of West Germany.

If this was an hour of moral triumph for Willy Brandt, kneeling in expiation before the monument to the fighters of the Warsaw Ghetto, it was also an hour

Signing the Warsaw Treaty, through which West Germany finally accepted Poland's western frontier on the Oder–Neisse Line, 7 December 1970. Chancellor Willy Brandt (left) shakes hands with prime minister Józef Cyrankiewicz. Gomułka stands between them. Behind Cyrankiewicz stands General Mieczysław Moczar, leader of the ultra-nationalist 'partisan' faction.

of political triumph for Władysław Gomułka. By sticking to his principles, in the teeth of West German hostility, the indifference of the NATO powers and the obstruction and suspicion of East Germany, he had overcome the basic constitutional dogma of the Bonn state and brought the most powerful economy in capitalist Europe to accept his terms for good relations. He had removed a threat to his country, and opened for it new horizons.

It was Gomułka's last appearance on the international scene. Brandt flew home. A few days later, on 12 December 1970, Warsaw Radio announced steep and sudden price changes. Some goods, like televisions and refrigerators, became cheaper. But food did not. Flour prices rose by 16 per cent, sugar by 14 per cent and meat by 17 per cent.

The case for price increases was sound enough. It was a part of the reform's intention to bring prices closer to production costs and reduce the heavy government subsidies which had been holding down the price of food in the shops. Something had to be done to bring supply and demand closer together again. But this time the method – overnight price rises – did not work. The Polish workers were already angry and nervous. These increases came just before Christmas, when Poles console themselves for the privations of the past year with family feasts of meat, fish and alcohol. What was a man to say to his wife and children, if he could not afford to give them a proper Christmas? The arrogance and the timing of the blow broke down all patience.

The increases were proclaimed on a Saturday. On the following Monday morning, thousands of workers from the Lenin shipyard at Gdańsk marched in protest to party headquarters. The police tried in vain to drive them back and fighting broke out in the streets. Next day, the Paris Commune shipyard at Gdynia stopped work. In Gdańsk, where a general occupation strike began, police opened fire on demonstrators and there were deaths on both sides.

Henryk Frankiewicz, on the march with the shipyard workers, saw the shooting begin. 'One of the commanders, the lieutenant, just simply shot at the crowd with his pistol. It was about an arm's length from me, and I only realised what had happened when I saw this squirt of blood. One of the lads from the shipyard had been hit straight in the larynx, in the artery, and the blood – you know – it spouted up about four feet. It was like oil on the flames, as we say in Polish: the people saw it, and they threw themselves at the police cordon. Then there was a massacre . . .

'The district hospital is nearby, and all the staff saw what was happening; they rushed out to the lad who had been shot. First we thought he had just been wounded, but they got there and looked at him and said he'd died. A Polish flag was found somewhere and the flag was soaked in blood: there was so much of it that it was all over the whole flag. And then, in that moment of passion, like in the riot, everyone turned round and said: "Let's march on the District Party Committee . . ."'' The party building was attacked and set on fire.

All along the Baltic coast, men and women downed tools at the news that Polish blood was flowing on the streets. The strike movement spread to Elbląg and Słupsk, then to the city of Szczecin far to the west.

At the first news from Gdańsk, Gomułka was not so much alarmed as enraged. In 1956, he had spoken of the 'justifed protest' of the Poznań workers; now he shouted about 'counter-revolution'. It was certainly Gomułka who, on Tuesday, gave the order to use force, though he may not have meant the police to shoot down unarmed demonstrators. His lieutenant, Zenon Kliszko, rushed down to Gdańsk, where he issued a string of panicky, incoherent orders. With him went Stanisław Kociołek, a young technocrat who had recently joined the politburo. Others were more prudent. Moczar, foreseeing a catastrophe he might turn to his own profit, went to ground and

December 1970: the workers' revolt in the Baltic ports. Men from the shipyard march through Szczecin.

stayed out of the crisis. General Wojciech Jaruzelski, the minister of defence, told Gomułka to his face that he would not allow regular army units to be used against the workers.

On Wednesday, the Gdańsk region was calmer, but the occupation strike of all factories and shipyards still held firm. Kociołek made a radio appeal for a return to work, discovering too late the same night that Kliszko had decided – on no evidence – that sabotage was planned and had ordered the security forces to bar factory gates to workers attempting to enter. Early in the morning of Thursday 17 December 1970, the morning shift of the Paris Commune shipyard at Gdynia poured off the train to go to work and met a blast of gunfire. Thirteen died. The same day, the workers at Szczecin rose; there was bloody fighting and scores more were killed.

By the weekend, although the fighting had died down, factories all over Poland were beginning to stop work. A general strike, which might well lead to a full insurrection throughout the country, seemed only hours away. On the Baltic coast, the workers were not only taking control of their plants but running their cities, through elected strike committees. From Szczecin came a list of twenty-one demands, including for the first time a call for 'independent trade unions under the control of the working class'.

In Warsaw, the remaining party leaders saw that the only hope of heading off disaster was to remove Gomułka. A message arrived from the Soviet politburo, advising a 'political' solution; in Moscow code this was a condemnation of Gomułka's attempt to solve the crisis by force. Over-wrought, Gomułka now suffered a minor cerebral haemorrhage, which partly blinded him.

On Sunday, with Gomułka fuming on a hospital sick-bed, the central committee met in emergency session. Most of them were determined to keep Moczar out of power. Instead, and probably with Soviet encouragement, they turned to Edward Gierek, a solid, reassuring presence with useful credentials as a man who had worked as a miner in the collieries of Belgium and France. Gomułka, Kliszko, Jaszczuk and Spychalski were deposed. Gierek was elected first secretary.

That night Gierek broadcast to the nation. The working class had been provoked beyond endurance, he said: the party had lost touch with the nation. He promised that there would be sweeping changes. A cycle had ended. Another, which would finish in an even greater crisis, was beginning.

'Poles are shedding Polish blood': workers from the Gdynia shipyard carry away a comrade shot by the police, 17 December 1970

8

From Gierek to Gdańsk: 1970–80

Outside the gates of the Warski shipyard at Szczecin, a large, grey-haired man, strikingly well-dressed, stood arguing with the pickets. Behind him, several other important-looking figures, one in a general's uniform, were climbing out of taxis. The big man insisted that he was the First Secretary of the Polish Workers' Party, Edward Gierek. The pickets at first thought he was a hoaxer. The party leader, politely asking to be allowed to talk to workers? That would be the day.

But it was Gierek, and the men with him included Piotr Jaroszewicz, the new prime minister, and General Wojciech Jaruzelski, minister of defence. It was the afternoon of 24 January 1971. The strikes which had calmed down after Gomułka's fall in December were breaking out again.

Promises of a wage rise for the low-paid and a freeze on prices had not been enough for the workers. For nearly a month, there had been angry debates in the factories, debates which had run far beyond the economic grievances which touched off the explosion of December. The Warski yard, which had gone back on strike two days before, now asked not only for the cancellation of the December price rises but for free elections in trade unions, 'reliable information' in the press, and the punishment of those who had fired on them four weeks before.

The Szczecin strikers had challenged Gierek to come and face them. But his decision to fly from Warsaw was taken so suddenly that the strike committee had only been warned by telephone a few minutes before the fleet of taxis arrived. After long hesitation, Edward Gierek had become convinced that this gesture was his last hope of staving off another working-class insurrection.

Thousands of men and women left their work and poured into the main shipyard hall at the news of his appearance. Then, for nine solid hours, Gierek and his team argued face to face with the class they were supposed to represent. He heard furious accusations, desperate appeals. But his reply, which he repeated the next day at the shipyards at Gdańsk, was both unexpected and disarming. He did not talk ideology or jargon. Instead, he proclaimed that he was a real worker too, a man who had dug coal for years in the collieries of France and Belgium. He asked the Polish workers to trust him and help him, as a patriotic Pole and as a leader who knew what poverty and toil meant.

'I say to you: help us, help me . . . I am only a worker, like you. But now, and I tell you this in all solemnity, as a Pole and a Communist, the fate of our nation and the cause of socialism are in the balance.' It was demagogic, but the workers wanted to believe in his sincerity despite themselves. Gierek spoke simply, at times with desperation in his voice. The astounding fact that he had come to them as a supplicant, not in the arrogance of power, moved them. At the end, when he had outlined what he meant to do and had promised to allow free elections to the shipyard's workers' council, he asked: 'Will you help me?' And they shouted: 'We will help!'

Did he mean what he said? Probably he did. Edward Gierek, who led his country into economic and political catastrophe, is reviled these days. But he was honest after his fashion. Certainly he was a complete contrast to Gomułka. Where Gomułka had been austere, remote, irascible, Gierek gave the impression of a good-hearted man of the world. Foreign statesmen and journalists liked him. He was affable, spoke good French, and clearly enjoyed comfortable living. He seemed to embody practicality and common sense.

'Help me . . . I am only a worker, like you.' Edward Gierek appealing to striking shipyard workers at Gdańsk, January 1971.

But Gierek was less worldly than he seemed. He 'knew the West', but knowledge of the West acquired by a foreign coal-miner during the Nazi occupation could hardly be extensive. He had indeed worked hard with his hands, but he had spent the last twenty-five years or so as a party bureaucrat. His years as party chief in the coal-mining basin of Upper Silesia, based on the city of Katowice, had been successful, in that the region had a rather higher standard of living than the rest of Poland and had come to regard Gierek as a good provider. Katowice, however, was not a good preparation for Warsaw. There, a comfortable and frequently corrupt party mafia had run affairs as it pleased, untroubled by rebellion or dissent. In Upper Silesia, with its grimy conurbations of brick buildings and cobbled streets, its rearing pit headworks, its pubs and its tall old factory chimneys gushing smoke, there was an almost Germanic solidity. But Warsaw, a capital seamed with intrigue and double-meanings, fascinated with the Romantic traditions of the anti-Russian struggle, was foreign territory to Edward Gierek. To help him find his bearings, Gierek brought many of his old cronies with him from Katowice to Warsaw. They were pragmatists who wanted a good life for themselves – and everyone else if possible. But neither they nor Gierek himself were politicians.

With the strike threat finally laid to rest, Gierek set to work. The first task was the usual formality: the party proclaimed that it would never lose touch with the workers again, promised to observe 'Leninist norms' in party life, threw out Gomułka's remaining placemen in the leadership, and offered the Poles new freedom to criticise and to reform society whether they were party members or not. It all sounded like the promises made by Gomułka in October 1956. But then the population had been enthusiastic, simmering with impatience and optimism. In 1971, the Poles were suspicious, resentful, and very tired.

Gierek set about building what he called 'a second Poland', a society utterly unlike the grim, stagnant country which Gomułka had produced. Economists silenced by Gomułka now bombarded Gierek with advice, and with exciting perspectives. There was to be a Polish 'Great Leap Forward'. The miserable standard of living was to be transformed; Western technology would revolutionise industry. It was all a huge calculated risk. Poland would borrow money from the West to import the machinery and know-how for a new export industry, whose profits would soon pay off the foreign debts.

And at first it went amazingly well. Real wages rose by forty per cent in Gierek's first five years. In 1972, national income rose by ten per cent, twice the planned target, and 1973 was even better. Under Gomułka, about $100 million a year had been spent on importing Western machinery. By 1974, Poland was spending $1,900 million. It was the steepest, fastest boom Poland had ever known.

For ordinary Poles, the early 1970s were good years. Poland had bought from Italy the licence to build two makes of Fiat car, the 125 and the baby 126. Within a few years, the gaunt outlines of Poland's streets vanished behind a rush of private cars, and behind the acid fog of low-octane petrol fumes. Waiting times for delivery were long, but they could be shortened by the use of black-market dollars, and the authorities no longer bothered to ask how those dollars had been acquired. Everyone was spending: on camping equipment, televisions, cheap foreign clothes and shoes imported to meet a demand Polish production could not fulfil, and, above all, on foreign holidays. In their new Fiats, with a few hoarded dollars or marks and equipped with Polish canned food to save hard currency, Polish tourists began to appear in western Europe. In return, the West began to visit Poland. Many of these visitors were Polish-Americans, who were now encouraged by the Polish government to return in old age to the land of their forefathers. There they were granted priority in building materials, to construct retirement cottages in the Carpathian foothills, and were allowed to draw their United States pensions at excellent rates of exchange. Given the colossal buying power of the dollar bill on the black market in Poland, it was a seductive scheme.

This was part of Gierek's *Polonia* policy. *Polonia* means the totality of all Poles on earth, whether they live in Warsaw, Chicago or Buenos Aires, as Australian farmers or as old-age pensioners in the western suburbs of London. In Gierek's version, it had a frankly nationalist appeal, which in effect said: 'Let us forget about political differences. We don't ask you to become Communists. We say there is a patriotism which transcends all beliefs. We are all proud of the same history. Come and visit Poland, as tourists or historians or to retire or to start a small business. If you can't come, help with your money to restore Poland's ancient buildings and monuments.'

As the political émigrés in London and Paris saw, there was calculation as well as generosity in this. In a way, it was following the example set by Moczar in the 1960s, when he had courted popularity by offering medals and war pensions to Polish veterans living in exile. Gierek was trying to present the West with a different image of Poland: a régime which was casual about ideology and founded its appeal on much more familiar values – prosperity and patriotism. *Polonia* responded; Poles living abroad gave valuable help to Poland's export drive, while much of the money raised to rebuild the Royal Castle in Warsaw, destroyed by the Germans, came from American Poles.

Gierek took the decision, not easy for a Communist, to give state support to private farmers. With higher wages, the Poles were eating more; the traditional Polish cuisine, which had become a mere memory, returned to the tables of better-off families with its marvellous cold summer soups, rich stews and dishes piled with breaded pork chops and puréed beetroot. To meet demand, the government bought quantities of food in the West and from the Soviet Union, running up new debts. But the real solution could only be helping

The Gierek boom years. Baby Fiat cars, made in Poland, spread across the land.

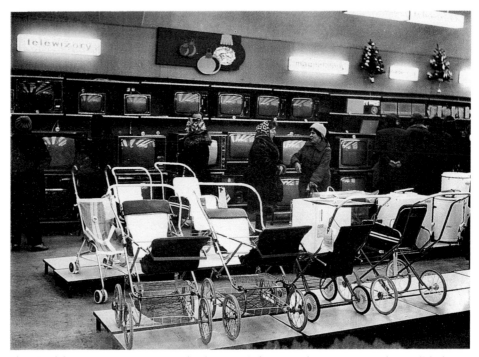

The Gierek boom years. Wages rise and industry switches towards consumer goods: a Polish shop in the mid-1970s.

Power for industry. The Turów power station in western Poland, fuelled by low-grade brown coal, comes on-stream.

Poland to feed itself, and that meant helping the peasants to grow more grain and raise more pigs.

In times of shortage, town-dwelling Poles enviously imagined their country cousins gorging on veal and ham, stuffing their mattresses with zloty notes. This was an illusion. Life for the peasant was tough. It meant toil from dawn to dusk, on thin medieval strips of land often miles apart. Tractors were rare, usually the privilege of big state farms. The private peasant relied on his blond-maned, chestnut horse, which pulled the plough and trotted the family cart to Mass on Sundays. The state paid miserable prices for what it bought; there was little incentive to grow more, and the productivity of the land was abysmally low. In addition, most peasant farms were worked by old men and women. Their sons and daughters had either migrated to the cities or were so-called 'peasant workers' who lived on the farm but commuted by motor-bike or rickety bus to some distant factory.

The government abolished compulsory deliveries of produce, paid more for what it bought, and began – stealthily, in case the Soviet Union disapproved – to sell more small tractors and agricultural machinery to the peasants. At last, the private peasants were allowed proper welfare and health benefits, and old-age pensions. With the help of some good seasons, agricultural production began to increase fast. And, with money in their pockets, peasants all over Poland began to pull down their cottages, often still thatched, and replace them by ugly but comfortable houses of brick.

But the great Gierek boom ran into problems. It was bad luck that in 1973 there was another Middle East war, which led to a colossal increase in world price of oil. This did not hit Poland directly; oil supplies came from the Soviet Union at controlled prices. But the industrial economies of the West plunged into chaos. Inflation suddenly multiplied the cost of the modern technology which Poland was importing, while recession in the West cut back the demand for Polish exports. Poland's hard-currency foreign debt, which had been only $100 million in 1971, was over $6 billion by 1975 and rising, almost vertically.

Poland was now importing inflation with every machine-tool or fertiliser plant bought in the West. But there was home-grown inflation as well. This was an old story, made worse by the worker uprising in December 1970. There had always been a recurrent problem of too much money chasing too few goods – especially food. Now, though, the workers had made themselves into a third semi-independent power in the land, joining the Catholic Church and the private peasantry. They demanded higher wages, but at the same time rejected any increase in prices – the women textile workers of Łódź had gone on strike in February 1971 and forced the new leadership to cancel the December price rises.

Anyone could foresee what would happen. With buying power running far ahead of supplies to the shops, there would be shortages. But Edward Gierek, for all his earnest bonhomie towards the workers, was too frightened of their power to take unpopular measures. The obvious answer was a slow, step-by-step increase in prices – meat prices, above all. Instead, the authorities did nothing, and went on paying a subsidy to keep the shop prices of food down which eventually became no less than forty per cent of the entire state budget. Meanwhile, reforms in the structure of the nationalised economy allowed groups of industries to decide on their own wages – and they took the easy course of paying the workers more every year.

The shops began to empty. Queues became a common sight again. In Warsaw, a foreigner visiting an apartment block would often find fresh blood on the stairs. This marked the tracks not of a murderer but of a peasant woman shouldering huge sacks of black-market meat, selling it from door to door at several times the controlled price. Meanwhile, the government sold more and more Polish farm produce to the West, in a desperate but vain attempt to keep up its falling export revenues.

Frantically seeking ways to mop up Polish purchasing power, the government persuaded the relatively prosperous German Democratic Republic to abolish visa requirements and open its shops to Polish visitors. The result was a stampede. Over seven million Poles went to East Germany in 1974 alone. The streets of East Berlin were lined with grimy Polish buses, while the big stores' stock-labels were printed in Polish as well as German. The Polish day-trippers emptied the shelves, the East German public grew enraged, and eventually the whole scheme was cancelled and visas restored.

The nightmarish imbalance between supply and demand grew worse. In a period of boom (in 1973 Poland had the third highest growth rate in the world), the Poles could find less and less to buy with their money. In despair, they stashed their earnings away in savings banks: the average proportion of income saved multiplied by five between 1970 and 1976. A frozen tidal wave of unspent cash began to tower over the economy.

By the mid-1970s, Gierek's promises of a more liberal, open, democratic Poland had long since faded away. Partly, this was because Gierek's whole strategy was double-faced. To cover his opening to the West, he felt obliged to show the Soviet Union that, in the ways that mattered, Poland was an orthodox Communist state. The censors zealously took up their red pencils and scissors once more: the daily papers and television became dreary and conformist, carefully giving much space and time to Soviet speeches and Soviet achievements. Commissions set up to investigate the December riots or to devise 'better methods of governing' were smothered. There was another change in agricultural policy, this time favouring the state farms against the private peasants who now found it harder to buy extra land, to leave their smallholdings to their children, and to get rare but vital supplies like chemical fertiliser.

No more was heard of offering non-party people responsible jobs, or letting the Sejm have more powers. Instead, the party interfered and dictated at every level. The workers on the Baltic coast lost their rights freely to elect their works' councils, and the leaders of the 1970 and 1971 strikes at Szczecin lost their jobs – several dying in mysterious, even suspicious, circumstances.

For the intellectuals of Warsaw and Kraków, these were despondent times. Their old patterns of life went on; they met in their favourite coffee-houses after Mass on Sunday mornings, sat and chain-smoked at their favourite table in the canteen of the Czytelnik publishing house, saturated themselves with gossip and vodka at Spatif, the actors' club. But there was nothing to read, except in foreign books and papers, and the intellectuals had a gloomy sense that they had lost their role. The workers had ignored them in March 1968; they, in turn, had stood by passively while the workers fought and died in December 1970. Unpublished writers, banned film-makers, professors who could not lecture about their theories, and editors with nothing to edit, the intellectuals felt like the 'superfluous people' of nineteenth-century Russian novels.

But in 1975, they were suddenly offered a chance to act. True to his policy of obsequiousness to the Soviet Union, Gierek now brought forward a new draft constitution, which included clauses about 'unshakeable fraternal bonds with the Soviet Union' and the 'leading role of the PZPR in the state'. There was a storm of intellectual protest, this time supported in public by the Catholic Church. The authorities backed down, and the offending phrases were softened until they were meaningless. It was an invigorating row for the intellectuals. It was also a sign that the Gierek régime, for all its noisy display of confidence, was afraid of a confrontation.

It was the same lack of nerve which had made the leadership put off the decision to tackle food prices. Frightened of how the workers would react, the politburo kept food prices frozen at the 1971 level for five years. Then, suicidally, Gierek and his comrades decided to solve the problem at one stroke. On 24 June 1976, Piotr Jaroszewicz, the prime minister, informed the Sejm that meat prices would rise by almost seventy per cent, sugar by one hundred per cent, butter and cheese by at least a third.

The next day, factories stopped work all over the country. In many towns, strike committees were set up on the model of 1970. There was a violent demonstration at Płock, the petrochemical centre on the river Vistula. In Warsaw, workers from the Ursus tractor plant blocked the main east–west railway line – the tracks which carried Soviet military supplies to East Germany. The worst outbreak took place at Radom, where a huge workers' demonstration marched into the city and besieged party headquarters.

A young dissident, Mirosław Chojecki, was on the scene soon afterwards, collecting accounts of events from eyewitnesses. 'Stones began to be thrown and windows were broken . . . Several people got into the buffet in the building. They started taking cold meat, sausages and ham outside, showing it to the demonstrators and shouting: "Look at the way these guzzlers live! And what about us?" The crowd began to invade the building. At about one p.m., systematic ransacking began. Television sets, desks and armchairs were

Radom, 25 June 1976. Workers protesting at price rises besiege party headquarters.

thrown out through the smashed windows. At about three p.m., a fire was started on the ground floor . . . Then a handful of people armed with large sticks appeared on Żeromski Street, making their way from shop to shop and breaking all the windows . . . At about five p.m., the crowd began to throw goods out of the damaged shops. Looting and wrecking commenced.' After a day of fighting the police, four people were left dead and the city centre was littered with stones and broken glass.

Gierek gave way so fast that there were no time for a national strike movement to develop. Jaroszewicz was pushed on to television that night to announce that the price increases would be withdrawn. It was a staggering humiliation, for which the government took its own revenge. Thousands of strikers were fired, and many were systematically beaten up, forced to run the gauntlet of a double file of policemen battering them with clubs. Radom was punished in medieval fashion, losing its state funds for education, health services and housing. Television showed scenes of grand loyalty rallies, in which thousands of party members proclaimed their faith in Comrade Gierek. Few Poles were fooled. As Szczypiorski wrote later, 'the year 1976 proved that Gierek was a stupid man and that his staff consisted of even greater imbeciles'.

In the aftermath of Radom and Ursus, a small group of men and women decided to organise private help for the victims of official vengeance: money for workers' families and for lawyers to defend those arrested. The Committee for the Defence of the Workers (KOR) was to become the best-known and most influential opposition centre in eastern Europe. But at first it was only a handful of intellectuals with no single ideology. It included old Edward Lipiński, a lawyer who had fought in the 1905 revolution, Jerzy Andrzejewski, author of *Ashes and Diamonds*, the actress Halina Mikołajska, two lawyers and a priest. There were several veterans of the Home Army resistance in the Second World War, including Józef Rybicki, a much-decorated officer who had commanded the legendary Kedyw diversionary special unit against the Nazi occupiers and who had spent many years as a prisoner in the Stalinist years.

But the most energetic element in KOR was formed by six young men who had been involved in the student revolt of March 1968. Its founder was Antoni Macierewicz, a young historian. Others included Jacek Kuroń, an irrepressible 'prison graduate' who had been one of the authors of the 'Open Letter' to the party in Gomułka's time, and Adam Michnik, a man whose angelic expression, curly hair and slight stammer concealed the most formidable, courageous and prolific revolutionary spirit which Poland had seen since the early days of Piłsudski himself. The ideas and the unbreakable determination of Kuroń and Michnik were to influence Polish history over the next ten years, and to make them famous far beyond Poland itself.

The aims of KOR were humanitarian, not political. But it was inevitably drawn into taking a political stand. The group campaigned for an amnesty for the imprisoned workers and for an enquiry into police brutality. In September 1977, KOR added the title of Committee for Social Defence, and began to agitate for freely elected workers' committees in the factories. To spread its ideas, KOR produced a single-sheet underground newspaper which it named *Robotnik (The Worker)* – significantly, the title of Piłsudski's clandestine socialist paper seventy years before.

Robotnik first appeared in September 1977, published once a fortnight. Just over a year later, it was running off 20,000 copies of twelve pages each, screen-printed in secret with the pages photographically reduced. Workers from different parts of Poland were recruited on to the editorial board, and created bodies of readers in their own plants and cities. *Robotnik* published the real facts about oppression and hardship on the factory floor, with hints on how to organise strikes and formulate demands on pay and conditions. In 1979, it carried a 'Charter of Workers' Rights', which called on its readers to organise 'founding committees of free trade unions' at their workplaces: 'Wherever there are strong, organised groups of workers able to defend their representatives if they are dismissed or arrested, committees of free trade unions should be formed . . . only independent trade unions . . . can constitute a force with which the authorities will have to reckon, and with which they will negotiate on a basis of equality.'

Opposition had revived. In 1977, other movements appeared, some of them taking an openly anti-Communist and nationalist line, others – like the Student Solidarity Committee – forming parallel bodies to existing official organisations. KOR, however, concentrated on the industrial workers, teaching through *Robotnik* its message that Poles should quietly but resolutely set up their own 'independent social organisations'. In 1978, tiny 'free trade union' groups began to meet in different cities, and in April 1978 a committee of workers and young intellectuals calling itself 'The Free Trade Unions of the Coast' issued its first bulletin at Gdańsk. KOR's real achievement was to overcome, very gradually, the gulf between intellectual opponents of the régime and the working class.

By 1978, there were something like nineteen different unofficial publications going from hand to hand. In a country where private persons were not allowed to possess printing equipment or duplicators, where supplies of paper and even printing ink were strictly controlled, this samizdat could only be produced in small numbers at erratic intervals. Some were smudgy and almost unreadable, closely typed pages softened almost to the texture of cotton by the hands of dozens of readers. Others were astonishing in quality and content. *Zapis* was a literary-historical review essential to every student of Polish culture. Nowa was a complete underground publishing house, which issued some fifty uncensored books by 1980 – including translations of George Orwell, Osip Mandelstam and Günter Grass. With this spate of publishing came the 'Flying University', a system of lectures and courses taught in private apartments.

LEFT: The new opposition: clandestine bulletins being printed. The operator wears the T-shirt of Nowa, an underground publishing enterprise.

BELOW: The new opposition: editors of Nowa. Left to right: Mirosław Chojecki, leader of the enterprise; Grzegorz Boguta; Konrad Bieliński.

In Warsaw, people were only half-joking when they compared the atmosphere to the German occupation: a rampaging black market, an underground press, a secret education system. But the penalties were infinitely less severe. All the same, the KOR people, the printers, the Flying University teachers and students had a rough time: they were constantly raided by the police, sometimes beaten up, often imprisoned for short spells.

For their raids, the police relied on gangs of specially recruited hooligans and thugs, rather than their own officers. One example among many is the wave of attacks against Flying University meetings organised in early 1979. On three occasions, lectures by Jacek Kuroń were invaded and broken up by men who beat up the audience and kicked the door down. A few weeks later, Kuroń was thrown downstairs at another lecture, and then Adam Michnik was beaten up before he could begin a talk. This particular wave of assaults came to a climax when a gang stormed Kuroń's apartment, knocked a visitor unconscious and attacked his family; the raiders, who wore black leather gloves, hammered his wife with karate blows, half-strangled her, and left their son with concussion.

Horrifying as this use of violence was, it was not enough to halt the lectures and debates or stem the flow of publications. This could probably have been achieved by the use of unrestrained state terror on the Soviet model: the arrest of thousands of people, followed by mass trials and prison sentences of many years. But Gierek, to the amazement and disgust of the security police, made no such serious effort to smash this opposition beyond recovery.

Why he restrained himself remains a mystery. Possibly he was unwilling to upset creditor governments in the West by an outburst of repression. Whatever his motives, Gierek badly underestimated the dangers of allowing the opposition groups to survive.

In a way, it was all absurd. A few hundred people, most of them boys and girls in worn jeans and sweaters, could scarcely menace the power of the state. The readership of *Robotnik* ran into thousands, but what was a tired coal-miner, engineering fitter or shipyard apprentice going to make of articles in minute type about Dmowski's politics or the aesthetics of the poet Słowacki? Unfortunately for Gierek, this sort of calculation was quite wrong. *Robotnik*, especially, was targeted with precision at a vital section of the working class: intelligent, well-educated men and women stuck in manual jobs because they had given political offence or because the way to promotion was blocked by untalented party appointees. They read, reflected, met the distributors and began to talk to them.

The new opposition was very different from the sceptical, leftish intellectuals who had mocked and criticised on the party's fringes up to 1968. These opposition groups, especially those to the right of KOR, were interested in traditional nationalism, in many cases, and were deeply impressed by the Church. In 1977, the Church began to form an informal alliance with these dissenters, sheltering hunger strikers and inviting several opposition figures to take part in a 'week of Christian culture'. Adam Michnik, who like Kuroń had been arrested in the student troubles of 1968, now wrote a widely read essay in which he argued that the failure of intellectuals to cooperate with the Catholic Church had been a fatal weakness of all opposition since 1944. The peasants, at least, had no such problem. In the late 1970s, parish priests were often the ringleaders of small 'farmers' self-defence committees' which began to appear in the villages of eastern Poland.

The violence of 1976 frightened the Polish government into a change of course. The brakes were slammed on to the economy, as investment was cut or transferred to producing consumer goods. Once again, the private farmers were offered easier access to fertiliser, tractors and extra land in the hope that food production would catch up with demand. None of these emergency measures worked. The boom ran down, stopped and went into reverse, until by 1980 national income and industrial output were actually falling.

Meanwhile the gigantic foreign debts began to fall due. All Poland could do was borrow more Western money to produce goods to export, in the hope that at least some of the interest could be paid. By 1980, the debt had spiralled up to $23 billion. Enormous, sullen queues waited in the sleet and snow for basic necessities like butter and sugar, to say nothing of meat. Machinery all over Poland began to break down, because there was no hard currency to import spare parts. Poland had imprudently let its pharmaceutical industry run down, assuming that everything could be bought abroad; now, with everything from antibiotics to soap unobtainable, public health began to collapse as infant mortality soared and diseases like infectious hepatitis spread. In the winter of 1979, the power stations ran out of coal and city people shivered in dark, unheated apartments. Cigarettes vanished: the machines had worn out. Even matches disappeared: the author remembers slicing the last book-match in his hotel in half with a razor-blade. Through the sheer incompetence of its rulers, Poland was now entering the worst economic disaster suffered by any European country for over thirty years.

Political authority was tottering. But with a strange, almost mad arrogance, the party refused to see what was happening. Instead, there was a 'propaganda of success', especially on the closely supervised state television, boasting about imaginery achievements, harping on social problems in the West and ignoring Poland's growing misery. This was a macabre game. Poles only had to listen to Radio Free Europe or the BBC to hear, in detail, what the real situation in their country was. In 1976, however, the director of Polish television claimed that his service 'satisfied eighty per cent of the spiritual needs of Poles', whatever that meant.

This walling-off of reality took a physical form. All over Poland, party chieftains were building themselves expensive private houses and villas, often with diverted public money. Early in the 1970s, the party journalist Mieczysław Rakowski had written a hopeful article suggesting that the party was at last uniting with the people: the local PZPR secretary was no longer a remote ideologue but a Pole who wanted what all Poles wanted: a car, a good life, a foreign holiday. Just the opposite happened. The party apparatchiks acquired a name for infamous corruption, and the people hated and despised them as never before. Edward Gierek lived in grand style, while others lived on bread, potatoes and inferior tea. But even he could not match Maciej Szczepański, the new director of Polish television, who ran a corrupt personal empire of yachts, Swiss bank accounts and call-girls.

Wherever the Poles fulfilled their spiritual needs, it was not through Szczepański's television service. Gierek had in fact tried hard to reach a fresh understanding with the Church, leading towards a formal settlement and diplomatic relations with the Vatican. Cardinal Wyszyński treated him with reserve, constantly asking for political concessions including a relaxation of censorship. It was a sterile process, which became irrelevant overnight on 16 October 1978.

On that day, to the amazement of the world, Cardinal Karol Wojtyła was elected Pope. As for the Poles, they poured into the streets, wept, opened bottles, kissed one another. Catholics and non-believers alike, they took this not just as a miracle but as a sign. Poland had been rewarded at last – by God, by a crew of old cardinals, it didn't matter – for all its sufferings, all its betrayals and disappointments.

The writer Andrzej Szczypiorski was in New York that day. 'There, in a small, stuffy hotel room, the telephone suddenly rang. I lifted the receiver. The man at the other end was a Jewish writer, a citizen of the United States who had left his native village in Poland forty years before. And this Jew, crying and laughing in turn, mad with excitement, was exclaiming: "We have our own Pope! Our own Pope!" . . . We spent the whole night in his home, speaking about Poland and her future, about the fact that the election of a Polish Pope might mean a change in the fortunes of the whole nation. If we could have been overheard by foreigners, they would have considered our views and prognostications as the babbling of madmen. But every Pole thought as we did . . .'[1]

A vast new confidence was born. Gierek did the only thing he could: his government sent a warm message of congratulation to Rome, celebrating the arrival on Peter's throne of 'a son of the Polish nation, which is building the greatness and prosperity of its socialist fatherland'. Privately, the régime was stunned. Optimists, like Edward Gierek himself, thought that a Polish Pope might be easier to deal with than the unbending Cardinal Wyszński. Pessimists saw that the spiritual and moral leadership of Poland had been transferred from Warsaw to the West, much as it had been in the Great Emigration after 1830. It was an unsettling comparison.

Seven months later, a wooden cross as tall as a house towered over Victory Square in Warsaw. Under it, his white robes dazzling in the hot June sun, Pope

1. Andrzej Szczypiorski, *The Polish Ordeal*, Croom Helm, London, 1982, p. 109.

John Paul II was speaking to half a million people. He talked to them about their motherland, about the blood spilled for liberty in every generation on every battlefield and in this city of Warsaw in 1944, 'a battle in which it was abandoned by the Allied powers'. He said: 'The exclusion of Christ from the history of man is an act against man. Without Christ it is impossible to understand the history of Poland . . .' He ended with these words: 'I cry – I who am a son of the land of Poland and who am also Pope John Paul II – I cry from all the depths of this millenium, I cry on the vigil of Pentecost: Let your Spirit descend, and renew the face of the earth – the face of this land. Amen.'

It was the first day of his nine-day pilgrimage through Poland. Perhaps a quarter of the entire population came to see and hear him. When he left, bidding farewell to the city of Kraków 'in which every stone and every brick is dear to me', men and women cried uncontrollably in the streets.

Something did indeed descend and transform the face of the land. It was an awakening. One boy said simply: 'Now I realise that nobody has ever talked to me before.' The Pope did nothing so crude as to attack the régime openly, or urge the people to rise. Instead, he spoke straight past the government to the real feelings, the real memories of the Poles. He evoked an ancient Christian nation, as if Communist rule was a transient phenomenon of little importance.

The Polish Pope returns to his country, June 1979. John Paul II praying at the execution wall, Auschwitz.

He blessed the struggle of every family towards happiness and justice, and told the Poles that their longings were righteous and would in the end triumph.

The state kept discreetly in the background, and it was young Catholic volunteers who organised the meetings and held back the crowds. Listening to the Pope and looking at these volunteers, Poles felt a surge of returning confidence. Given freedom, the people could organise Polish life for itself, true to its own sense of what was just and appropriate. The visit was morally cathartic; John Paul seemed to draw out of the crowds their individual and collective sense of humiliation and failure, and to exorcise it. Hatred of the authorities almost dissolved, to be replaced by something even more ominous: a contemptuous indifference. The Pope's visit reinforced the message which KOR and the rest of the opposition had been trying to put across: that the Polish nation was mature and strong enough to take its own choices. The Communist authorites should be tolerated as long as they did not obstruct this inner independence, but there was no longer any reason to respect their wisdom or to fear their power.

The Pope flew back to Rome; the Poles blinked and looked around them again. It was plain to every thinking person that a new crisis or explosion was approaching. In October, Nowa's underground duplicators issued the report of 'Experience and the Future', a symposium of about a hundred well-known personalities recruited to examine the future of Poland.

Though the symposium enjoyed a degree of official sponsorship, the authorities had refused to publish the report. This was hardly surprising. The participants concluded that the whole post-war period had failed to produce any fundamental agreement between rulers and ruled, that the bureaucracy and the party élite were threatening to become a new hereditary class through their monopoly of wealth as well as power, and that official lying had become so prevalent that even the authorities no longer knew the difference between truth and propaganda.

The 1970s were ending badly – and not only in Poland. East–West relations were turning sour, and the optimistic climate of détente – crucial to Poland, which had become so dependent on the West – was beginning to freeze up. In December 1979, NATO took its decision to station a new generation of medium-range nuclear missiles, Cruise and Pershing II, in western Europe. At the very end of the year, Soviet troops poured into Afghanistan.

Within Poland, the decade closed on a scene of approaching catastrophe. Shortages of food and all consumer goods were growing steadily worse; industry was running down and many plants were turning out only a fraction of their capacity. Unrest and work stoppages began to take place in the factories. The government's hand-to-mouth response was to rush extra meat supplies down to the plants where protests broke out.

It was on the factory floor, above all, that party morale now began to crumble away. When local party meetings were held to prepare for the Eighth

Congress of the PZPR in February 1980, there were furious protests from the membership against the shortages, against the privileges of the salaried party officials (the 'apparatus') and against the suffocating censorship. But when the congress met, Gierek diverted the attack from himself by putting the blame for failures on the government rather than on the party, although everyone knew that the PZPR nominated the government and dictated its policies. Piotr Jaroszewicz, the unpopular prime minister, was forced to resign.

This manoeuvre merely enraged the rank and file of the party. They had hoped to force through sweeping democratic reforms of party behaviour and structure. Instead, Gierek was proclaiming against all the evidence that there was nothing basically wrong with the party, whose 'correct' policies had been distorted by the government. This was too much to swallow, and thousands of PZPR members, especially factory workers, began to turn in their party cards.

The new prime minister, Edward Babiuch, introduced fresh cuts in government spending and prepared to slow down wage increases. Meanwhile, there was an attempt to stifle the opposition groups. Jacek Kuroń and some of his colleagues were detained, and charges were brought against Mirosław Chojecki, the head of the unofficial Nowa publishing house. Then, on 1 July 1980, the government introduced a complex but very gradual system to increase the shop prices of better-quality meat.

This was the sort of modest measure which should have been taken years before. But now it was too late. The workers carefully worked out the new regulations; when they had understood what they implied, spontaneous strikes began. They were orderly and they were not coordinated. But they were effective. Work would stop, a strike committee would appear, a wage demand would be made – and at once granted. Then everyone would go back to work again. At first, the government refused to admit in public what was happening. But as July went on, more and more plants joined in this process, some striking for a second time to win yet another wage rise. By the end of the month, over 150 plants had taken action, and the rate of pay increases had risen from about five per cent to an average of ten per cent – twice that, in some cases. The newspapers began to mention 'interruptions of production'.

In his father's ground-floor apartment on Mickiewicza Street in Warsaw, Jacek Kuroń and a girl assistant were living by the telephone day and night. KOR was acting as news centre, gathering news of every strike and every award and relaying it through foreign journalists to radio stations in the West; the broadcasts were heard throughout Poland, and gradually transformed the patchwork of isolated incidents into a national movement. With pay demands, political demands began to be raised. At Lublin, strikers from many enterprises, including the railways, asked for the abolition of press censorship, family allowances equal to those for the police, and trade unions controlled by their members.

Authority in Poland was beginning to fall apart. But Gierek made no effort to take charge – he could easily have ordered the suppression of KOR's 'information exchange', for example – and on 27 July he left on holiday for the Soviet Union. The spate of brief strikes ran on; demands steadily escalated and gathered cohesion. Then, on 14 August, workers on the early shift at the Lenin shipyard at Gdańsk failed to start work. They had been met by three boys sent into the yard by the Free Trade Unions of the Coast, carrying leaflets which demanded the reinstatement of Anna Walentinowicz, a crane driver who had been sacked for her militant opposition to the management.

There was a spontaneous march within the yard, which became a disorderly mass meeting in the open air. The manager, standing on a bulldozer, was making some headway with his arguments for a return to work. Then an unemployed electrician named Lech Wałęsa was hoisted over the shipyard fence by his friends. He jumped up on the bulldozer to face the manager: 'Remember me? I gave ten years' work to this yard. But you sacked me four years ago!' Seizing his chance, he turned round and spoke to the astonished crowd of grey-overalled men and women below, many of whom knew him well. He called for an immediate occupation strike. There were cheers. More workers joined the crowd. Then they went indoors to the hall of the shipyard's health and safety centre, and sat down to elect a strike committee and work out a list of demands. They were soon asking not only for better pay and conditions but for an uncensored press and free trade unions.

The next day, the other Gdańsk shipyards, the Paris Commune shipyard at nearby Gdynia and the dockers in both cities joined the strike. All Poles knew that this was a crisis of a quite different order. The Baltic port cities were in revolt again; given the history of the shipyard rebellions in December 1970, this would not be a matter of a brief stoppage to be ended with a pay award. This was the start of a full-scale showdown with Poland's party and state. The long-predicted explosion was taking place.

Out of this confrontation, just over two weeks later, there emerged the 'independent, self-managing trade union' Solidarity. By the end of the year, the official trade union structure had dissolved while Solidarity was well on its way to a membership of some ten million, dominating a turbulent and revolutionary scene in Poland for the fifteen months of its legal existence and fascinating, through copious television coverage, the entire world.

There were two immediate causes for the birth of Solidarity without bloodshed. One was that Gierek and most of his colleagues, after opening government negotiations with Wałęsa and the Inter-Factory Strike Committee at Gdańsk, realised that if they did not settle on something close to the twenty-one Gdańsk demands, or if they tried to suppress the strike by force, there would be a national insurrection, probably ending in Soviet military intervention. The second was the patience and self-control of the workers and their leadership, not only at Gdańsk but at Szczecin and at Jastrzębie in Upper Silesia, where separate but parallel negotiations with strike committees were soon in progress.

The birth of Solidarity, August 1980. Workers at the Lenin Shipyard, Gdańsk, listening as the negotiations between strike leaders and the government are broadcast. The Factory Council notice has been crossed out.

The birth of Solidarity. Striking shipyard workers at Gdańsk sleep on the yard floor.

The birth of Solidarity. Lech Wałęsa kneels at Mass during the strike. Beside him is Anna Walentynowicz, the crane driver whose sacking touched off the strike at Gdańsk.

At Gdańsk, government ministers and strike leaders negotiated nose to nose in a small room. Workers and journalists peered at them through a large glass window, while their words were broadcast to all the factory strike delegations sitting in the main hall next door and to the shipyard workers standing, sitting or lying in the dusty gardens outside. The shipyard gates were hidden by flowers, posters, and pictures of the Black Madonna or the Pope. Beyond them, a huge crowd of workers' families and sympathisers waited for the moment each day when Lech Wałęsa would be lifted to the top of the gates and – after the cheers and songs had died down – give them the news of deadlock or progress. Once a day, the gates would open to admit a priest, who would hear confessions and give absolution to the workers as they knelt on the asphalt roadway.

Too much has been made of individuals in the strike, of the role played by KOR in preparing it and of Wałęsa himself. Sooner or later, given the combination of economic crisis and government inertia, the Polish working class would have rebelled anyway. Equally certain, they would have demanded independent trade unions when they did so. The importance of KOR, and of the groups of independent intellectuals called in to advise the strikers in negotiation, was that they helped to draft the political demands and – above all – had a gift for compromise. The intellectuals and the government negotiators, divided as they were politically, sprang from the same Warsaw milieu and spoke the same language.

Wałęsa spoke a different language. He came from a poor peasant background, but he had an unerring instinct for sensing and voicing the feelings of his fellow workers. His speeches were extempore affairs, veering from the aggressive to the clownish, combining Catholic patriotism with a defiant loyalty to his class. Perhaps his fundamental driving emotion was anger and shame about the martyrs of the December 1970 fighting, in which he had taken part; Wałęsa had been in constant trouble with the police for trying to hold illegal public ceremonies at each anniversary. He had been repeatedly fired from one Gdańsk factory after another for organising protests on behalf of his workmates. Though the Gdańsk workers knew him for a troublemaker, they trusted him as a loyal friend, as a good Catholic and as an incomparable fighter.

The Gdańsk Agreement was finally signed on the morning of 31 August 1980. Mieczysław Jagielski, a member of the politburo, set his name to it. Wałęsa took up an outsize souvenir pen bearing the Pope's picture and did the same. He proclaimed the strike over. With Wałęsa leading them in his tuneless voice, the negotiators, the exhausted delegates of the Gdańsk factories in the hall, and the workers massed outside broke into the national anthem – 'Poland has not perished, while we are alive'.

In the end, there were three main agreements. The Szczecin Agreement had been signed the day before. The bargaining at Jastrzębie, covering the coal-mining region of Upper Silesia, did not end until 3 September. Taken together, they committed the Polish government to an astonishing agenda of reforms, bringing justice, equality and democracy into almost every corner of Polish life.

In the first point of the Gdańsk Agreement the workers won the right to set up new, independent trade unions of their own alongside the official unions. The right to strike was recognised. Censorship would be restricted to protecting state and economic secrets. State radio would broadcast Mass to the nation every Sunday: a thank-offering to their church by a Catholic working class.

The government promised a rise in the minimum wage, and a complete reform of welfare allowances and pensions. The Gdańsk text included a long, detailed list of improvements in the health service, and women won an assurance of more pre-schools and better maternity leave. The Jastrzębie Agreement ended all Saturday and Sunday work for miners – a concession which was to cut deeply into Poland's export earnings. And the government was forced to agree to fundamental and rapid reform of the whole management of the economy, with trade unions helping to draft new rules for workers'

After the Agreements. Lech Wałęsa, as head of the 'independent, self-managing trade union Solidarity', is welcomed in Kraków.

self-management. Then came another fundamental point. It was agreed that from now on, the management in all state enterprises would be chosen on the basis of ability alone. At a stroke, this robbed the party of one of its most effective instruments of power: the *nomenklatura*, which meant the practice of naming its own trusted people to commanding positions throughout Polish society.

These were stupefying documents. Not since the revolutions of the nineteenth century had a European people forced such a treaty on its own rulers. In a Communist system, in a country which formed part of the Soviet alliance, the agreements were almost unimaginable. They were possible only because, in Poland, Communism had ceased to be totalitarian in all but its ideology. Especially since Poland's successful defiance of Soviet domination in 1956, the party's 'leading role' in society had become an official sham. The reality was a sort of crude pluralism, an undefined contract under which the Communist authorities retained political power as long as they did not violate the fundamental interests of the Catholic Church, the private peasantry and the industrial working class. It had in fact been true for many years that, faced with determined and organised challenge from one or more of these three great blocks of opinion, the régime would have to give in or risk insurrection and civil war.

It soon became clear that the agreements were only the beginning. Ten days later, Wałęsa and his committee set up the headquarters of the new Solidarity trade union in a shabby Gdańsk hotel. At first, it seemed that Solidarity might be only one of many independent unions up and down the country. But as one strike committee after another all over Poland adopted the outline of the Gdańsk Agreement, adding local points of their own, Solidarity swelled into a nationwide organisation.

Most trade union federations are 'vertical' – an alliance of separate unions each based on one type of employment and each with its own national structure. Solidarity, however, was quite different. It consisted of 'horizontal' bodies: in each region, workers of all trades belonged to a single union branch. This was the shape of a political movement rather than of a normal trade union. It allowed the better-paid and better-organised to help low-paid colleagues in other trades and it gave Solidarity the power to bring enormous strength to bear at short notice, in any local dispute.

Outside Poland, foreign statesmen and sympathisers wrung their hands, expecting Soviet invasion at any moment. But inside Poland, people were at first surprised and then irritated to be asked about this peril. In their excitement, absorbed by the tasks of joining unions, drawing up demands, electing representatives, reading newspapers and magazines which had suddenly begun to report the truth and – while rushing from one packed meeting to the next – trying to grab a glass of tea, a piece of bread and a cigarette, the world outside Poland seemed almost unreal.

Their irritation was understandable. Spinechilling talk about 'a national tragedy' (code for Soviet intervention) had for so long been an official trick to discourage Poles from trying anything new. All the same, the threat was there, even though it was a few months before it became visible. The elderly Leonid Brezhnev was reluctant to move against Poland. He foresaw a prolonged and bloody conflict which would wreck what remained of détente, ruin the world reputation of the Soviet union for a decade and – not least – saddle the Russians with the entire cost of the shattered Polish economy and its debts. None the less, if the Polish crisis flared up into an open struggle for political power – a 'counter-revolution' – then Soviet intervention could not be avoided.

Meanwhile the Polish party leadership went into deep shock. Edward Gierek, whose appeals to the strikers had been totally ignored, vanished from the public eye. His colleagues had expected him at least to go on television after the agreements and appeal for national self-restraint. Instead, he acted as if the ship were already sinking. The rest of the politburo decided that he would have to go.

Tens of thousands of ordinary party members were now pouring into Solidarity and being elected to its committees. Some tore up their party cards. But most saw no reason why they should. If the place of a Communist was not with the working class, where was it? Indeed, several of Wałęsa's colleagues on the original Gdańsk strike committee, like the young engineer Bogdan Lis, were members of the PZPR.

The Sejm building in Warsaw is an odd but graceful white building, with a pointed roof like a marquee. On 5 September, it lived through one of its most splendid and theatrical days. The deputies had gathered to discuss the crisis and the August Agreements and, for the first time in most of their memories, they found themselves taking part in a real parliamentary debate. There were speeches of accusation, speeches of self-reproach, speeches of prophetic force and vision. But Edward Gierek was not there to listen to them. Late in the afternoon came the news that he had suffered a heart attack on his way to the Sejm, and that his chauffeur had rushed him to hospital.

Poles are sceptical about coincidences, especially in politics. But it was a genuine coincidence that three successive Polish leaders were struck down by illness precisely when their political time was up: Bierut, Gomułka, and now Gierek. The central committee of the PZPR went into emergency session. In the small hours of the next morning, they deposed Edward Gierek and chose as the first secretary of the party Stanisław Kania.

He was the son of a peasant, a sturdy, good-natured man of the 'apparatus' who for years had been in charge of internal security. In the morning, long and excited queues jostled at the newspaper kiosks to discover what had happened. But many Poles shook their heads and laughed when they read Kania's first speech as leader. It was 1956 and 1970 all over again. The protest of the working class was 'justified'. A minority of 'anti-socialist agitators' had tried to misuse a genuine protest for their own ends. 'Leninist norms' of party life would be restored. The party would never again lose touch with the masses. And so on, in the customary manner.

But Kania, at first, was optimistic. He announced a grand 'renewal' programme, to overhaul the party and the state. As for Solidarity, he thought that the worst of the crisis was now over; the workers would gradually simmer down as they had before, and 'social unity' – a euphemism for the party's monopoly of power – would reassert itself. This was hopelessly wrong. In the next few months, Poland stumbled along the edge of disaster, as Solidarity and the authorities collided again and again.

In the weeks following the agreements, strikes continued to break out all over Poland. Most had two things in common: demands for higher wages and demands for the sacking of local government or party officials. The government's delay in agreeing to wage increases enraged the Solidarity rank and file, who pushed Wałęsa and the union's provisional executive into calling a one-hour general strike on 3 October. Then, on 23 October, the judge handling the legal registration of Solidarity ordered the union to include in its statutes a recognition that 'the Polish United Workers' Party exercises the leading role in the state'.

In one sense, this meant little. If the clause had stated that the party had the leading role in 'society', this would have implied its right to lead and control Solidarity. But to say that it led 'the state' was only repeating the obvious, and anyway the phrase had been included – rather unwillingly – in the Gdańsk Agreement. The sense of outrage and fear that gripped the union after the court's decision sprang not from the words but from the way they were inserted. The authorities were violating the independence of Solidarity and the whole spirit of Gdańsk, acting as if they alone would decide the union's statutes and its policies.

This was a far more serious confrontation. Solidarity concluded that the régime was about to revoke the agreements altogether, and prepared for a general strike – this time, unlimited. The Gdańsk branch threatened to return to the Lenin shipyard and defend itself; others prepared to go underground if a state of emergency was declared. In return, the government threatened to conscript strikers under military discipline, and Kania flew to Moscow for advice.

In the end, the authorities backed down; a compromise was found on the statutes and Solidarity was registered on 10 November 1980. There was relief and rejoicing; Wałęsa was guest of honour next evening in the Warsaw opera house for a special programme of patriotic songs and recitations. But the respite was short. Only a few days later, police raided the offices of Mazowsze, the Warsaw branch of Solidarity, seized papers, and arrested a union worker named Jan Narożniak.

The registration crisis had been about the union's life or death. This, in contrast, was a symbolic matter. Narożniak was only one of those who lent a hand with the Mazowsze duplicators, and the police were looking for a document leaked from the public prosecutor's office. But, slight as it was, the raid snapped nerves already taut. Zbigniew Bujak, a young worker from the Ursus tractor plant who was now the Mazowsze chairman, threatened a strike in Warsaw if Narożniak and Piotr Sapieło, a clerk in the prosecutor's office alleged to have purloined the document, were not released. The police refused. The whole Ursus plant struck, and Bujak served the authorities with a list of demands going far beyond the immediate cause of the strike and including a full public enquiry into the workings of the security police.

Again, Solidarity prepared to go to the barricades. Speakers urged the workers to 'die on their feet rather than live on their knees'. After hectic negotiation, the two men were freed. But the big Warsaw steelworks, Huta Warszawa, refused to return to work until, after sleepless nights and days of argument with Wałęsa and his advisers, the strike accepted a government promise (which came to nothing) that there would be talks about the enquiry into the police.

It was the end of November. The three nerve-racking months since the Gdańsk Agreement had left Poland more divided than ever. Both sides drew frightening conclusions. Solidarity had set out to be an independent trade union and no more, leaving politics to the existing régime. It wanted no share in government; it was the job of the authorities to carry out the provisions of the agreements, while the union would use its collective strength only to remind them of their duty. Instead, the régime seemed to be fighting the union at every step and every level, giving the impression that it would repudiate the agreements and even destroy Solidarity if it could.

Meanwhile, the union itself had turned into an enormous popular movement for democracy. Through strikes or the threat of strikes, it had secured the dismissal of a third of Poland's regional party secretaries and governors, and its appetite was growing. More ominous still, the mass membership was not only very young but far more militant than Wałęsa and the provisional leadership of Solidarity, who spent much of their time whirling round the country trying to urge moderation. Already there had been ugly scenes when other Solidarity members had accused Wałęsa of weakness, even of selling out.

The party was badly divided. A few 'liberals' like Tadeusz Fiszbach, party secretary at Gdańsk, still argued for an honest partnership with Solidarity, a partnership on which a real transformation of Poland – political, economic and social – could be built. But after the registration crisis, the mass of the permanent party officials – the 'apparatus' – gave up all such hopes. This was a fight for power, they concluded: if the party could not destroy Solidarity, then Solidarity would destroy the party. At the local level, they did everything they could or dared to obstruct the union.

But there was a third group in the party to contend with. In the factories, many of the worker-members had become enthusiastic supporters of

Solidarity. Now they began to hold debates and form alliances with PZPR branches in other factories, agitating for a complete democratic upheaval in the party. This was 'horizontalism', a mortal sin against the rules of a Leninist party which prescribe that a branch can relate to the district party organisation above it but never to another branch. Decisions were supposed to flow vertically. The 'horizontalists', who intended to smash for ever the power of the 'apparatus' by making all posts temporary and all party elections secret, were undermining the whole authority structure of the PZPR.

Above these struggles – but not as far above them as it might have wished – the Catholic Church peered into the turmoil. Many things had happened which warmed the hearts of Cardinal Wyszyński and his bishops, and of the great Pole away in Rome. The workers had shown from the first hour of the 'self-limiting revolution' that they were loyal sons and daughters of the Church. Solidarity had brought the Mass on to the radio; the crucifix was on the wall of every Solidarity office, of every school and lecture-room, even in institutions of the atheist state like the post offices. Intellectuals from the Catholic lay societies were taking part in all the strike negotiations.

Abroad, many concluded that Solidarity was a Catholic movement. Sir Harold Macmillan, a Conservative ex-prime minister of Britain, observed that it was wonderful to see the workers on their knees. On the other wing of politics, many British trade unionists saw Solidarity as a right-wing, reactionary affair dominated by superstition. The Polish bishops knew better. The truth of the matter was that the Church was being dragged along in the train of

Economic crisis. All through the Solidarity period, the shortages grew worse. Food queues at Gdańsk.

a revolutionary upsurge. The workers, for most of whom patriotism and the Catholic faith were inseparable, simply assumed that because they had acted for Poland, the Church must be behind them.

It was not so straightforward. The Church was at once delighted and alarmed by what was happening. Its fundamental interest was in a concord between Church and state, allowing the faith to be maintained without impediment. Its deepest fear was of civil conflict, which might provoke – with or without Soviet intervention – the suppression of all the Church's hard-won rights.

During the Gdańsk strike, Cardinal Wyszyński warned that, although the workers' demands were just, there were faults on both sides and long stoppages could damage the nation. This bewildered the workers, who had expected his unqualified support; they decided that reports of his sermon must have been censored. But Wyzsyński, whose favourite word was 'prudence', used all his authority to establish a personal relationship with Wałęsa himself, and in the chaotic months that followed, constantly edged him towards compromise rather than challenge. Not all the hierarchy were as cautious. Archbishop Gulbinowicz of Wrocław and Bishop Tokarczuk of Przemyśl gave vigorous support to Solidarity, both behind the scenes and in their public sermons. Many of the parish priests, who saw themselves as 'Poland's soldiers in black uniform', were more radical still.

Poland's Communist neighbours watched developments with growing horror. At the end of October, both Czechoslovakia and East Germany closed their frontiers to almost all visitors from Poland, and began noisy press and radio campaigns against 'counter-revolutionaries' in Solidarity. The Bulgarians talked about the duty of members of the 'socialist community' to rescue one another when in danger. Some Czech and Slovak newspapers openly compared the Polish crisis to the Prague Spring of 1968, and warned that it might have to be solved in the same way. Even in Hungary, now an easy-going society a long way down the track of economic reform, the trade unions' chairman warned that 'a strike is not a means of socialist construction'.

In contrast, Soviet comment was at first careful and restrained. Brezhnev seemed inclined to let Kania solve his own problems. But in early December, with the clamour of alarm from his allies reaching a peak, the Soviet armed forces began to move. On 2 December, East Germany closed its border region next to Poland to Western military attachés. Swedish and American intelligence began to gather evidence that Soviet forces in East Germany, Czechoslovakia and the western USSR were advancing to positions on the Polish frontiers. There was a partial call-up in the Ukraine and the Baltic republics.

The West had a bad conscience about 1968, when the Warsaw Pact invasion of Czechoslovakia had taken NATO by surprise. Now there was an uproar of protest and official warnings to the Soviet Union, while the Western media were encouraged to announce that Soviet armed intervention was imminent.

At first, the Poles were incredulous. Early December was a moment of calm after twelve weeks of storm; for the first time in three months, Wałęsa could announce that there were no strikes in Poland. Instead, both Solidarity and the party were talking hopefully about a new mood of 'national unity'. But the news about Soviet troop movements was becoming hard to ignore. On 4 December, the party issued an 'appeal' to the nation, proclaiming that 'the fate of our nation and this country is in the balance. The persistent unrest is pushing our fatherland to the brink of economic and moral annihilation . . .'

The following day, there was an emergency summit of the Warsaw Pact in Moscow. Brezhnev and his colleagues acted as silent judges, while the East Germans read out an interminable attack on Kania and the PZPR which accused the Polish leaders of 'objective' anti-Communism because they tolerated open criticism and Solidarity agitation. Meanwhile, there were unusual Soviet naval movements in the Baltic, and several Soviet army divisions – in bitter winter weather – camped in tents on the eastern border of Poland. On 7 December, the United States announced that Soviet preparations for military intervention in Poland were complete.

But it did not take place. Possibly Brezhnev was deterred by the volume and violence of Western warnings. More probably, he was following a typical Soviet 'two-track' policy, using the threat of armed force to back up the political argument at the Moscow summit, and to reassure Erich Honecker and Gustav Husak, the panicky party leaders of East Germany and Czechoslovakia.

Slowly, the international tension drained away again. Brezhnev departed to visit India, while Soviet diplomats in the West remarked that 'the Poles are big enough to handle their own problems'. But it was in a chastened mood that the Poles approached the 'week of commemoration', the ceremonies planned on the Baltic coast to mark the tenth anniversary of the slaughter of December 1970.

Everyone – the Solidarity leaders, the Catholic bishops, the party and the government, even the heads of Poland's armed forces – was now talking about the need for 'unity', for a 'national accord' between the contending forces to save the independent existence of Poland. The ceremonies of December were deliberately planned to make this point. Andrzej Wajda, the great film director, was invited to create and produce the main celebration at Gdańsk on 16 December.

It was an unforgettable, dream-like moment. Outside the gates of the Lenin shipyard, the workers had erected a steel monument to the dead 140 feet high; at its tip were three crosses and at its base were metal reliefs, crumpled as if by the fire of the riots, showing men and women at work in the yards. Around it, that winter night, stood the Establishment of the new Poland: Professor Jabłoński, the head of state, ministers and members of the politburo of the PZPR, generals and admirals, the Cardinal Archbishop of Kraków – and

Gdańsk, 16 December 1980. At a great ceremony of 'national unity' outside the Lenin Shipyard the monument to the dead of December 1970 is consecrated.

mingling with them, men and women who a few months before had been the régime's enemies: the workers who were now the officials of Solidarity. Beyond them in the frosty darkness stood hundreds of thousands of ordinary Poles, who had come from all over the nation to be present at this moment of history.

The sirens of the factories sounded to mourn the dead, joined by locomotives, bus horns, ships in the docks and at anchor around the mouths of the Vistula. An orchestra and choir played Krzystof Penderecki's 'Lacrimosa'. The actor Daniel Olbrychski read out the names of the twenty-seven men known to have been shot at Gdańsk in 1970, and after each name the choir chanted: 'He is still with us!' Then a man with a bushy moustache, wearing a brown anorak, climbed out of the crowd of uniforms and official suits. Lech Wałęsa took a welder's torch and lit the eternal flame.

In some ways, the grand commemoration with its floodlights, rituals, and music was unreal, a tremendous stroke of theatre. The ordinary people who had brought all this about by their determination to live in dignity and honesty stood in the outer darkness as spectators. Meanwhile, the speakers around the monument proclaimed their own myth surrounding the martyrs of 1970. They did not die just for cheaper food or better wages, because they tried to burn party headquarters or even because they wanted a normal life for their children without lies and fear. They sacrificed their lives for the unity of the nation. That was the new myth.

For the Polish Establishment – the secretaries, ministers, bishops, and even the Solidarity chiefs – December 1970 was too important to be left to the people. This was another way of saying that August 1980 was also too important to be left to the masses. Not only Solidarity but the Polish United Workers' Party had to survive. This meant a national compromise, and the reining-in of vengeful militants on both sides.

And yet it was strange to hear orators from the government, especially, appealing for national unity. For the crowds listening to them, unity already existed. In a sense, it had been Solidarity's central moral aim to break down artificial barriers between Poles: barriers of money, of class or caste, of region, of skill and profession. The summer upheaval had given back to Poles their feeling of community and common interest: the existence of a free, self-managing trade union and the fact that it was called Solidarity was only one of the results of that. If there was a division in Poland to be overcome, it was between the people and those who had tried for so many years to divide them: the leadership of the Polish United Workers' Party.

But in spite of these ironies, there was a solid reality about the Gdańsk ceremony as well. Everyone had met to remember that, ten years before, Pole had killed Pole. A thousand years of history, and especially the last two centuries, had shown that other states were only too eager to destroy this nation. They had failed because the Poles themselves, for all their own quarrels, had stood together and persisted in the struggles for Poland.

'Poland had not yet been destroyed', begins the national anthem. Only the Poles themselves could do that, by destroying themselves through merciless internal conflict. Understanding that, the nation and its leaders had never pushed any confrontation to its logical extreme. This inner tolerance, which had made Poland such a mature society in comparison to Germany or Russia, had led to a history of half-measures, of belligerent words and symbols accompanied by only hesitant deeds. The nation had suffered for this, but because of this it had also survived.

In the crowd at Gdańsk on that December night, there were many who feared that the Solidarity era might end in violence. Perhaps a few who were present hoped that it would. But all accepted the unwritten law underlying Polish attitudes and actions: whatever was done must be done to help the nation endure. That law had always held, and it was to hold even through the tragic years that lay ahead.

On his visit, Pope John Paul II had picked up a small girl and asked her: 'Where is Poland?' She stared at him, bewildered. Then he placed his hand gently over her heart, and said: 'Poland is here.'

9
Solidarity, Martial Law, and Beyond: 1980–86

On 13 December 1981, a young Pole living in a tower block near the centre of Warsaw overslept. 'When I woke up, I tried to ring the office, but the phone was dead. I thought: some sort of power cut. I looked out of the window and saw military trucks standing everywhere in the snow. I thought: some sort of manoeuvres. Then I turned on the radio and there was no news, no chat shows, nothing but Chopin, Chopin and more Chopin. And suddenly I knew what had happened.'

A few hours later, the police came to search the flat. The young Pole's wife managed to eat the latest Solidarity bulletin, and threw the others out of the kitchen window. General Wojciech Jaruzelski, now not only minister of defence but prime minister and first secretary of the party as well, had declared a 'state of war' and imposed martial law.

The brief Solidarity period lasted for just under a year after the ceremony of 'national unity' at Gdańsk. That hopeful mood evaporated only a few weeks into the New Year. Mutual mistrust wrecked all efforts to reach a durable compromise between Solidarity and the régime, while in late 1981 the economy had almost completely broken down. By the autumn, both sides had almost abandoned hope of reaching agreement. Solidarity prepared openly for political action. General Jaruzelski laid secret plans to solve the crisis by force.

The truce had ended in January 1981, as the government announced that it could not fulfil its promise in the Gdańsk Agreement to end all Saturday work. Strikes broke out in several cities and towns, ending with a compromise at the end of the month which allowed the Poles three free Saturdays out of four. At the same time, a long sit-in strike at Rzeszów in south-east Poland marked the start of a campaign for a 'Rural Solidarity' of private farmers, which won the open support of the Church.

On 19 March, security police burst into the prefecture at Bydgoszcz and beat up a group of Solidarity members who were negotiating there. Whether this was an act of local stupidity or a deliberate provocation engineered by hard-line party leaders in Warsaw is still not clear. But it led to the most violent upsurge of protest since August 1980. Solidarity took the Bydgoszcz incident as a direct challenge to its existence. A countdown to a general strike began as union members and supporters prepared the factories for siege.

Once again, Soviet troops began to move, and there were fresh warnings from the West. General Jaruzelski had become prime minister on 9 February, and had appointed Mieczysław Rakowski, the editor of *Polityka* who was generally seen as a party 'liberal', as deputy prime minister in charge of negotiation with Solidarity. The Pope and President Reagan appealed for restraint and compromise. Then, only a day before the strike was to begin, Rakowski and Wałęsa managed to make a shaky deal.

The police action at Bydgoszcz would be investigated. More importantly, Rural Solidarity would be allowed to exist. This was an enormous concession, and a perilous one. The Soviet Union might tolerate independent unions for the working class, but in the Soviet view private peasants were a reactionary and anti-socialist element in society. In the event, Rural Solidarity spread rapidly throughout the countryside, and by the eve of martial law was beginning to look very much like a revival of Mikołajczyk's old Peasant Party under another name.

By calling off the strike, Wałęsa provoked a furious backlash in the union against his own authority. The rank and file had wound themselves up for what

The year of Solidarity. General Wojciech Jaruzelski, prime minister and minister of defence, and Stanisław Kania, first secretary of the Polish United Workers' Party, April 1981.

was to be the decisive trial of strength. Many felt that Wałęsa had let them down. And in hindsight, after the union was suppressed, they continued to believe that March 1981 had been the right moment for a confrontation, when Solidarity still had the initiative and the government had not yet organised its forces for a contest. After Bydgoszcz, Wałęsa had to defend himself against a radical opposition within Solidarity.

On 13 May, the Turkish fanatic Ali Agca shot and gravely wounded the Pope on St Peter's Square in Rome. Two weeks later, with the Pope still dangerously ill, Cardinal Stefan Wyszyński died at the age of seventy-nine. A quarter of a million people, with the leaders of party, state and Solidarity, gathered at his funeral in Warsaw. There was a sense of bereavement, and of fear for the future. From Rome, the Pope called for thirty days of calm and mourning. Early in July, after long hesitation, Pope John Paul II announced Wyszyński's successor as Primate of Poland: Archbishop Józef Glemp, a modest, cautious personality with none of the princely flair and charisma of his predecessor.

Most of June was taken up with party preparations for an emergency congress. This time, the membership made sure that the process of electing delegates and committees was genuinely free and democratic. There was a great slaughter of the old guard. When the congress met in July, seven out of every eight members of the old central committee were thrown out, including seven out of the eleven members of the politburo and forty out of forty-nine district party secretaries.

This looked like a true 'renewal'. But the new central committee and politburo turned out, unexpectedly, to be even more passive and disorganised than the last one. There was an ironic reason for this. The ultra-democratic voting system made it easy to block an opponent but difficult to elect a friend. As a result, most of the best-known party veterans and the most prominent reformers managed to knock each other out of the lists. Those who were elected tended to be nonentities, who proved easy for the surviving party 'apparatchiks' to manipulate.

The new party leadership and the government remained paralysed. Jaruzelski's appointment as head of the government had raised some hopes of a fresh, military vigour at the top. But nothing coherent was done to halt the steady slither of the economy into disaster. As a result, Solidarity finally began to lose patience with its own original idea of a sort of 'dualism' in Poland: the régime governing and applying the Gdańsk reforms, while Solidarity restricted itself to the business of a trade union. If the government refused to act, then – so, increasingly, the argument went – Solidarity had a responsibility to take action and save the nation by its own initiatives.

Solidarity held its own first congress at Gdańsk in September and October. Some 900 delegates from all over Poland assembled in the bleakly modern Olivia sports hall, which became a living theatre of the nation as speeches, pageantry, desperate arguments, ceremonies to welcome veterans of Polish history, messages from foreign guests, recitations of poetry or epic prose, debates and elaborate ballot after ballot filled the days. Outside the Olivia, small crowds listened to the speeches relayed from the hall, or shopped in the flea-market of Solidarity badges and leaflets. Inside, the delegates struggled to agree on a permanent structure for Solidarity, and on a platform over which the nation could be led to safety.

It was a lengthy, confused, noble affair. The elections suffered from the same problems of ultra-democracy encountered by the PZPR congress in the summer. In addition, manual workers – and women – showed great reluctance to run for office in the union, preferring to vote for intellectuals or for white-collar workers. The permanent bodies of Solidarity turned out to have a high proportion of writers, professors and unemployed young graduates – who were far more politicised and radical, in many cases, than the working-class membership.

At the congress, Solidarity set out on a new track. It would not wait for the authorities to act, but would act itself. It called for free elections to the Sejm. It agreed to make a start on the economic reforms at factory level, without delaying any longer for the government. 'We are the only guarantor for society, and that is why the union considers it to be its basic duty to take all short-term and long-term steps to save Poland from ruin, poverty, despondency and self-destruction.' And the congress, on an impulse, issued an appeal to the workers of the Soviet Union and eastern Europe, calling on them to follow Solidarity's example of free trade unions.

TASS, the Soviet news agency, retorted that this 'villainous appeal' had been drafted by 'a whole conglomerate of counter-revolutionaries, including agents of imperialist secret services'. The régime was terrified. It condemned the appeal to workers in other socialist countries as 'an insane act', and accused the congress of 'breathing hatred' and of 'declaring war on the government of its country'. A week later, the despairing Stanisław Kania was induced to step down and was replaced as party leader by General Jaruzelski.

Poland was on a collision course. It was probably now that Jaruzelski, with all power in his hands, began the detailed plans to impose martial law. On all sides, there were calls for a new authority in Poland, a powerful and almost dictatorial coalition including Communists, Catholics, Solidarity leaders and the heads of the armed forces in a 'government of national salvation'. Even in Solidarity, there were some who argued that the best solution might be an army takeover. There was a blind faith, based on Polish wishful thinking rather than on Polish experience of history, that the army was a non-political, patriotic force which would put the national interest above all ideologies.

By now, the economy was approaching final breakdown. The factories were stopping for lack of spare parts, raw materials and fuel. The currency was losing all value, and urgent transactions were being done with dollars or by barter. People slept on the pavements to keep their places in the food queues.

The writer Kazimierz Brandys came back to Warsaw in the autumn of 1981, after a long visit abroad. He found it 'a phantom capital . . . along the buildings, lines of people hunched like strips of some congealed matter. From a distance, a line looked like an unhealthy growth clinging to the base of a wall, the way wild vegetation sometimes fastens on to the base of a tree. Lines adhering to walls, swelling out, tripling, quadrupling, their ends catching on to each other.'[1]

He found the queues themselves 'living, allegorical images' of Poland's past. In the cheese line, Brandys saw dismissed cabinet ministers, a former member of the politburo with a bulging black briefcase, and one of the Home Army chiefs who had been abducted to Moscow and tried in 1945. In the line for chicken, he recognised a woman whose ancestor had been hanged for treason by the Warsaw Jacobins in 1794, behind the wives of 'bricklayers who had been awarded decorations for helping to rebuild the Old City after the war'.

By the late autumn of 1981, General Jaruzelski was operating on two levels. In public, he issued a series of calls for a new 'national accord' and a 'unity front' to include Solidarity and representatives of the Church. In secret, he drove ahead with the planning of martial law. Solidarity, admitting that it was beginning to lose control of its followers, responded to his public appeal, and on 4 November Wałęsa, Jaruzelski and Archbishop Glemp met in Warsaw for two hours of talks.

For a few days, there was hope that a real 'national accord' was near. But strikes continued to break out, and the régime accused Solidarity of launching a campaign to evict party cells from their offices in factories throughout Poland.

Suddenly the government began a series of sharp actions against Solidarity, apparently aiming to provoke the union into acts or words which would justify the imposition of martial law. Riot police stormed the Fire Brigade Academy in Warsaw, where a strike was in progress, on 25 November. Solidarity retorted by threatening a general strike and by again demanding free elections to the Sejm. At a meeting of the union executive in Radom, Wałęsa was reported to have said that confrontation was now inevitable, while others – according to the official media – called for the overthrow of the government and the formation of a workers' militia.

The 'national committee' of Solidarity met at Gdańsk on 11 December. A confused two-day debate began, some calling for a truce with the authorities, others suggesting a referendum to seek a vote of no confidence in the government. It was decided to call a day of national protest on 17 December.

In the last hours of 12 December, Jaruzelski struck. A 'state of war' was proclaimed. All Solidarity buildings were seized, most of the leadership was

1. Kazimierz Brandys, *A Warsaw Diary 1978–81*, Chatto & Windus, London, 1984, p. 203.

On the anniversary of the outbreak of the Warsaw Rising, the city honours its martyrs and their struggle for freedom: 1 August 1981.

rounded up at Gdańsk by riot police, and there were mass arrests through-out Poland, as tanks and armoured vehicles poured out into the streets. All telephone and cable links with the outside world were cut, the entire civilian telephone network was dis-connected, and a curfew was im-posed.

In the morning, Jaruzelski told the nation that he had installed a 'military council of national salvation'. Soli-darity 'extremists' had been interned, but so, too, had a group of Poland's pre-1980 leaders, including Edward Gierek. Jaruzelski insisted that he had acted to prevent a 'national catas-trophe' and that the course of reform and renewal would go on.

Martial law. On 13 December 1981 General Jaru-zelski announces on television the imposition of a 'state of war'.

In the short term, the coup was completely successful. Solidarity was taken utterly by surprise, and there was no coherent resistance or general strike. But Poland did not escape bloodshed. In many places, workers defended factories and mines against the ZOMO riot police. Tanks were used to storm the Lenin shipyard at Gdańsk, and at the Wujek colliery near Katowice seven miners were killed. Miners in several other collieries began underground occupation strikes, which lasted until 28 December. The total death roll, in these first weeks and in conflicts through the next twelve months, was probably between fifty and a hundred. Over 10,000 people were confined in internment camps or prisons, including Lech Wałęsa himself.

Seen in longer terms, however, martial law was a failure. It was another example of a Polish half-measure. It was carried out with a brutality which appalled and alienated the nation, and yet it was not brutal enough to terrorise the Poles into passivity. Within a short time, Solidarity set up a clandestine provisional committee led by Zbigniew Bujak, who had escaped arrest in December 1981 and was able to elude the police for no less than four-and-a-half years.

Jaruzelski's real self-justification, which was difficult to state openly, was that by crushing Solidarity he had prevented a power struggle which would have led to civil war and Soviet intervention. He almost certainly believed this. In the years that followed, he was to be accused of being 'a Russian in Polish uniform'. A stiff, reserved figure behind his black spectacles, Jarulzelski – who had been a forced labourer in the Soviet Union after his family were deported

Martial law. Jacek Kuroń, one of Solidarity's chief advisers, in the exercise yard of Białołęka prison, summer 1982

Martial law. Solidarity internees tackling prison diet.

from eastern Poland in 1940 – bitterly resented this, and continued to insist that he had acted as a patriot to ensure the survival of his country.

Not much came from his promises to carry on the 'renewal'. Worst of all, the military government wasted its chance to force through a sweeping reform of the over-centralised economy while the nation still lay under the anaesthetic of martial law. Some prices were increased, and a little progress was made towards introducing the laws of supply and demand into economic management. But when the Poles came round from the anaesthetic, they proved uncooperative. The creative intellectuals and a large part of the technical intelligentsia refused to help; the working class was mutinous; old vested interests in heavy industry revived and were able to slow the reforms down into insignificance.

The West was outraged by martial law and the crushing of Solidarity, and declared a wide range of economic and political sanctions against Poland. Although these were at first welcomed by many Poles as a token that they had not been forgotten, the sanctions made Poland's dire economic condition even worse. For the next few years, a lifeline of food, clothing, and medical supplies brought in by Western voluntary organisations and mostly distributed by the Catholic Church helped to hold in check the worst of the malnourishment and epidemics. But Poland felt degraded and humiliated. The author visited Polish hospitals in this period; sights like critically ill children sleeping in corridors because of gross overcrowding in the wards, or surgeons washing over and over again masks, needles and catheters made for one-time use, or old razor-blades being used to take skin grafts while microtomes stood by unusable for lack of spares – these were the normal conditions of medical care.

Helped by strict rationing and steep price rises, the economy eventually stabilised at a low level. A gradual start was made on rescheduling Poland's enormous foreign debt.

Martial law finally ended in July 1983, after a second papal visit to Poland, although it was replaced by a battery of almost equally severe emergency laws. A general amnesty for political and other prisoners followed, which opened the way for a resumption of political contact with the West. But Jaruzelski was unable to achieve his main political aim of a 'national reconciliation' which excluded veterans of Solidarity and the opposition.

His problem was how to build a power base wider than the mere armed force of the state. Military government through an army junta was completely alien to Communist tradition. Jaruzelski had ignored advice to abolish the PZPR at the same time as Solidarity, but the party had been pushed out of power, a demoralised and resentful rump of apparatchiks which was no longer considered fit to hold the 'leading role' in society. In 1982, Jaruzelski sponsored the Patriotic Front of National Rebirth (PRON), supposed to be a grand movement of independent opinion from all sectors of Polish society. But – with most educated Poles maintaining a boycott of official institutions –

PRON never acquired any convincing life of its own. After 1983, the army formally withdrew from politics, and Jaruzelski continued to govern through a curious junta, elected by no one, composed of generals, journalists and professors. Without the party or the army, his only tool of government was the state – which often meant the security police.

Martial law and its aftermath did not really destroy the pluralism of Polish society. The Solidarity atmosphere persisted; although the press was tightly censored, people continued to say what they thought without inhibition, and little was done to silence them. With Solidarity gone, except as an illegal opposition, the influence of the Catholic Church increased enormously. Although Archbishop – now Cardinal – Glemp made himself unpopular through his caution, the Church repeatedly called for the restoration of Solidarity and civil rights, carried the main burden of supporting the internees and their famililes, efficiently distributed foreign aid to the poor, and gave discreet assistance to the underground opposition.

On his visit to Poland in 1983, Pope John Paul II tried to urge those who were hostile to the régime to move towards the protection – and the restraining control – of the Church. By now the possibilities and limits of opposition were becoming clear. After a long series of demonstrations, usually ending under

Opposition revives. Demonstrators and riot police in Warsaw on the second anniversary of the Gdańsk Agreements. The photographer blanked out the face of the man at right to prevent identification.

the clubs of the ZOMO, people were becoming less willing to take mass action in public. Instead, an unofficial publishing industry had revived on a much larger scale than that of the 1970s, while Solidarity survived mostly in the form of secret workers' groups in the factories which supported workmates in political trouble and distributed opposition literature.

There was talk of setting up an underground 'alternative society', on the model of the wartime resistance or the nineteenth-century conspiracies. To some extent, this came about. But the opposition admitted to a lack of clear perspectives. Its activists could neither prepare insurrection nor expect foreign liberation. The best they could do was to preserve independent thought and discussion, publish as many facts and figures about the past and the present as they could, and wait patiently for something to change.

It was a deadlock. Meanwhile, the Jaruzelski group tried uneasily to combine harsh repression of 'extremists' with an appearance of broad tolerance towards the majority. The contradictions in this approach broke surface in October 1984, when a gang of secret policemen from the religious affairs department of the ministry of the interior abducted and atrociously murdered Father Jerzy Popiełuszko.

'Father Jerzy', a modest, intense young man, was the best known of the radical priests who had become famous in the post-Solidarity period. His 'Masses for the Fatherland' attracted huge crowds of Solidarity supporters to the church in north Warsaw where he worked – much to the alarm of Cardinal Glemp. For over a year, he had been the target of press attacks and police harassment.

His murder outraged the entire nation. Jaruzelski, desperate to show that he bore no responsibility, ordered a long public trial of Popiełuszko's killers, attended by the press. It emerged from the trial that the murderers had enjoyed some encouragement from senior officials in the ministry, but – although there was strong suspicion that powerful hardline figures in the party had provoked the murder to wreck Jaruzelski and his policy of national compromise – guilt stayed with the men in the dock.

Father Popiełuszko became a martyr; his funeral in Warsaw in a sea of flowers and patriotic banners was attended by Lech Wałęsa and many other former leaders of Solidarity. Before nearly half a million mourners, Wałęsa spoke his own farewell. 'Rest in peace. Solidarity is alive, because you have given your life for it.'

This was true, and yet less than the truth. From the murder, the active opposition gained a new moral intensity. But the death of Father Jerzy also revealed the limits of what was possible in Poland. On the one hand, there were elements in the régime prepared to kill rather than to lose control, and this fact – reinforcing the lessons of December 1981 – told the opposition that the price of all-out resistance was too high. On the other hand, the régime was tacitly admitting that the price of reducing Poland to conformity and obedience was

Father Jerzy Popiełuszko, murdered by secret policemen on 19 October 1984. He is seen comforting the mother of the student Grzegorz Przemyk, who died of injuries received in police custody in 1983.

also too high. It would have to be paid in blood, and possibly with the loss of Poland's independence.

Solidarity and martial law, in other words, had not really changed the Polish rules. They had neither brought Poland full independence and democracy, nor strengthened the grip of the Communist system on Polish society. Instead, they had shown that an informal, unstable, bad-tempered 'national compromise' did exist – had, in fact, always existed.

Piłsudski had not put his enemies to death, and Bierut had spared the nation the worst of Stalinist tyranny. Solidarity had tried to make a 'self-limiting revolution', and tolerate a government it instinctively detested. Even Jaruzelski's 'state of war' could not be compared to the years of state terror inflicted on the Hungarians after 1956, or to the stifling dictatorship which the Czechs and Slovaks endured for over a decade after 1968.

The struggles for Poland will go on. They are no longer struggles for basic national existence: Poland's neighbours have abandoned their centuries of effort to delete the Polish state from the map. Instead, they are a struggle to establish a truth. This courageous and experienced people in the heart of Europe will never be calm until it is allowed to solve its problems in a way which satisfies its own – very exacting – sense of morality and fairness.

The Poles have often been criticised by foreigners who find them 'romantic' or 'quixotic', obsessed by their own history and insisting on the impossible. But appeals from the space between Germany and Russia go unheard if they are not proclaimed loudly and with drama. And what is being asked for amounts, in fact, to the minimum for a decent national life: a society free of external threat, whose political currency is truth and whose citizens are free to combine on their own initiative for the improvement of their lives. Not much. And yet, so far, too much. It is over a hundred years ago that the poet Cyprian Kamil Norwid asked why so many 'vast armies and valiant generals' gathered against Poland to suppress 'only a few ideas: none of them new'.

Further Reading

1. General Works

Norman Davies, *God's Playground: A History of Poland* (2 vols.), Oxford University Press, Oxford, 1981.

Norman Davies, *Heart of Europe: A Short History of Poland*, Oxford University Press, Oxford, 1986.

Aleksander Gieysztor, Stefan Kieniewicz and others, *History of Poland*, PWN, Warsaw, 1979.

2. Later Partition Period, up to Independence (1863–1918)

R. F. Leslie (ed.), *The History of Poland since 1863*, Cambridge University Press, Cambridge, 1980.

Józef Piłsudski (Darsie Gillie, ed. and trans.), *Memoirs of a Polish Revolutionary and Soldier*, Faber & Faber, London, 1931.

3. Poland Between the Wars (1918–39)

Norman Davies, *White Eagle, Red Star: The Polish–Soviet War 1919–20*, Macdonald, London, 1972.

Antony Polonsky, *Politics in Independent Poland 1921–39*, Oxford University Press, Oxford, 1972.

4. Second World War and Occupation (1939–45)

Jan Ciechanowski, *The Warsaw Rising of 1944*, Cambridge University Press, Cambridge, 1974. (Politics of the Resistance.)

Józef Garlicki, *Poland in the Second World War*, Macmillan, London, 1985. (General history.)

Gustaw Herling, *A World Apart*, Heinemann, London, 1986. (Experiences of a Polish deportee in Soviet labour camps.)

Jan Nowak, *Courier from Warsaw*, Collins, London, 1982. (Poland under Nazi occupation.)

Edward Rozek, *Allied Wartime Diplomacy*, Wiley, New York, 1958.

5. *Post-War Poland* (1945–80)

Nicholas Bethell, *Gomułka: His Poland and His Communism*, Pelican, London, 1972.

Maria Kuncewiczowa (ed.), *The Modern Polish Mind*, Secker & Warburg, London, 1962.

Czesław Miłosz, *The Captive Mind*, Penguin, London, 1981.

Andrzej Szczypiorski, *The Polish Ordeal*, Croom Helm, London, 1982.

6. *The Solidarity Period* (1980–   )

Neal Ascherson, *The Polish August*, Penguin, London, 1981.

Tim Garton Ash, *The Polish Revolution: Solidarity 1980–82*, Jonathan Cape, London, 1983.

Denis MacShane, *Solidarity: Poland's Independent Trade Union*, Spokesman Books, Nottingham, 1981.

Kevin Ruane, *Polish Challenge*, British Broadcasting Corporation, London, 1982.

Index

Numbers in *italics* refer to illustrations

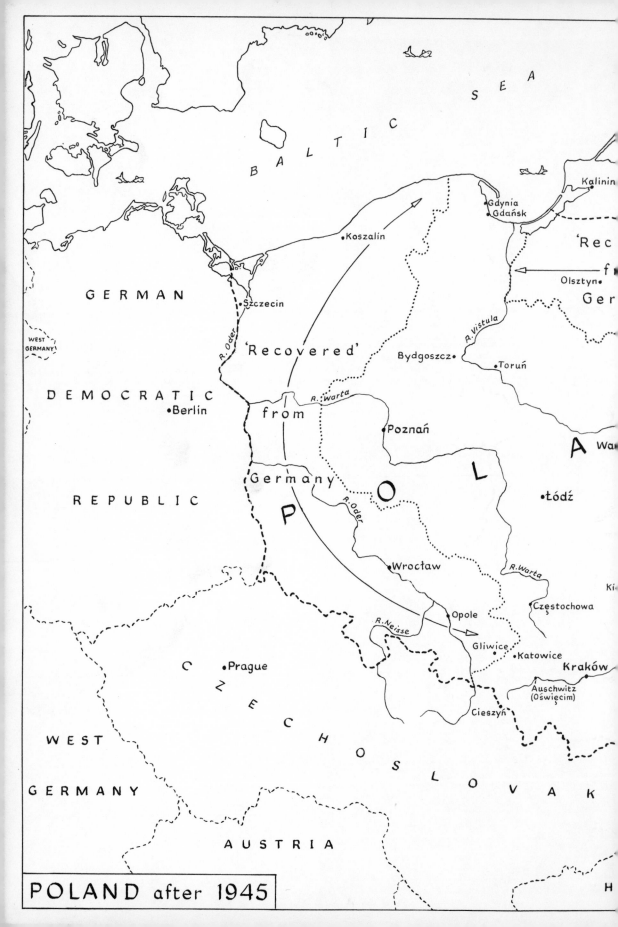

BALTIC SEA

Kalinin

Gdynia
Gdańsk

Koszalin

'Rec

f

GERMAN

Olsztyn

Ger

WEST
GERMANY

Szczecin

R. Vistula

'Recovered'

Bydgoszcz

Toruń

DEMOCRATIC

•Berlin

R. Warta

from

Poznań

A

Wa

R. Oder

Germany

O

L

REPUBLIC

P

Wrocław

R. Oder

Łódź

R. Warta

Ki

Częstochowa

Opole

R. Neisse

Gliwice

C

•Prague

Z

E

C

H

O

S

L

O

V

A

K

Katowice

Kraków

Auschwitz
(Oświęcim)

Cieszyn

WEST

GERMANY

AUSTRIA

H

POLAND after 1945